PROMETHEISM

This book is dedicated to my fiancée Nassim,
Who was drawn to me through the
Promethean fire in her own soul.

Let's set this world ablaze together, beloved!

PROMETHEISM

JASON REZA JORJANI

ARKTOS
LONDON 2020

ISBN	978-1-912975-89-1 (Paperback)
	978-1-912975-90-7 (Hardback)
	978-1-912975-91-4 (Ebook)

| **EDITING** | John Bruce Leonard |

| **COVER & LAYOUT** | Tor Westman |

🌐 Arktos.com   ❖ fb.com/Arktos   🐦 @arktosmedia   ◎ arktosmedia

CONTENTS

"Prometheus, teacher in every art, brought the fire that hath proved for mortals a means to mighty ends."

— Aeschylus

Introduction

THIS IS A DECLARATION OF WAR. In the name of our creator, we declare a revolutionary war against both the gods and those titans who were gods before them! In the name of our liberator, we declare a revolutionary war against fatalism and every other form of tyranny! We think from out of the end of all things, with an indomitable will to achieve either victory or a martyrdom that inspires enduring rebellion in those to whom we pass the torch of our example.

Of all the ancient myths that still have vital force, that of Prometheus is set apart as the most powerful because it is also the most ominous. In a world where the majority of people have been brainwashed into believing that their creator is a jealous and tyrannically wrathful God-Father, archetypally identical to Zeus, the myth of Prometheus as the creator of Man is a meteor that threatens an entire Cosmos with the spectre of deranging its constellations of belief.

That Prometheus bestowed a soul on the human being in the form of a butterfly already suggests that he is not only the creator, but also the liberator of Man.[1] When Zeus punishes Prometheus for attempting to secure his creation a life beyond sacrificial servitude, the rebel titan takes his revenge against the God-Father by gifting mortals with the fire of the forge and the light of knowledge. The fire that he steals from

---

1   Kerényi, Carl. *Prometheus: Archetypal Image of Human Existence* (Princeton University Press, 1997).

Olympus in the fennel stalk is emblematic of the power of technological science to free us from imposed scarcity and enforced ignorance.

We see the most defining characteristics of Prometheus reflected
in the kind of projection that is involved in the framing of Nature by
every scientific theory, and the provision for the future that is made
possible by technological innovations that are developed on the basis
of these theoretical models. The very name of "Prometheus" is derived
from the Greek words for forethought and prevision.[2] This archetypal
creator and liberator of Man epitomizes the intrepid spirit of thinking
ahead by envisioning futures and preparing provisions with a view to
making sure that the best possible future unfolds. That he is punished
by having his ever-regenerating liver perpetually pecked at, suggests
that even the God-Father wants to know the things to come as clearly
as Prometheus sees them: the archaic Greeks used the liver for fore-
telling the future.

Prometheus is the first freedom fighter. The archetype of
Prometheus tacitly reflects a recognition that *freedom is the most
fundamental fact in the Cosmos.* The Cosmos is inconceivable without
consciousness, which presupposes intentionality. Some degree of free
will, however conditioned, is a prerequisite of anyone being personally
accountable for meaningful actions. A Cosmos in which our creative
acts do not add anything that was not predetermined, and that could
not have been foreseen or anticipated — even by the Providence of a
deity — is a world that is not worth living in.

Prometheus is, of course, also the deity who most fully epitomizes
foresight. His name means to "think ahead" and when Zeus chains
him to a rock in the Caucasus, the eagle pecking out his liver is a
symbolic expression of Zeus seeking to devour and appropriate the
superior power of precognition, projection, and anticipation that
is characteristic of Prometheus. However, the purpose of this definitively Promethean power is to expand our scope of free will and

---

2   Ibid.

self-determination, not to constrain it with a sense of inexorable fate. Foreseeing *possible* futures — whether by the intuitive means of precognitive clairvoyance or through rational projective analysis, or a balance of both — actually affords us the opportunity to become the masters of our own destiny.

Various factors do condition thought, constrain the will, and limit the imagination, but the capacity to exercise individual freedom at some level despite these factors is a *sine qua non* of any meaningful conception of existence. Only a discontinuous and somewhat internally dissonant cosmic structure, which always preserves a degree of chaos, allows for this kind of creative individuality. Understanding such a structure precludes, and is mutually exclusive of a putatively 'scientific' commitment to mechanistic reductionism, religious faith in an omniscient and omnipotent God, and the belief that there should or ever can be an end to violent struggle and strife. Any entity falsely claiming omniscience and omnipotence, so as to demoralize people by subjecting them to the illusion of the futility of resistance, is simply "Zeus" by another name.

Prometheus redefines the preconceived limits of the possible, making the putatively impossible possible by means of technological science. The Prometheist has the strength to grasp the burdensome fact that the *truth is what works*. Knowledge is not the mirroring of an objective 'Reality' by a subjective cognition that only needs to be rendered more perceptive and precise, like a mirror that requires polishing. Knowledge is radically pragmatic, because technology is ontologically prior to science — which is inseparable from the technology that makes theoretical research possible and renders knowledge discoverable. Rather than distinguishing Science from Technology, and misconstruing technology as applied science, we should always conceive of them as the unified phenomenon of Technoscience, wherein *theoria* is inconceivable apart from *praxis*.

Scientific knowledge is the white light of molten metal in the forge of industrious innovation. Science ought not to be confined within any particular paradigm, which also constrains technological innovation. Instead, various paradigms, and the theories that they make possible, ought to be seen as different scientific models that each offer us the potential to craft certain types of technological tools for handling things better and, ultimately, for expanding the horizon of our achievable aims. Multiple and mutually inconsistent paradigms can be exploited simultaneously for the sake of their power to foster discovery and act as a framework for invention.

As the deity whose mind races ahead to survey the most distant horizons of possible futures, Prometheus also offers us inspiration as a sacred fountainhead of creativity. *The inspirational power of beauty is an expression of the evolutionary force.* A seduction to surmounting perceived limitations is what ought to resonate within oneself in the face of the harmonic proportionality or dynamic tension of an aesthetic work, whether in literature, painting, architecture, music, or performance art. Aesthetic experience should be an encounter with an expression of ascendant life, not for the sake of inspiring an awe that suffocates and dwarfs the soul, but with a view to kindling personal genius. Inspiration always involves a feedback loop with possible futures, so that the creativity it affords us can generate forms and architectonics that are never merely a repetition of the past. This also means that, however archaic certain elements of an aesthetic work may be, an orientation towards the future is necessary for it to be rightly deemed beautiful, rather than awe-fully monstrous in its titanic brutality.

Brutalism in architecture, which is kindred in spirit to industrial techno music, can positively reveal certain elemental techno-scientific forces more nakedly than any other aesthetic orientation, but it ought not to be accepted as anything like the crystalline perfection of what Hugh Ferriss characterized as "power in buildings." Whether Frank Lloyd Wright will be seen as a herald of the archeo-futurist architectonic to come, or whether it will take shape in a fashion that was more clearly anticipated by the post-metropolitan bio-mechanical abodes that H.R. Giger depicted, evolutionary openness and an overcoming of alienation *without the loss of individuality* is characteristic of Prometheist aesthetics.

The willingness of Prometheus, as a loving father, to sacrifice himself as a martyr for the sake of emancipating his children, makes him the most ethical of all deities. While this tragic martyrdom is certainly a symbol of salvific forbearance, that it is suffered and endured as a punishment for offering us techno-scientific empowerment and unleashing our artistic creativity, should also be read as a recognition of the fact that *cultivating ethos, personally and socially, is about the pursuit of excellence.*

This means that the Prometheist will have no tolerance for the putatively moral outrage that calls for so-called 'social justice' by valorizing disability and resentfully desecrating and destroying everything that memorializes the achievement of those who excelled in various endeavors. It also means that any morality that demands adherence to a code of conduct that is arbitrarily imposed, as in a religious "revelation," or affirmed merely on the basis of ossified customs and in the name of ancestral authority, is fundamentally unethical. Individuation is indispensable to being an authentic and conscientious person who can contribute to fostering an ethical society, which in turn provides children with an environment that encourages them to excel.

An ethos — a character or moral fiber — geared toward the progressive enhancement of capacities for creative expression does depend, to some extent, on embracing a mythos. Personal meaning cannot be forged by fiat from out of a cultural-historical vacuum. Individuals need to draw from the mythic structures of living traditions, and the archetypes that sustain these structures on the level of the collective unconscious. But ethical conduct always involves a situational adaptation and appropriation of this heritage, not a subservience to it that is tantamount to a tyranny of the past over present and future generations. Our traditional heritages ought to inspire us in a daimonic fashion rather than subject us to demonic possession.

With a view to these psychological and sociological considerations, the mythos of Prometheus is the most progressive archetypal basis for an ethical society.

Prometheus rebels against his fellow titans on behalf of the Olympians and then rebels against these gods, who prove equally tyrannical, for the sake of man. Resistance to any authority that is perceived to be arbitrary and illegitimate is integral to the Prometheist ethos. *Governments are legitimate power structures only insofar as they serve to secure industrious and exploratory enterprises.* The only justification for sovereign power, namely the force of law over the lives of citizens in any state, is to secure the liberty of those individuals to pursue their projects. A Prometheist government would unchain all productive economic forces while protecting the industrious individual, who ought to be superhumanly empowered thereby, from an instrumental dehumanization and existential degradation.

It is not the business of government to legislate morality or propagandize about the meaning of life. The liberty of individuals is limited with justification only when that constraint serves the purpose of ultimately securing citizens freedom from collective coercion and freedom for the personal pursuit of meaning, purpose, wonder, and creative power. The constitutional order of any regime should reflect this conception of Justice — in the sense of the justification of state power that is deemed to be legitimate. Every other political order or disorder ought to be considered a type of tyranny to be resisted, or an anarchy that invites tyranny.

A (r)evolutionary spectre is haunting the whole of terrestrial humanity, the Posthuman spectre of Prometheism. When Karl Marx identified Communism as a spectre, he was right. He may have been mistaken about how it would end, but the spectre of Communism did dominate half of the planet for most of the 20th century. In the mid to late 1800s, when modern Communism was still a fringe sociopolitical movement, this was hardly conceivable. That is why, despite his avowed atheism, Marx deserves his place among the ranks of prophets. The Prometheist will be as seductive, powerful, feared, and hated in the 21st century as the Communist was in the 20th century.

That is because the 21st century will undoubtedly be the epoch of the technological Singularity. What this "Singularity" signifies is the acceleration and convergent culmination of scientific discoveries and technological innovations in a catastrophic situation that faces us with the end of a recognizably human life. At a certain point, within the next several decades, the exponential increase in the rate of technological advancement and the expansion of scientific knowledge will no longer represent an upward curve on a graph, allowing us to extrapolate the future from the past; it will instead become a spike, a point past which the "history" in question is no longer "human," and even what counts for "reality" may be radically redefined. When faced with the prospect of the end of humanity, the end of history, and the end of reality, we can either reactively retreat from the Singularity, and attempt to indefinitely delay it, or we can embrace and even embody the spectral essence of technology bringing it about. The latter is the Promethean attitude, and this book shamelessly advocates assuming it.

The book begins with a consideration of the first thinker who seriously contemplated an apocalyptic culmination of the developmental trajectory of technological science: Martin Heidegger. In Chapter 1, titled "Shamelessly Promethean", we see how Heidegger conceived of the essence of technology as holding sway before and beneath theoretical science, driving scientific discovery toward a catastrophic future moment when humanity will have to confront the prospect of total instrumentality. Technological science or Technoscience is, in Heidegger's view, an inherently apocalyptic force. While Heidegger could only see the apocalypse that it would bring about through a glass darkly, he presciently delineates a handful of characteristics of the techno-scientific Apocalypse that remain relevant for any attempt to seriously think through the technological Singularity. These five insights will be examined one by one.

At least as important as these specific characteristics of Technoscience, which destine it to be apocalyptic, is Heidegger's suggestion that, true to any "apocalypse" worthy of the name, the coming revelation could also be the coming of a god — if we properly prepare to be "saved" by that god.[3] Paradoxically, there are hints to the effect that the archaic god whose future return he envisioned is none other than Prometheus, the god — or rather, the titan — of technology. True to the structure of Heideggerian thought in general, only that power responsible for the catastrophe that we are about to face can save us from being annihilated by it. No merely human effort will suffice. The Promethean spectre of Technoscience needs to be owned, reclaimed, and redirected from out of its own essence, which was initially intended to be salvific.

To be sure, this is a very controversial interpretation of the theology implicit in Heidegger's reflections on what he calls "the question concerning technology."[4] It is, however, supported by the Promethean preoccupation of two Heideggerian thinkers on technology, Günther Anders and Bernard Stiegler. Anders was a student of Heidegger who went on to develop the concept of "Promethean shame" as a way of understanding how technological development threatens to redefine the human being's existential relationship to the being of manufactured things.[5] Bernard Stiegler most extensively engages with the myth of Prometheus in his attempt to radicalize Heidegger's existential analysis of temporality in relation to the evolution of technology.[6]

---

3   Heidegger, Martin. "Nur noch ein Gott kann uns retten," ("Now Only A God Can Save Us") in *Der Spiegel*, 31 May 1976.

4   Heidegger, Martin. *The Question Concerning Technology* (Harper Torchbooks, 1977).

5   Anders, Günther. "Promethean Shame" in *Prometheanism*, edited by Christopher John Müller (Rowman & Littlefield Publishers, 2016).

6   Stiegler, Bernard. *Technics and Time, 1: The Fault of Epimetheus* (Stanford University Press, 1998).

Building on Anders and Stiegler, Chapter 1 thinks through and beyond Heidegger in order to contemplate "the end of all things" by deconstructing the radical distinction between things and persons.[7] In this way it sets up the main theme of this book as a whole: a contemplation of the end of humanity, the end of history, and the end of reality as three facets of a unified phenomenon that involves a deconstruction of the distinction between things and persons or technology and nature, between what is designed to be manufactured and what is born to evolve.

That having been said, a few words of warning are in order. Chapter 1 is uniquely abstract and technical. It is written with a view to situating the subject matter of this book in the context of the concerns of academic Philosophy — especially in the Continental tradition that culminates in Heidegger and his heirs. Those who take the time and care to read through it could be able to understand the rest of this book, and the project of Prometheism as a whole, on a much deeper level. However, for someone with little to no background in academic Philosophy, it is not strictly necessary. The lay reader should certainly not be put off by this chapter from reading what follows, which is written in a much more colloquial style and is far more concrete in terms of its subject matter.

Chapter 2 focuses on "The End of Humanity." It begins with the observation that Genetics, Robotics, Information, and Nanotechnology (GRIN) threaten all of the boundary conditions that have hitherto defined human nature.[8] Genetic engineering promises to drastically extend the human lifespan, eliminate all heritable diseases, boost the immune system, make it easier to build muscle mass, and most importantly, increase mathematical and spatial reasoning as well as memory capacity to superhuman levels hitherto only achieved by computers. At the same time, the robotics revolution finally promises to bring all

7   Heidegger, Martin. *Poetry, Language, Thought* (Harper Collins, 1971).
8   Garreau, Joel. *Radical Evolution: The Promise and Peril of Enhancing Our Minds, Our Bodies — and What It Means to Be Human* (Doubleday, 2005).

human drudgery to an end. When combined with advances in information technology that are yielding specialized AI or "expert systems", robots will be able to outperform humans in every field of labor that does not involve the most dynamic forms of creativity and the artful imagining of new ideas.

When one considers the potential of Nanotechnology, the projected impact of this robotics revolution on economics and industry becomes mind-blowing to contemplate. Ultimately, almost anything could be manufactured by anyone through the re-arrangement of feedstock on a molecular level inside of tabletop machines that are the successors of today's three-dimensional printers.[9] Meanwhile, if biotechnology has not cured cancer, even the most metastasized cases of it, including those affecting the brain and spine, could be dissolved by nanobots performing hitherto impossibly precise surgery at a molecular level under superhumanly intelligent control. The cybernetic combination of biotechnology, including cloning, and robotics at a nano-scale of engineering will make any damage to the body possible to repair and any organ easy to replace.[10] Taken together it seems that Genetics, Robotics, Information, and Nanotechnology promise us an evolution into a race of Supermen.

On the other hand, the GRIN technologies confront us with the prospect of bringing about an "end of humanity" in ways that are much more deeply disturbing, disconcerting, or even horrifying. At the very least, genetic engineering will bring an end to the exclusive sexual dimorphism that has thus far been characteristic of the human species. The psychological power of archetypal androgyny is such that, in the context of contemporary hormone replacement therapy and plastic surgery, it has already led to the rapid rise of a transsexual

9   Drexler, Eric. *Engines of Creation: The Coming Era of Nanotechnology* (Anchor, 1987).

10 Mulhall, Douglas. *Our Molecular Future: How Nanotechnology, Robotics, Genetics, and Artificial Intelligence Will Transform Our World* (Prometheus, 2002).

community. Consequently, the widespread CRISPR-style gene hacking of tomorrow, when taken together with cybernetic modifications by means of nanotechnology, will undoubtedly yield veritable hermaphrodites as a significant subset of the (post)human population.[11] Much more disturbing is the prospect of the splicing of human and animal genes, leading to the transformation of certain species of animals into chimera that possess quasi-human (or even superhuman) characteristics. What was envisioned in *Planet of the Apes* pales in comparison to some of the monstrous possibilities in play here.

Then there is the attempt to replicate human intelligence inside of a silicon-based neural network. The *Terminator* franchise has made it clear what a Frankenstein's monster Artificial Intelligence could become, especially if the murderous Posthuman AI in question has a race of inhuman robots under its control. What if this AI could also hack programmable nanobots? Instead of an accidental or randomly generated 'virus' that results in nanobots melting the molecular structure of everything in the world, our bodies included, into a "grey goo," what if an AI were to seize control of these nanobots and use them to recode the molecular structure of the natural world, cityscapes, and even our own brains, in ways that suit purposes that remain inscrutable to merely human minds?

The *Terminator* films also contemplated AI and robotics in the context of Time Travel. This science-fictional projection is perfectly reasonable considering the fact that the problem of manipulating the space-time continuum is one of the achievements that has eluded mere mortals, and one of the higher goals that a superhuman intelligence could be expected to set for itself. Whether travel through time is accomplished by purely mechanical means, such as the shearing of the space-time fabric by a device like the infamous "Bell" developed by the SS in Project Chronos, or whether it is partly or wholly psychical in nature, time travel confronts us with the prospect of "The End

---

11   Farrell, Joseph P. and Dr. Scott D. de Hart. *Transhumanism: A Grimoire of Alchemical Agendas* (Feral House, 2012).

of History." This is the focus of Chapter 3, which has as its point of departure a return to the work of Bernard Stiegler (whose *Time and Technics* will have been introduced in Chapter 1) with a view to what the "speed" of modern technology reveals to us about the nature of time.

In the history of Philosophy "the end of history" has signified an abstract concept for the culmination of a teleological or purposive, goal-directed process of historical progress. G.W.F. Hegel conceived of this in terms of the evolution of consciousness by means of dialectical tensions at work in the psycho-social structure of all domains of human life, from religion and science, to artistic styles and political systems.[12] Karl Marx reinterpreted this dialectical development in reductively material terms, seeing the change in economic systems and the human relations involved in various modes of production as the key to all other transformations, whether scientific, religious, or political.[13] He endeavored, by means of this reductive analysis, to render History as scientific as other domains of knowledge. Friedrich Nietzsche altogether rejected the Hegelian and Marxist conception of a law-like material *and moral* progress toward a utopian "end of history."[14] Rather than seeing any logical process of progression as intrinsic to psycho-social development, Nietzsche saw a struggle for power (not mere "survival" as Darwin had postulated) as characteristic of the evolutionary life force.[15]

If there is an "end of history" it is that moment when techno-scientific development, driven solely by the will to power, reaches a point past which it affords us the practical capability to transform ourselves into superhuman beings whose projects are supported by an equally

12   Hegel, G.W.F. *Phenomenology of Spirit* (Oxford University Press, 1977).

13   Marx, Karl. *Economic and Philosophic Manuscripts of 1844 and the Communist Manifesto* (Prometheus, 1988).

14   Nietzsche, Friedrich. *On the Advantage and Disadvantage of History for Life* (Hackett Publishing Company, 1980).

15   Nietzsche, Friedrich. *The Will to Power* (Vintage Books, 1968).

Posthuman species of subhuman robots. Nietzsche was one of the first thinkers to envision what is now widely referred to as the "artificial speciation" of humanity into more than one Posthuman species. So to him "the end of history" meant the end of human history and the beginning of the "higher history" of the Promethean Superman who has murdered God.

With H.G. Wells writing *The Time Machine* just five years before Nietzsche's death, and five years after the philosopher had been presumptuously declared insane and literally straight-jacketed, it could hardly have been conceivable to Nietzsche how much "higher" than human history the Superman's mode of life may be. Interestingly, *The Time Machine* (1895) also involved a Nietzschean artificial speciation of humanity into two different branches of a transhuman society, the godlike Eloi and the monstrously subhuman and subterranean Morlocks.[16] But what remained inconceivable to Nietzsche, and even to H.G. Wells, was that the "higher" history of the Superman would mean a fifth-dimensional existence encompassing a plethora of 4-D space-times.

Even if we take the simplest and most uncontroversial type of time travel, namely travel into the future through space travel at near the speed of light, the psycho-social and biological implications force us to think beyond human limits. A civilization that routinely sent spaceships out from the Earth, or any other colonized planets, at near the speed of light and then had them return from these missions, would be so radically different from any society known to history that it would have to be considered post-historical, if not Posthuman, by comparison. Hundreds or even thousands of years would elapse on the home world whereas only a few years, or in the case of cryogenic hibernation, maybe only a few days, would have passed for those on board the spaceship before they returned to their point of origin.

---

16 Wells, H.G. *The Time Machine* (Penguin Classics, 2005).

A society capable of fielding such missions would require a political stability so far exceeding that of any society known to history that it is almost unthinkable. Try to imagine a government capable of sustaining hundreds of Apollo-type projects that would each span thousands of years before the astronauts sent out on each mission could be safely returned. For one thing, this would be impossible without a significant extension of the human lifespan through genetic engineering. Even then, analyzing—let alone managing—the psychological and social factors involved in fielding such enterprises of exploration and exploitation demands a superhuman intelligence.

This is, however, nothing by comparison to the complexity involved in time travel to 'the' past—or, rather, to what had been the past before being altered by the time travelers.[17] Despite the protests of overly rationalistic logicians, it may be possible to retroactively change history in a manner akin to retro-active collapse of the wave function in the case of Schrödinger's cat with its cells suspended in a ghostly quantum superposition between life and death. The Mandela Effect suggests that it is not the case that only unobserved past 'events' are susceptible to retro-PK.[18] Moreover, there are tantalizing physical traces suggestive of time travelers who may have already effaced a different version of the present or futures that may now never come to pass. The capability to Time Travel, whether by mechanical or psychical means, or some synthesis thereof, would indeed be the greatest weapon in the most terrible war of all: the Change War.

What human being could bear the thought of being subjected to repeated revisions of the timeline of his life, tragically losing what would have been lifelong loves or facing the horror of holocausts that, in an earlier version of history, had not shattered all his hopes? Who could tolerate being the plaything of fifth-dimensional gods? No one

---

17 Nahin, Paul J. *Time Machines: Time Travel in Physics, Metaphysics, and Science Fiction* (Springer, 2001).

18 Wheeler, Jay. *Alternate: The Mandela Effect* (Amazon, 2018).

other than the Prometheist who joins their ranks himself, perhaps with much nobler ideas about how to shape histories.

It is possible that this means something like hacking through the coding matrix of a simulation and becoming one of its programmers. That possibility is explored in Chapter 4, which focuses on "The End of Reality." The Simulation Hypothesis offers us the most coherent ontological explanation of what it would mean to "change the past," and one which, unlike the Many Worlds Interpretation of Quantum Theory, manages to also preserve some degree of free will. In line with the hypothesis that we are living in a computer simulation, changing the past would be a question of gaining access to an archived past state of play and replaying the simulation forward again in a different way from how the game was played out the first or second or thirty-second time.[19]

One reason why denizens of an advanced civilization might design simulations on the scale of our own world is to develop a science of history of the kind that, as suggested above, Hegel and Marx were aiming at. The only way to really develop scientifically rigorous models of historical change in societies of a certain type, and to predict their transformation into other types or stages of societies, would be to simulate a variety of alternate timelines. Changing variables over and over again would afford the programmers the opportunity to observe how the conscious artificial intelligences inside the simulation, namely beings such as we might be, would react differently on a psycho-social and inter-societal level. Eventually, these observations could lead to the development of testable hypotheses about what kind of trajectories could be expected of certain types of societies and how these societies could be reengineered in relatively predictable ways by altering particular variables.

Different scales of time-dilation on various levels of layered simulations, comparable to the incommensurate time-scales of dreams

---

19 Virk, Rizwan. *The Simulation Hypothesis* (Bayview Books, 2019).

within dreams, could allow the programmers to observe these simulated histories in something akin to "fast-forward" mode. Working through avatars of putative "time travelers" to manipulate variables within many such parallel processed simulations, laws of history could emerge from out of the computer systems of the programmers in a fraction of the time it took for the "psychohistorians" of Isaac Asimov's *Foundation* to arrive at a scientific understanding of historical phenomena.

Whether such a lofty goal motivates the programmers of our simulation or whether it is just a gigantic arena of entertainment for sadistic archons who enjoy entering into games like the Second World War, there are, unfortunately, good reasons to take the Simulation Hypothesis seriously. Numerous hitherto puzzling aspects of quantum physics make much more sense when they are set in the context of what we know about how computer games work. So-called "quantum superposition" and "wave/particle duality" may just be optimization functions of a computer system that does not render any part of the coding matrix that is not being observed by at least one conscious participant inside the simulation. That would afford quite a lot of optimization indeed, and save a great deal of processing power, especially if it were the case that most of the 'people' inside the simulation are actually Non-Player Characters (NPCs) rather than conscious AIs or avatars of the programmers.

The quantized quality of space-time itself, which is counter-intuitive based on our experience of spatial continuity and our experiential time continuum, is exactly what one would expect of a pixelated world. The "plank length" of quantum physicists could just be describing the magnitude of a single pixel. What Einstein found objectionable as the "spooky action at a distance" of "quantum entangled" particles might simply be a coding sequence akin to the kind of instruction programmed into video games to make sure that when a certain set of pixels change against a fixed background another seemingly disparate grouping of them always also changes at the same time.

In other words, while seeming to be distinct pixels — or, as the case may be "particles" observed by quantum physicists — these 'entities' are actually images projected from a deeper and hidden level, namely that of the programming code, wherein they are not as distinct as they seem to be. David Bohm referred to this deeper sub-quantum level of the universe as "the implicate order" and compared it to the seemingly chaotic swirl of interference patterns on a piece of holographic film that is only unfolded into a holographic projection when subjected to a beam of laser light.[20] Bohm saw many of the properties of a hologram at work in the more paradoxical non-locality and entanglement of quantum physical phenomena. He ultimately concluded that we are living inside something like a dynamic hologram, a holographic universe. We truly arrive at "the end of reality" when we realize that holographic universes may be nested within one another, the way that dreams can sometimes be.

Many phenomena hitherto deemed "paranormal" make sense in the context of the Simulation Hypothesis, whether in the form of the Holographic Universe theory or in terms of other models of global (if not cosmic-scale) simulation. Telepathy, Clairvoyance, Precognition, Psychokinesis, Teleportation, Reincarnation, and even Astrology are no longer "anomalous" once we accept that putative "laws of nature" are just programming code in the physics engine of a game and that meaning-structures such as karma and synchronicity are part of the story-telling fabric of a cosmos that has an intrinsically and intentionally narrative structure. Such a world is very much akin to Heraclitus' concept of the Cosmos as *Logos*. The question is how much control we dare to demand over telling the story that we are a part of. Before assuming a Promethean stance with respect to that question, we would first have to face "the end of reality." Realism and rationalism that is based on a verificational conception of truth as an adequate mirroring of objective reality by acquired knowledge has to be abandoned

---

20 Bohm, David. *Wholeness and the Implicate Order*. (Routledge, 1994).

in favor of radical pragmatism. The "truth" is what works — *what we have the power to make happen* and, as Arthur C. Clark prophetically claimed, "Any sufficiently advanced technology is indistinguishable from magic."

How many people are ready to live in a world that is undeniably recognized as magical, especially if it requires swallowing the bitter "red pill" that those who currently control this prison planet are black magicians? What if these occulted techno-priests even have the power to pull the plug on our simulation if those within it aspire to break out or simply demand a world that is on par with that of the programmers — and therefore a world too taxing for whatever information processing system is the substrate of this virtual reality?

Considering this prospect of the controlled demolition of our nascent planetary civilization on the brink of the technological Singularity brings us to the Breakaway Civilization. Chapter 5, "Atlas Never Shrugs," explores the idea that an elite group of techno-scientific thinkers, military-industrialists, corporatists, and masterminds of intelligence operations and psychological warfare may have foreseen the coming catastrophe and made the decision to break away from the civilizations of Earth before deliberately demolishing them in order to indefinitely delay the Singularity. Seeing themselves as the only people capable of enduring Singularity-level technological breakthroughs, they achieve these before anyone else and deny them to everyone else. Their occulted world of "black projects" becomes, first, a society unto itself, and then, eventually, a self-sufficient civilization.

Meanwhile, nearly everyone left behind on the Earth is regressed to a feudal, pre-industrial level of culture. From pandemics that demand "social distancing" to earthquakes and tsunamis that destroy infrastructure and knock out electricity, these and other apparent 'disasters' will strongly discourage people from living in cities and their commuter suburbs. Instead, a neo-agrarian life on isolated homesteads will be promoted — a form of social organization that would be prohibitive of political protest and make atomized individuals and disconnected families easier to control, especially if a severe solar storm or other EMP event were to knock out the electronic cyberspace that would be the only tenuous web connecting these isolated individuals.

In the concluding chapter, it will be argued that this patronizing regression ought to be resisted at all costs. The sixth and final chapter endeavors to render the evolutionary revolution of Prometheism more tangible, if not programmatic. In Chapter 6, "(R)Evolutionary Spectre," the idea of a "Spectral Revolution" from *Prometheus and Atlas* (Arktos, 2016) is revisited and revised in a constructive critique that incorporates the consideration of certain technological advances first contemplated in *World State of Emergency* (Arktos, 2017) and further explored in this book. Emphasis is placed on the social and political implications of affirming the convergence of technological breakthroughs into a Singularity that represents the end of humanity, history, and reality. Embracing this greatest of all revolutionary transformations means taking an evolutionary leap detrimental to the vast majority of a (mere) 'humanity' that will experience this revolution as an extinction event. Only a small minority of individuals, comparable to Magneto's band of rebel mutants, will be strong enough to take the leap into a positively Posthuman future. As much as it demands an indomitable will, this leap is also a leap of faith. It means having faith in Prometheus by redefining one's relationship to him as a spectre — in the very concrete sense of empowering an egregore that is based on an archetype.[21] Chapter 6 discusses the difference between egregores and archetypes, with a view to elucidating what was meant in *Prometheus and Atlas* by the characterization of Prometheus as the apocalyptic "spectre" of technological science.

Instead of averting the Singularity by indefinitely delaying certain revolutionary, and convergent, technological breakthroughs, we ought

---

21 Stavish, Mark, *Egregores: The Occult Entities That Watch Over Human Destiny* (Inner Traditions, 2018); Jung, C.G., *The Archetypes and the Collective Unconscious* (Princeton University Press, 1990).

to forthrightly face the spectre of the end of humanity, the end of history, and the end of reality — the spectre of the titanic trickster who is destined to bring about the end of all things. The survivors of this technological apocalypse ought not to be a self-appointed 'elite' of soulless corporatists, arms dealers, bankers, and second-rate sellout scientists. Rather, the future should belong to those with the Prometheist ethos and the creative genius to craft a positively Posthuman community from out of the Singularity's fiery forge.

CHAPTER 1

Shamelessly Promethean

THE FIRST THINKER of the apocalyptic essence of technological science is Martin Heidegger. The failure to free oneself from Heidegger's bewitching language has been a significant cause for the inability to think beyond him. Heidegger's insistence, anticipating McLuhan, that the medium cannot really be separated from the message, and that we are shaped by the cultural-historical particularities of language on an existential level, has not helped those who wanted to think through and after him. Many of these would-be philosophers even accepted Heidegger's absurd claim that ancient Greek philosophy, or for that matter his own German thought, could not be translated and had to be read in the original to be understood at all. One must bear in mind that Heidegger's almost medieval manner of expression was shaped by studies of Thomas Aquinas and extensive meditations on Meister Eckhart. One has to cut through this scholastic and mystical language to see that Heidegger has a handful of insights that are astonishingly prescient and even "futuristic" in a sense that the Italian futurists of his own early-to-mid twentieth century milieu would have appreciated.

The first part of this chapter presents five fundamentally novel insights that Heidegger has about the essence of technology. The first of these is that technology is ontologically prior to science, rather than being a practical application of what is known about objective 'reality' by means of theoretical science. The most shocking implication of this is that the physical universe does not preexist our tools in an 'objective' fashion, since any and all knowledge we can have about it is the result of technology and is fundamentally conditioned by the modalities of experience afforded to us by crafted things. The second is that humans have a unique relationship to technological science, one which could be described as co-constitutive, and this renders our existence uniquely problematic and dangerous — not just dangerous to ourselves but to the cosmos or Being-as-such. The universality of this threat brings us to Heidegger's third revolutionary insight, which is that technological science has the power to assimilate, encompass, reorganize, and eclipse all that is seemingly natural — not just 'human nature' but "the worldhood of the world" as such. Here Heidegger is anticipating not just biotechnology, but also virtual reality (i.e. "the World *as* Picture") and contemplating their significance on an existential level. The fourth thesis of Heidegger's interpretation of technological science is that its development is not only teleological (purposive, goal-directed), but also apocalyptic. It destines us, through meaningfully successive epochs, to an end of history, after which our existence will be almost inconceivably transformed. Moreover, this end of history is not subjectively relevant to *Homo sapiens* on the planet Earth. It is, as Heidegger imagines it, the ultimate "event" in the history of Being and of Being's revelation of itself in different modalities and in the guise of various worldviews. Fifth, and finally, this apocalypse is also a "revelation" in the original Greek sense of that word. Heidegger thinks that "only a god" can save us from the danger of total instrumentality and the most degrading objectification of (a no longer) 'human' existence. The irony is that, as I argued in *Prometheus and Atlas*, the same deity that can save us if we consciously recognize its power is the titan that is the spectre driving technological-scientific evolution throughout the epochs, leading up to the end of history.

The second section of this chapter focuses on the Promethean in the context of Heideggerian thought, especially as it has been understood by the French philosopher Bernard Stiegler. In an attempt to think beyond Heidegger, Stiegler claims that the prosthetic is existentially constitutive of being human. In the context of the myth of Prometheus and his brother Epimetheus, Stiegler argues that humans would not be human without the technology that threatens to dehumanize them — or give them the power to become superhuman. We are not just the recipients of the gift of Prometheus, namely *techne* (art/craft), but also truly the children who were made by him in his own divine image.

The third and last section of this chapter, from which the chapter as a whole derives its title, is an exploration of the psychological dimension of this Promethean inheritance. It focuses on the idea of "Promethean shame," which Günther Anders develops and contrasts with the classic understanding of Promethean pride or the hubris of attaining god-like power through technological science. Anders' thoroughly Heideggerian analysis of Promethean shame, which is our shame in the face of the competence and excellence of manufactured things, builds on a phenomenological analysis of shame-in-general. Anders argues that by allowing ourselves to feel humiliated in the face of designed things and the machines that manufacture them, we are divesting ourselves of the humanistic pride that was originally characteristic of the Promethean ethos. I offer a running critique of his characterization of the alienating effects of modern technology, suggesting that it suffers from a failure of imagination.

Anders generalizes the characteristics of a certain era in the development of technology, the heavy industry of the 1950s together with the passive television viewing experience of the time, as definitive of the impact of technology on human existence. As I suggest toward the end of this chapter, and as we shall see throughout the rest of this book, technologies are developing in ways that will allow a total fusion of man and machine and the abolition of the distinction between what grows organically and what is made mechanically. This end of all (objective) "things" in their alienation from our (subjective) person-hood can be accomplished through an orgiastic fusion of technology with the most primal and primordial aspects of our existence. That would mean an overcoming of Promethean shame and its dialectical reversal back into a Promethean pride that is more shameless than ever before.

1.1 Apocalyptic Technoscience

The first of Heidegger's astonishing insights is that technology is ontologically prior to science. This runs contrary to the commonly accepted view, both in his own time and even still in ours, that tech-nology is applied science. Heidegger argues that technology is not an assemblage of tools, and technological innovation is not simply a practical application of theoretical principles discovered by scientists through their experimental investigation of nature.[1] Nor is it merely the case that all scientific theorization is dependent upon certain tech-nologies, which chronologically preceded science before entering into an innovative feed back loop with scientific research. Rather, there is something essential about the crafting and use of technology that is hidden behind scientific theorization and that only reveals itself in time, over the course of history, as this theorization becomes less metaphysically abstract and more nakedly pragmatic.

Heidegger understood that even the most metaphysical abstrac-tions of early scientific theorization, on the part of scientists who still considered themselves "natural philosophers," were sublimated and occulted expressions of what Nietzsche aptly characterized as "the will to power."[2] The objectification of nature for the sake of its control was always what scientific theorization was aiming at. It was dominated,

---

1   Martin Heidegger, *Basic Writings* (HarperCollins, 1993), 312–313.

2   Martin Heidegger, *The Question Concerning Technology* (Harper Torchbooks, 1977), 140.

from the outset, by the essence of technology which is "craft" not simply in the sense of the Greek word *techne* but also in the sense of the Greek word *mekhane*, from which we derive "mechanical," but which suggests a more primordial "machination" or "contrivance." Science is always already technological. It is, in effect, "Technoscience." Heidegger did not come up with this neologism, but when he used the hyphenated term "technological-scientific" he was the first to deeply think through what subsequent writers would attempt to convey by deploying it.[3]

Heidegger's second insight, which is as astonishing as the first, is that the being who develops technology has a uniquely problematic existence on account of the danger of total instrumentality. The early modern attitude toward the development of tools was that, by freeing us from a thoughtlessly animal struggle for survival, technological development is what first made us properly human. There may be a certain anthropological truth to this claim, since rudimentary tool use has been observed even in higher primates, and it was, undoubtedly, early technologies such as bone and stone, and using flint stones to make fire, that conditioned our evolution into fully upright *Homo sapiens*. For example, on account of the invention of fire and of cutting tools, we no longer needed massive jaws with molars capable of crushing food. But at a certain point, technological development reveals its essence as the will to all-encompassing control or universal 'mechanization' in the sense of machination (in other words, in a deeper sense that includes genetic manipulation and not just industrial machinery or robotics).

The essence of technology, taking possession of us and acting through us with a kind of daemonic power, not only challenges every natural being with the prospect of becoming a controllable thing,[4] but it also threatens to turn people into things, so that our existential

---

3   Heidegger, *Basic Writings*, 448.

4   Ibid., 305, 308, 313–314.

relation to them becomes akin to that which we have with tools. Rather than "being-with" others, we increasingly treat them as if they could just be "present at hand" (which even when it comes to tools, is a deficient mode of relating to them as compared to their being "ready to hand").

Considering the global implications of this objectification brings us to the third of Heidegger's insights that was way ahead of its time. The network of instrumentality inevitably extends itself over the entire planet, enmeshing what were once meaningfully differentiated locales into an integrated matrix of calculation and manipulation.[5] Since the experience of authenticity is defined by meanings that are historically inherited and culturally specific, this leads to an increasingly intense sense of unreality. Significant places are demolished through industrial power generation, which demands running power lines through cleared forests or damming up rivers.[6] Superhighways suburbanize towns, and radio broadcasts destroy places by fusing them into a uniform space that information can cross virtually instantaneously.

The final stage of this that Heidegger was able to witness in his own lifetime, was the broadcast of moving pictures (a Nazi German invention, I might add). Heidegger presciently predicted that, with the invention of the television or "far-seer" (*Fernseher* in German), the characteristics of a movie production would increasingly encompass the 'real' world and turn it into a simulacrum.[7] Just as a movie director gives directions to actors on a set, the television was destined to become a medium by means of which our lives would become directed acting that is taking place within a set up where we are never really at home and everything is as fake as a movie prop. Heidegger called this the "Age of the World Picture" — in other words, the epoch wherein the world itself becomes a moving picture produced by an

---

5   Heidegger, *The Question Concerning Technology*, 168.

6   Heidegger, *Basic Writings*, 296–298.

7   Martin Heidegger, *Poetry, Language, Thought* (Harper Collins, 1971), 163.

all-encompassing information processing network of ever more autonomous mechanical production.[8]

What is most insidious is that, unlike in the case of the movie
production, there is no identifiable director who is directing our lives
within this "set-up" or *Gestell*.[9] Rather, we are being set up or framed
by a network that is monstrously headless and that, in proportion to
its increasingly powerful representation of everything, is also depriv-
ing us of the capacity to reflect on our situation. This is true even in
science, which Heidegger remarks is rapidly losing the capacity for
reflection. Research programs are determined not by the spirit of
discovery, but by a "cybernetic" relationship to the technical problems
posed by certain technologies — problems whose solutions are always
assumed to also be technological.[10]

The "Age of the World Picture" is the culminating epoch in
the historical process of Technoscience revealing its own essence.
Heidegger's fourth visionary insight is that this historical process is
not only teleological, but apocalyptic. Heidegger identifies at least
three epochs prior to this one. The first is the archaic age of Pre-
Socratic Greek thought. The second is the epoch of Platonism in the
broadest sense of transcendentally abstract rationalism. The third is
the medieval epoch of Christian theology, Heidegger's characterization of which would hold equally true for Islamic Iran during the
same period. The latter was as much an inheritor of the archaic and
classical Greek heritage and also pioneered rigorously mathematical
theoretical science not only on the basis of pagan Greek thought but
also, as in Medieval Europe, with a view to a monotheistic theology
with a post-pagan notion of man as a created or manufactured being.
The turn toward the World Picture Age comes with Descartes, specifically with his redefining truth as *veritas* or representational adequacy

---

8   Heidegger, *The Question Concerning Technology*, 130–132.

9   Ibid., 126–127.

10 Heidegger, *Basic Writings*, 434, 448–449.

or verisimilitude as compared to the Greek understanding of truth as *alethea* or "discovery" (literally un-concealment or un-forgetting).[11]

Ironically, defining truth — namely the end or aim of science — as the adequacy of a subjective representation of a putatively objective reality was destined to so thoroughly objectify every thing and person that it would abolish 'reality.' This destiny was already implicit in Descartes' shocking doubts about the real existence of the external world, including the reality of what appeared to be his own physical body. These were doubts that, in the context of his biography, were suggested to him by creepy encounters that he had with early automatons in a wonderland-type theme park during a period in his life when he was suffering a mental breakdown. What lies concealed behind Descartes' doubts about the reality of perceived phenomena is a terrifically violent will to define as "real" only that which can be instrumentally manipulated on account of being mathematically calculable. The "deceiving demon" that Descartes conjures in his *Meditations* is a projection of the daemonic essence of Technoscience, which denies 'reality' to any Being other than what we can, under controlled conditions, render calculable, re-produce, or manipulatively manufacture.

This brings us back to the relationship between Being and beings. Heidegger realizes that we are not only in danger of treating ourselves as just another type of beings, alienated from our own Being. Rather, this existential threat is on such a scale — and at such a depth — that it is a threat to existence itself. That is what is meant by "Age of the World Picture." Rather than being in a world that culturally and historically conditions our existence and offers us certain possibilities for flourishing, the "worldhood" of the world itself is assaulted with the prospect of total objectification. Heidegger suggests that, at this moment of gravest danger, the "saving power" that we have to decide in favor of becoming the Guardians of Being also reveals itself.[12] This is,

---

11 Heidegger, *The Question Concerning Technology*, 127.

12 Ibid., 313–317.

as it were, the angelic rather than the demonic aspect of the teleological force of Technoscience. It is *apocalyptic* in the original Greek sense of that word, namely "revelatory." Technoscience is radically religious insofar as contemplation of its essence offers us the ultimate revelation, and does so precisely on the precipice of our descent into hell.

The fifth and final insight of Heidegger, which seems even more striking today, is that salvation from the total eclipse of existence can only come through a return of the gods. This thought is not only post-apocalyptic, it is also Posthuman, since Heidegger is conceding that human beings will not be able to save themselves. The "new beginning," as he calls it, would take place after human history has ended apocalyptically. Moreover, it is possible that the gods will never come and only oblivion awaits us. The best we can do is engage in a kind of prayerful thought that prepares the way for these deities, thereby entreating or inviting them. In his last interview, which he instructed to be posthumously released, Heidegger seems to have the coming of a particular god in mind:

> But the greatest need of thought consists in this, that today, so far as I can see, there is still no thinker speaking who is 'great' enough to bring thought immediately and in clearly defined form before the heart of the matter [seine Sache] and thereby [set it] on its way. For us today, the greatness of what is to be thought is [all] too great...

> Philosophy will not be able to bring about a direct change of the present state of the world. This is true not only of philosophy but of all merely human meditations and endeavors. ... Only a god can save us now. ... I think the only possibility of salvation left to us is to prepare readiness, through thinking and poetry, for the appearance of the god or for the absence of the god during the decline: so that we do not, simply put, die meaningless deaths, but that when we decline, we decline in the face of the absent god.

> ...It is not simply a matter of just waiting until something occurs to man within 300 years, but rather to think forward without prophetic claims into the coming time in terms of the fundamental thrust of our present age that has hardly been thought through at all. Thinking is not inactivity, but is

itself by its very nature an engagement that stands in dialogue with the epochal moment of the world.[13]

While Heidegger is not explicit about just what "god" (lowercase "g") he has in mind, it is absolutely clear that he is envisioning a return to pagan spirituality. The teleology of Technoscience begins with Platonic idealism, whose will to truth is proto-Christian and takes an essential turn with the Jesuit Descartes; it then undergoes an inversion in Nietzsche that, as it were, turns it inside out and exposes its guts as "the will to power." Philosophy of the kind that Plato forwarded was destined to culminate in a technological science hell-bent on all-encompassing instrumentality and total objectification. So the god that Heidegger seeks is Pre-Platonic or Pre-Socratic. It is a god of what Nietzsche called "the tragic age of the Greeks," the age of Heraclitus and Aeschylus. Moreover, it is a god that has something to do with thinking ahead or having an anticipatory concern with the future, which the Greeks called *prometheia*.

In fact, Heidegger does once let slip the unspeakably holy name of the god whose return he wants us to prepare for. This happens in the infamous address that he gives when he assumes the position of Rector of the University of Freiburg on behalf of the Nazi Party. Note these lines from his speech, "The Self-Assertion of the German University":

All science is philosophy, whether it knows and wills it—or not. All science remains bound to that beginning of philosophy. From it science draws the strength of its essence, assuming that it still remains at all equal to this beginning.

Here we want to regain ... the original Greek essence of science for *our* existence.

An old story was told among the Greeks that Prometheus had been the first philosopher. Aeschylus has this Prometheus utter a saying that expresses

13   Martin Heidegger, "Nur noch ein Gott kann uns retten," ("Now Only A God Can Save Us") in *Der Spiegel*, 31 May 1976.

the essence of knowing: 'Knowing, however, is far weaker than necessity' (Prom. 514, ed. Wil.). That means that all knowing about things has always already been surrendered to the predominance of destiny and fails before it.

Precisely because of this, knowing must unfold its highest defiance. ... Science is the questioning standing of one's ground in the midst of the constantly self-concealing totality of what is.[14]

1.2 Thinking Beyond Heidegger

Prometheus and Atlas (Arktos, 2016) was not the first philosophical text to associate Heideggerian thought with Prometheus. Although I confess to having been unaware of it when I wrote that book, the French philosopher of technology, Bernard Stiegler, had already done so. Stiegler did not, however, go so far as I did, namely to suggest that Prometheus is "the god" who Heidegger believes "can save us now."

In *Time and Technics*, Stiegler explains how inorganic but organized beings, namely designed things, are a genre of beings between the organic life that is the domain of Biology and the inorganic beings that Physics focuses on.[15] This third class of beings is, moreover, related to the biological through a dynamic of "technical evolution" and also to the physical insofar as it has the potential for rupturing the continuum that defines events in space-time.[16] In both respects, the speed of innovatively produced things or designed devices involves a "process of deterritorialization" — an uprooting from, and even an annihilation of, *places* that were once proper to things and to the people(s) who meaningfully interacted with them.[17] The term

---

14   Martin Heidegger, "The Self-Assertion of the German University" (1933) in *Martin Heidegger and National Socialism* (Paragon House, 1990), 5–13.

15   Bernard Stiegler, *Technics and Time, 1: The Fault of Epimetheus* (Stanford University Press, 1998), 17.

16   Ibid.

17   Ibid.

"evolution" is not a mere analogy when it is employed in the conception of a "technical evolution" proper to inorganic but organized beings. Rather, as Stiegler puts it, "technics is the pursuit of life by means other than life."[18] In this sense also, crafted things or designed devices are a mediate phenomenon that is both more fundamental and also "older" than the phenomena that are the subject matters of the domains of Physics and Biology—namely inorganic beings and organic life forms. What Stiegler means by "older" is more "primordial" in the Heideggerian sense of ontological priority.

Technics is often thought of as supplementary or prosthetic, but Stiegler's analysis reveals it to be elementary.[19] The anticipation that is reified in the projection, planning, and programming of modern technology is actually nothing other than "the possibility of possibility" that is fundamental to our existence.[20] A "prosthesis" is "what is placed in front, that is, what is outside" but since prostheses are constitutive of human existence, "the being of humankind is to be outside itself."[21] As Heidegger had emphasized in many of his writings and lectures, this is, of course, what it literally means to ex–ist. To put it in mythological terms, as Stiegler does, "to make up for the fault of Epimetheus, Prometheus gives humans the present of putting them outside themselves."[22] This also means throwing them ahead of themselves by imagining (*mekhane*) and striving to realize what we imagine. Language and reason are existentially grounded on this being-outside and being-ahead of humans, so that *logos* is inextricable from *techne*.[23]

This is true of *logos* in all of the forms that it takes: "The *logos, qua* religion, *qua* politics, is (on the basis of the fault) wholly technical,

18   Ibid.
19   Ibid., 183.
20   Ibid.
21   Ibid., 193.
22   Ibid.
23   Ibid.

fruit of an originary incompleteness of technical being."²⁴ The *hermeneia* of hermeneutics is "made up unquestionably of *prometheia* and *epimetheia*."²⁵ It is because man is without the positive qualities of animals, and therefore fundamentally prosthetic, that humanity is also unbound by the natural predestination that drives animal life; consequently, man bears both the burden and the gift of innovative invention.²⁶ Stiegler comes right out and describes this being without qualities as a "Promethean condition" that he takes to be synonymous with what has been called "the human condition."²⁷

Stiegler characterizes his philosophy of technology as "a confrontation between the Heideggerian existential analytic and the myths of Prometheus and of Epimetheus in their most known versions (Hesiod, Aeschylus, Plato)."²⁸ This confrontation hinges on the concepts of *prometheia* and *epimetheia*, which are two fundamental modalities of "temporalization" or our existential relationship with time.²⁹ The ideas are from the tragic age of the Greeks, not only preceding Platonic metaphysics but also contradicting it in the essence of the protophilosophical mythology of Prometheus.³⁰ The archaic Greek mind in its astonishment at the incipient phenomenon of technics notices something about the Promethean *hubris* and "the violence of man against *phusis* when he considers himself a god" which is lost on more rational thinkers in the wake of Plato, such as Aristotle.³¹

The most prominent version of the Prometheus myth that includes his brother Epimetheus is the one presented by Plato in his dialogue *Protagoras*, to whom, not incidentally, classical authors attributed the

24 Ibid., 194.
25 Ibid., 201–202.
26 Ibid., 193.
27 Ibid., 199.
28 Ibid., 16.
29 Ibid., 16, 185.
30 Ibid., 185.
31 Ibid., 186.

maxim: "Man is the measure of all things." In this dialogue, Plato has Protagoras recount the myth as follows:

> Once upon a time, there existed gods but no mortal creatures. When the appointed time came for these also to be born, the gods … charged Prometheus and Epimetheus with the task of equipping them and allotting suitable powers [*dunameis*] to each kind. Now Epimetheus begged Prometheus to allow him to do the distribution himself— 'and when I have done it,' he said, 'you can review it.' So he persuaded him and set to work. In his allotment he gave to some creatures strength without speed, and equipped the weaker kinds with speed. Some he armed with weapons, while to the unarmed he gave some other faculty and so contrived means for their preservation. To those that he endowed with smallness, he granted winged flight or a dwelling underground; to those which he increased in stature, their size itself was a protection. *Thus he made his whole distribution on a principle of compensation, being careful by these devices that no species should be destroyed.* …
>
> Now Epimetheus was not a particularly clever person, and before he realized it he had used up all the available powers on the brute beasts, and being left with the human race [*non-aloga*] on his hands unprovided for, did not know what to do with them. While he was puzzling about this, Prometheus came to inspect the work, and found the other animals well off for everything, but man naked, unshod, unbedded, and unarmed, and already the appointed day had come, when man too was to emerge from within the earth into the daylight. Prometheus therefore, being at a loss to provide any means of salvation for man, stole from Hephaestus and Athena the gift of skill in the arts [*ten enteknen sophian*], together with fire—for without fire there was no means [*amekhanon*] for anyone to possess or use this skill—and bestowed it on man. … Prometheus, so the story says, thanks to Epimetheus, had later on to stand his trial for theft. (Plato, *Protagoras*, 320d–322a)[32]

We are, therefore, the "fruit of a double fault" as Stiegler puts it, "an act of forgetting, then of theft" for which Epimetheus and Prometheus are

---

32 Ibid., 187–188.

respectively responsible.[33] The forgetting of Epimetheus in this myth is an archaic understanding of the exceptionally unprepared, un-equipped, and vulnerable condition of human beings at birth as com-pared to all other animals.[34] It is almost as if we are born premature, naked, and without any means of defense, so that technical develop-ment is existentially fundamental to the human being. Without *techne* we cannot even survive, let alone thrive. Stiegler describes the fault of Prometheus as a "fall" and explicitly associates this with "the one that Heidegger's existential analytic will attempt to think."[35] Stiegler goes so far as to claim that "Heidegger's question, put from the very begin-ning in terms of a hermeneutic, moves toward, and is already moving within, the Promethean question."[36]

Prometheia, the mentality that defines Prometheus, is a thinking-ahead that advances with concern for the future and develops projects based on foresight: "*Prometheia* is the anticipation of the future, that is, of danger, foresight, prudence, and an essential disquiet: some-body who is *promethes* is someone who is worried in advance."[37] By contrast, *epimetheia*, which mentality is embodied by his idiot of a brother, Epimetheus, is an "unconcerned distraction" that learns only from the experience of failures and hardships that result from this, so that its 'wisdom' born of the folly of an idiot is always only an "after-thought."[38] It is "knowledge that arises from the accumulation of experience through the mediation of past faults."[39] Stiegler takes *epimetheia* to be that mode of being that Heidegger calls "withdrawal," concealment, or forgetfulness — the archaic Greek *lethomai*, from out of which the privative of *alethea* or "truth" is constructed.

---

33 Ibid., 188.
34 Ibid.
35 Ibid., 191.
36 Ibid., 199.
37 Ibid., 202.
38 Ibid., 16.
39 Ibid., 184.

Epimetheus accepts the *gift* of Pandora, the first woman, from
Zeus.[40] What is sealed up in Pandora's box or jar is not only all of the
ills that will afflict humanity, but also *elpis* — meaning both hope and
fear (as contrasted with *phobos*, which is fear in the sense of terror).[41]
With reference to the idea of "anticipation" in Heidegger's existential analytic of Dasein, Stiegler explains that "*Elpis* could be seen as
(the relation) to the indeterminate, that is (the anticipation of) the
future, and as such, "the essential phenomenon of time."[42] Stiegler
thinks that the meaning of "what occurs with Pandora is the jar, and
the meaning of the jar is *elpis*: anticipation, time … *temporality is
thought here not only in terms of mortality but also in terms of birth
qua sexual differentiation*."[43] It would follow that the reversal of sexual
differentiation is a necessary, even if not a sufficient, condition for the
attainment of that immortality hitherto reserved only for the gods.[44]
We will revisit this idea of alchemical androgyny in the next chapter.

Human existence involves a dialectic between "the Promethean
advance and the Epimethean withdrawal" and it is "their inextricability which gives mortals *elpis*, both hope and fear, which compensates
for their consciousness of irremediable mortality."[45] But would this
also be true of a race of immortals, or is it only characteristic of *human* existence? Is biotechnology a new form of alchemy that offers us
a path to finally becoming shamelessly Promethean?

Stiegler agrees with Heidegger that death is unknown to animals,
so that "being-towards-death" is existentially characteristic of a being "*between* god and beast, neither beast nor god, neither immortal
nor prone to perish, sacrificial beings…"[46] Animals may perish in

---

40 Ibid., 195.
41 Ibid., 197.
42 Ibid., 198.
43 Ibid., 196.
44 Ibid.
45 Ibid., 16.
46 Ibid., 198.

nature, or prey upon one another, and whole species of them might face a catastrophic extinction, but they "do not destroy themselves."[47] Another uniquely defining feature of human existence is that because of its radical dependence upon technics, the human being is prone to self-destruction: "Mortals, because they are prosthetic in their very being, are self-destructive."[48] For example, the wooden leg of Captain Ahab in *Moby Dick* is symbolic of the prostheses that render human existence uniquely dangerous and self-destructive.[49]

1.3 The Orgiastic End of All Things

The very idea of a "prosthesis" only makes sense in a context where things are clearly differentiated from persons. The evolution of technics confronts us with the spectre of the end of all things, in the sense of an annihilation of the distinction between things and persons that would be the *telos* — end or purpose — that culminates the destiny of Western metaphysics. Heidegger already went so far as to think that the structure of Being has no spatial matrix prior to the cultivation and construction of things. We are be-thinged [*bedingt*] or conditioned beings, and we should leave behind any presumption of an unconditioned ontological core.[50] The irony is that the Cartesian-Newtonian attempt to transform or translate all places or locales into abstract spaces ultimately brings about the end of all "things" as such.

In his essay "The Thing," Heidegger claims that a universal, mathematically conceived and precisely measurable spatial extension cannot accommodate "things" anymore than it can contain "places." For example, a wine jug that is being filled is no longer that "thing" it was once it is turned into a topological hollow, the air molecules of which

---

47 Ibid.

48 Ibid., 198.

49 Ibid., 198–199.

50 Heidegger, *Poetry, Language, Thought,* 179.

are displaced by a spreading liquid.[51] Heidegger points out that the meaning of "thing" in Old High German is *that-which-is-a-gathering-together*, a subject matter (related to the Greek *hypokeimenon*), by which he means to suggest it is the fourfold that the thing gathers together, and the fourfold of earth, man, sky, and gods that is occluded in the destruction of the thing.[52] In his reflections on "The Question Concerning Technology," Heidegger writes that "spaces receive their essential being from locales," and the locales in turn are able to be such only on account of *things* designed in such a way as to properly gather together and preserve the fourfold in a bounded, unevenly finite horizon.[53] The horizon of our so-called 'spatial' experiences of "nearness" and "remoteness" have this uneven character. "Nearness" and "remoteness" do not primarily signify intervals of intervening space. Only abstraction turns them into this.

In "The Thing," Heidegger elaborates on this by phenomenologically differentiating spatial nearness from the existential experience that he termed "de-severence" in *Being and Time*, whereby something is brought close to one by one's attention or concern no matter how far away it appears to be to an 'objective' observer.[54] With regard to "The Thing," Heidegger claims that technology's "frantic abolition of all distances brings no nearness; for nearness does not consist in shortness of distance. What is least remote from us in point of distance, by virtue of its picture on film or its sound on the radio, can remain far from us."[55] What is incalculably far from us in point of distance can be near to us. Short distance is not in itself nearness. Nor is great distance remoteness. Heidegger goes on to claim that the "merging of everything into" what he describes as "uniform distancelessness" is more "unearthly" than the "bursting apart" caused by the atom bomb, even

51 Ibid., 168.
52 Ibid., 172, 175.
53 Heidegger, *The Question Concerning Technology*, 356.
54 Martin Heidegger, *Being and Time* (Harper and Row Publishers, 1962), 134–148.
55 Heidegger, *Poetry, Language, Thought*, 163.

when the design of the latter is enhanced so as to transform it into a doomsday device capable of ending all life on Earth. The detonation of such devices cannot be more terrifying and unsettling than "the annihilation of the thing" that has long since been accomplished.[56]

In "The Question Concerning Technology," Heidegger describes this as "the profundity of the world shock that we [should] experience every hour..."[57] In "The Thing," Heidegger identifies the television, which in German is called *Fernseher* or "far-seer," as the epitome of this development. Note this passage from "The Thing":

> All distances in time and space are shrinking. Man now reaches overnight, by plane, places which formerly took weeks and months of travel. He now receives instant information, by radio, of events which he formerly learned about only years later, if at all. The germination and growth of plants, which remained hidden throughout the seasons, is now exhibited publicly in a minute, on film. Distant sites of the most ancient cultures are shown on film as if they stood this very moment amidst today's street traffic. Moreover, the film attests to what it shows by presenting also the camera and its operators at work. The peak of this abolition of every possibility of remoteness is reached by television, which will soon pervade and dominate the whole machinery of communication.[58]

The last line here is clearly envisioning the emergence of Cyberspace and its eventual predominance as the primary means of communication, one that also represents a culmination of the annihilation of what "distance" always meant for human existence. In Heidegger's view this fundamentally compromises "nearness," including and especially in the sense of intimate communion with others rather than mediated communication with them — even if this communication takes the form of cyber sex.

56 Ibid., 164.

57 Heidegger, *The Question Concerning Technology*, 157.

58 Heidegger, *Poetry, Language, Thought*, 163.

Günther Anders forwards Heidegger's contemplation of the transformative power of radio and television on our being-in-the-world at an existential level. Anders studied under Heidegger before emigrating to the United States in the 1940s. He is best known for "On Promethean Shame," published in 1956 as the first of four essays to appear in the book *The Obsolescence of Human Beings, Volume 1: On the Soul in the Age of the Second Industrial Revolution.*[59] We will come to this meditation on the Promethean and modern technology shortly. The second of the essays in that volume is titled "Die Welt als Phantom und Matrize: Philosophische Betrachtungen uber Rundfunk und Fernsehen," which was translated into English by Norbert Guterman and published in the magazine *Dissent* under the title "The World as Phantom and Matrix."[60] There can be little doubt that the title of this piece inspired the Wachowskis to name their masterpiece about the world as a simulacrum, *The Matrix.*

Let us begin with what Anders writes about the radio in this meditation on media and simulacra. Music played on the radio destroyed, in short order, the culture of bringing musicians into one's home.[61] Anders thinks that the radio already degrades our range of linguistic expression, and that as a consequence of it language has become cruder in every 'advanced' country.[62] This is not just a matter of eloquence, because our consciousness is fundamentally shaped by language.[63] Consequently, the impoverishment of language is a degradation of our selfhood. When we are together, we have less to say to each other, because each of us is tuned into what the anonymous public voice on

---

59 Günther Anders, "Promethean Shame" in *Prometheanism*, edited by Christopher John Müller (Rowman & Littlefield Publishers, 2016), 15.

60 Günther Anders, "The World as Phantom and Matrix" in *Dissent* 3.1 (Winter 1956).

61 Ibid., 18.

62 Ibid., 18–19.

63 Ibid., 19.

the radio is saying.[64] Our own expression is reduced to an occasionally interjecting commentary on this voice, and this modality becomes normal even when the radio is off. Not only does this damage the capacity for intellectual or aesthetic conversations amongst friends, or members of a family, it also damages the relationship between lovers.

Anders sees couples who bring a radio along on their outings, such as a walk by a riverside, not as akin to walking a dog but as akin to their being walked by the dog that, by analogy, is the radio set.[65] Even lovers, who are supposed to have the most intimate rapport, show this same horror of that vacuum which the radio has defined as the negative space (and time) opened up by its silence.[66] Couples even make love to the sound of the radio in the background. Unlike the torchbearers of Roman times, who would be hired to illuminate lovers in their bedchambers, the radio offers not only 'illumination' but also the warmth of assimilation into the public-ness of mass man — what Heidegger called *das Man* or "the They" — even in what is supposed to be the most intimately private moment shared by two individuals.[67]

The television effects an even more radical reorientation of our existence. Whereas movie theaters still brought families together for an outing, in a context where they would also encounter others in their society, the television atomizes the consumer of that mass 'culture' which it broadcasts.[68] The television set has replaced the family table or the hearth of the home, around which the kindred of two or more generations would gather to speak with one another and entertain each other.[69] Whereas the family table had a centripetal force, Anders describes the television as impacting those gathered around

---

64   Ibid., 18.
65   Ibid.
66   Ibid.
67   Ibid.
68   Ibid., 14–15.
69   Ibid., 16–17.

it with a centrifugal force.[70] If they ever say anything to one another, while trying not to miss a moment of the 'show', this is an interruption in the process whereby the television isolates each of them. Each feels as if he is addressed personally, and addressed by personalities that — although they are in fact perfect strangers — have adopted a manner of communication that is as frank and "chummy" as what would be expected from a lifelong friend.[71] Not only newscasters and entertainers, but even public officials adopt this tone.[72] What this mirage of familiarity insidiously conceals is that the individual is being fundamentally conditioned as a mass man and a consumer of events that have been transformed into commodities: "When the event is no longer attached to a specific location and can be reproduced virtually any number of times, it acquires the characteristics of an assembly-line product; and when we pay for having it delivered to our homes, it is a commodity."[73] It is astonishing how it can be lost on people that the "program" is programming them.[74]

Things seen on the television screen are phantoms, but they become more real than what happens in the world outside the home that is now a box containing one's channel to 'the world.' Anders describes this experience of one-way visibility, without any possibility of interaction with this "phantom world," as something that turns each of us into a "Peeping Tom."[75] He writes:

> Since the world comes to us only as an image, it is half-present and half-absent, in other words, phantom-like; and we too are like phantoms. When the world speaks to us, without our being able to speak to it, we are deprived of speech, and hence condemned to be unfree. When the world is

70 Ibid., 17.
71 Ibid., 22–23.
72 Ibid., 22.
73 Ibid., 20.
74 Ibid., 18.
75 Ibid., 22.

perceivable, but no more than that, i.e., not subject to our action, we are
transformed into eavesdroppers and Peeping Toms.[76]

Such passages demonstrate a failure to imagine the interactivity of
media today, especially social media and multiplayer immersive simulations. Heidegger may have been more insightful when he predicted
that the mode of being of the motion picture would pervade *all forms
of communication*. That sounds more like virtual reality than the phenomenology of the increasingly disembodied television-viewer that
Anders offers us. Nevertheless, Anders does write insightfully about
television's transformation of our experience of place, and of our capacity to experience anything at all.

It used to be that one had to travel in order to gain life experience — and not travel on airplanes with television screens to standardized hotels with television sets that endeavor to level every different
locale into somewhere that makes you feel "at home."[77] By uprooting
the most disparate events from their proper places (and times), the
television delivers a 'world' of representations that is no longer an
authentic world at all. This annihilation of reality becomes complete
when what were once 'real events' are expected to conform, in advance, to the representations of them that have to be manufactured
like things on an assembly line.[78] This turns the event into a matrix for
the production of representations, such that the world as phantom has
perversely become the prototype for the manufacturing of 'reality' by
the demiurge of industrial machinery — in this case, the machinery
of the industry of television news and entertainment (which become
hardly distinguishable from one another).[79]

> When the actual event is socially important only in its reproduced form,
> i.e., as a spectacle, the difference between being and appearance, between

76   Ibid., 20.

77   Ibid., 20–21.

78   Ibid., 20.

79   Ibid.

reality and image of reality, is abolished. When the event in its reproduced form is socially more important than the original event, this original must be shaped with a view to being reproduced: in other words, the event becomes merely a master matrix, or a mold for casting its own reproductions. When the dominant experience of the world thrives on such assembly-line products, the concept 'the world' is abolished in so far as it denotes that *in which* we live. The real world is forfeited; the broadcasts, in other words, further an idealistic orientation.[80]

Anders describes this development (or devolution) as "idealistic" in the sense that "When the phantom becomes real, reality becomes a phantom."[81] This is also the most extreme and yet most insidiously unnoticeable form of alienation, which masquerades as the total familiarity of everything wherein nothing is alien: "When that which is remote becomes familiar, that which is familiar becomes remote. … Although we actually live in an alienated world, this world is presented to us in such a manner that it seems to exist for us, as though it were our own and like ourselves."[82] Anders evokes Descartes' deceiving demon in his characterization of how diabolical and demonic this destruction of the real world is: "Such a situation points to a mode of existence, a relation to the world so extraordinarily perverse that even Descartes' malicious demon would be incapable of devising a comparable deception."[83]

If "The World As Phantom and Matrix" is thinking toward the "demonic" possibility of Virtual Reality, then the essay "On Promethean Shame" that precedes it in *The Obsolescence of Human Beings* thinks ahead to the implications of biomechanics or what Anders calls "human engineering." Here Anders defines "Promethean shame" as "the shame when confronted by the humiliatingly high quality of

---

80 Ibid.

81 Ibid., 16–17.

82 Ibid., 16, 21–22.

83 Ibid., 21.

fabricated things (*selbst-gemachen Dinge*)."[84] Designed products are, through and through, immaculately designed, whereas people who are "naturally grown" by means of "the highly archaic process of procreation and birth" owe their existence "to the blind and uncalculated."[85] "Promethean" has usually been used to describe an attitude of defiance on the part of one who refuses to owe his existence to anyone else. Promethean pride is the sense that everything is ultimately one's own achievement, including one's self. It is epitomized by the modern will to "become a self-made man."[86] Consequently, Promethean shame involves a dialectical reversal wherein "the Prometheus of today" is indignant, not that he was made by a God or gods other than himself, to whom he would owe his existence, but because as someone who was naturally born and grown he was "not made at all" and is therefore inferior to everything fabricated in accordance with a design.[87]

Anders sees in this a reiteration of the scholastic Catholic heresy of the confusion of creator and creation, and the idolatrous worship of the created artifact rather than the creator who deserves credit for it. He thinks that Promethean shame in the face of the supposed superiority of manufactured products is a degradation of humanity, wherein human beings deny themselves the recognition that they deserve as the creators of these things.[88] Promethean shame involves a vicious circle, a cycle wherein the more humans fail to keep apace with their machines, the more machines are produced to mediate the relationship between humans and the machines that they are incapable of manning.[89] This, in turn, makes humans even more miserably incompetent in managing an intricate bureaucracy that eventually becomes a network of machines and sub-machines. Anders would not live to

---

84 Anders, "Promethean Shame" in *Prometheanism*, 30.

85 Ibid., 30.

86 Ibid., 31.

87 Ibid.

88 Ibid., 32.

89 Ibid., 39.

see the "internet of things" that is now taking shape, but he would
have seen it as the culmination of what Heidegger called the *Gestell*.

What Marx had called the alienation of labor has reached a
qualitatively different level. Anders points out that even those with
expertise in the production of certain designed objects, let alone the
mere workers involved in the mechanized production process, do
not identify with these products.[90] No one sees these devices as the
product of their "own labor." The labor and even the creative ingenuity
of the human individual seems alienated from the "world of machines
and products as a whole" to the point where it renders ridiculous
the "Promethean glory" that once hallowed the productive power of
mankind or the creative vision of the genius. Anders makes the witty
observation that if anyone were to react to the fantastic capabilities of
a machine by exclaiming something like "Aren't we great guys, to be
capable of this!" that person would be seen as "a clown." The normal
reaction is to be as disturbed as one is astonished, and while shaking
one's head as if put to shame by one's relative inability, murmur something like, "My god, it's incredible what *it* — the machine — can do!"[91]

Promethean shame is much more than another iteration of the
phenomenon of the "reification and objectification of the human."[92]
Marx and others who analyzed this phenomenon understood this
treatment of the human being, as if the human being were a thing,
as a dehumanization, which is lamented by those same objectified
individuals who are subjected to it. By contrast, the person who feels
Promethean shame laments being a person and has contempt for himself as such. He wants to be as much like a perfectly designed thing as
possible, and feels shame before the superiority of these things that
he idolizes.[93] Reification and objectification have reached a new level,

90 Ibid., 33.

91 Ibid., 34.

92 Ibid., 35.

93 Ibid.

not just quantitatively but in terms of a qualitative transformation, which defies the logic of a Marxian analysis.

This also involves a reversal of the classic economic relationship between supply and demand. Instead of the supply produced through mechanized industry meeting a human demand for certain things, what is supplied makes demands on the human being to conform itself to the supply.[94] Furthermore, the supplied things inculcate desires in the persons on whom they make demands, which means that what is being supplied is generating its own demands for what it will supply in the future. Consumers are, as Anders sees it, "terrorized or flattered into their needs" by the machinery of a production process, which captivates the human and makes him duty-bound "to supply everything the machine needs to function as well as it 'could' function."[95] The charge of being a "luddite" is enough to silence any critics of this dreadful situation, or at least to stop the public from listening to them.[96]

Anders thinks that in our epoch what it means "to live as one with the gods" is to attain "co-substantiality with technological instruments" rather than "to accept the stubbornness and inability of the human body as to settle once and for all for human inferiority and retardation."[97] Where he is badly mistaken is in believing that this "remains wishful thinking" since for "humans, true integration into machinery" is not possible, insofar as "Machines are once and for all ontologically superior to beings who are born."[98] Anders seems to have no concept of a machine that is born and capable of growth, nor of how genetic engineering or "biomechanics" could transform mankind.

---

94 Ibid., 43.
95 Ibid.
96 Ibid., 44.
97 Ibid., 40.
98 Ibid.

Nevertheless, he goes on at length about a "human engineering" that is intended to modify men in order to integrate them into machinery. Anders aptly describes the "torture-like experiments" of human engineering as an "investiture" comparable to archaic initiation rituals and rites of passage.[99] He remarks: "*The experiments that make up 'human engineering' are* in fact *the initiation rites of the robotic age.*"[100] The neophytes who endure this ordeal are aiming to leave the "childhood" of their humanity behind. Anders sees the old Marxist concern with how workers are being exploited by their working conditions as quaintly naïve and harmless by comparison to this "*climax of all possible dehumanization.*"[101]

The purpose of "human engineering" is to identify the weaknesses of the human being through tests of its corporeal limits, to catch "soft parts" in their inadequacy, and then to train or replace them in order to better adapt people to "the demands of machines."[102] These experiments effect a transcendence of the human being into "the realm of the hybrid and artificial" through a metamorphosis that aims to strip humans "of all that is fatal."[103] In Anders' original German, the word *fatal* also means "really embarrassing." Anders sees this torturous and "masochistic" process as Puritanical, in an apparent attempt to connect the "residual energy generated by the puritan hatred of the body" with the so-called Protestant work ethic that fueled the Industrial Revolution.[104] The technology of human engineering aims to radically reshape the body in ways that fit the ever-changing specifications of various machines. Anders uses an almost alchemical metaphor to describe how the pre-given human form is melted down into prime matter and re-formed into something that can fit into the assemblage

99 Ibid., 44.
100 Ibid.
101 Ibid.
102 Ibid., 41.
103 Ibid., 42.
104 Ibid.

of machinery, which process is also a deconstruction of the putative *eidos* or ideal form of humanity:

> Moreover, every pre-given form turns out to be 'wrong' and 'already pressed into the wrong shape,' because in each instance the actual form machines require varies. In 'human engineering' people attempt to 'melt down' this 'misshapen form' in order to retroactively source the material from which the required shape at any particular time can still be made.
>
> The fact of 'having already been formed in the wrong shape' is the main defect that the human engineer seeks to address and the main reason for 'Promethean shame.' It is only the main source, however, for he has many deficiencies that 'generate shame.' It would be impossible to compile a list of all these shameful shortcomings because this would correspond to a list of the virtues of all existing and potential machines.[105]

Anders sees Promethean shame as ironically more presumptuous than Promethean pride. He sees it as "unreasonable to dispute that the attempt to turn us humans into machine-like beings is monstrous."[106] For him, that goes without saying. But what Anders finds really appalling is that the "human engineer" has an attitude that is "self-deprecating" at the same time as it is overconfident. It is an attitude of "arrogant self-degradation" and "hubristic humility."[107] That makes it in some ways similar to the attitude that leads to a serious attempt at suicide. Suicide has been banned by the 'revealed' religions because the suicidal man is arrogant enough to assume that he is his own property to do away with, in disregard of the debt of gratitude that he owed to his creator. Meanwhile, the suicidal person is also beyond humble; he is in fact so self-deprecating that he is ready to do away with himself. However, the will to "the annihilation of the human *as* human" is even more hubristic than suicide, because whereas a suicidal person wills to choose the time of something that will happen anyway, by the

---

105 Ibid., 51.
106 Ibid., 49.
107 Ibid.

decree of God or Nature or Fate — namely his death — the "human engineer ... invents something new."[108] This is really what Anders cannot forgive, because in his view it is equivalent to the incarnation of a Gnostic demiurge by means of which humanity enslaves itself:

> To the injuries he must expect from above, to hardship, illness, ageing and death he now masochistically adds a further one: self-reification. This is how one might imagine a theological account reflecting on this in the year 2000: 'Because the daemon or Marcionist God who condemned humans to a machine-like existence or turned them into machines did not exist, humanity invented one. Yes, humans were even presumptuous enough to cast themselves in the role of this additional deity. They assumed this role, however, only to damage themselves in ways that they could not suffer from any other gods. Humans turned themselves into masters only to find a new way to become slaves.'
>
> It may be true that humans are doing all this in the blind hope, or at least on the pretext, that this self-reification will reduce or even abolish all other forms of human frailty and degradation. But what counts are not reasons, but, rather, what is actually done: in order to combat the limitation of their liberty, humans limit themselves in a new way.[109]

It never occurs to Anders that his logic is faulty — or that his 'argument' is emotional moralism devoid of any sound logic — since, if it were indeed possible to "reduce or even abolish" human limitations such as "hardship, illness, aging" and other "forms of human frailty and degradation," then the technological transformation of the human condition would not be just another degradation, namely that of "self-reification." What if all of this is not a "blind hope," but an achievable Posthuman future?

Anders claims not to confuse the existent or the natural order of things with the "good" by interpreting it as a "preordained order of things" such that "what 'is as it is' ... must so be.'"[110] He also denies

---

108 Ibid., 49–50.

109 Ibid., 50.

110 Ibid., 47.

being "someone who infers what is allowed and forbidden from the given order of things."[111] In an effort not to appear naïve, Anders even goes so far as to admit that because "of the natural sciences, the world has transformed itself for us into a thing that is 'beyond good and evil.'"[112] He is clearly glossing Nietzsche when he adds that "moral problems, and not only theoretical 'problems,' but above all *our own* '*moral*' and '*immoral*' *deeds*, are now, whether we like it or not, *drifting without roots in the ocean of morally indifferent being.*"[113] The reference is to Nietzsche's description, in *The Gay Science*, of the situation in which we find ourselves after having murdered God.

Since "nature itself is clearly open to mutation" Anders supposedly recognizes that it is not legitimate for him "to regard the form (*eidos*) or morphological fixedness of existing 'species' (the 'human' species included) as 'sacrosanct' or 'good' … or condemn their transformation as a 'cosmic prohibition.'"[114] Here is the key passage on which Anders stakes his argument in *On Promethean Shame*:

No, the alteration of our body is not fundamentally new and vile because we are abandoning our 'morphological destiny' or transcending the assigned natural limitation of our capabilities. It is despicable, rather, because we are undergoing this transformation of the self for the sake of machines and because we employ these as blueprints and models for our own modification. We hence relinquish ourselves as our measure as humans and with this gesture we either restrict or give up our freedom."[115]

In other words, Promethean shame in the face of putatively superior machines is a perverse devolution of the classical Promethean hubris of making man the measure of all things and seeing the human being as the creator of himself—i.e. man as made in the image of

111 Ibid.
112 Ibid., 48.
113 Ibid.
114 Ibid.
115 Ibid.

Prometheus, who is none other than the archetypal Man — with no debt owed to Zeus or any other deities.

The most striking example that Anders uses to illustrate Promethean shame concerns General Douglas MacArthur. During the Korean War, MacArthur advocated the use of nuclear weapons in order to secure victory. The President and the Pentagon questioned whether this was a sound strategic decision, and they put this question to a computer — or what they at that time called an "electric brain."[116] When Anders writes that these men "transferred the responsibility and answerability" to the computer, the word "answerability" is a translation of *uber-antwortet* in German and a reference to the idea of *Überantwortung* or "being delivered over and made answerable" in Heidegger's *Being and Time*, specifically his discussion of existential "thrownness" and "facticity."[117]

What Anders finds particularly remarkable is that the computer could not answer any questions having to do with whether MacArthur's proposed strategy, or even the war in general, was a just or unjust war.[118] All ethical considerations had to be set aside. Instead the question was put to the electric brain in the only terms that it would be able to 'understand' — or rather to calculate and analyze. They asked whether MacArthur's strategy would be economically profitable or unprofitable. The computer came back with the answer that MacArthur's strategy for winning against both North Korean and Chinese communists would result in a nuclear Third World War that would be financially ruinous for the United States. It might destroy the American economy, even if a "victory" were secured on the battlefield or in the ideological conflict with Communism.[119] So for the first time in history, a decision as consequential as the very survival of

---

116 Ibid., 58–59.

117 Ibid., 58.

118 Ibid., 60.

119 Ibid., 60–61.

humanity was deferred to a computer whose judgment was accepted over that of a five-star General. Anders contemplates the tremendous and terrifying significance of this development in terms of a perverse rupture in the ontological relationship between the thing and persons:

> It is irrelevant that the machine's verdict on this occasion was a veto and a reprieve, for it still constituted *a death sentence, precisely because the source of possible reprieve had been transferred to a thing.* The status of humanity was not decided by the machine's positive or negative answer but rather by the fact that this question had actually been submitted to the thing and the answer abided by.[120]

MacArthur was so humiliated that he resigned from the military but, as Anders recounts, that is not what makes this such a striking example of Promethean shame. MacArthur rejoined the sphere of civilian life by accepting a job as an executive of Remington Rand, the corporation that made the UNIVAC computer that humiliated him.[121] What makes this an example of Promethean shame is that it is humanity that took decisive responsibility, and in this case even answerability for its own existence, away from itself to put it in the 'hands' of a machine:

> After all, the power wresting the decision from MacArthur was not some superhuman authority, no 'Moira,' 'Tyche,' 'God' or 'history,' but *humanity itself.* In a sense humanity used its right hand to rob its left, offering up the booty — its own conscience and freedom to decide — on the altar of machines. With this, humanity proved that it had submitted itself to this man-made calculating robot and was willing to accept this machine as a substitute for its own conscience and acknowledge it as an oracle-machine and even as a machinic eye of providence. ... *For the first time humanity didn't feel any shame at publicly humiliating itself.*[122]

---

120 Ibid., 61.
121 Ibid.
122 Ibid., 59.

Anders concludes this example by looking at MacArthur's decision to
become an executive at Remington Rand through the lens of Hegel's
dialectical analysis of mastery and slavery in *The Phenomenology
of Spirit*.[123] It is his contention that by putting himself in a decision-
making position at the corporation that manufactured the computer
entrusted with the decision that had been his to make during the
Korean War, MacArthur was a former master who had been reduced
to slavery, now attempting to become the "master of the master" in a
machination that only serves to underline the profundity of his humiliation and the depth of Promethean shame.

Shame is a phenomenon that undergoes a dialectical reversal. The
person who is ashamed wants to disappear or become invisible, to
"sink into the ground" as it were, but in view of the impossibility of
this, she conceals the shame by appearing brazen and assuming the
attitude that "I couldn't care less."[124] Shame is a reflexive act that fails,
because the self encountered in this act seems not to be oneself but
rather an "it."[125] For this reason shame never comes to an end in the
sense of being able to "get over it." Instead, it has a quality similar to
distraught astonishment, confusion, despair, and disorientation.[126]
Unlike sadness, it does not fall over one gradually, because it lacks the
reflective capacity of sadness; it overcomes a person in an instant, the
instant in which one feels one's will to self-determination frustrated
by an "impotence" and "inability" that feels "fatal"—in the sense of
a fate that one can do even less about than the fatality of one's eventual death.[127] It also builds on itself frenetically, as shame about being
ashamed.[128]

123 Ibid., 62.
124 Ibid., 35.
125 Ibid., 63.
126 Ibid., 63, 67.
127 Ibid., 66.
128 Ibid., 67.

Shame has a "double intentionality" that is directed not only toward the self (which it never successfully encounters as itself), but also toward an authority before which one feels ashamed.[129] It has what Anders calls a "*coram*," a Latin term meaning "in the presence of" or "before," as in standing before the law or being in the presence of the public. The authority is unsolicited and therefore evaded, so that the intentionality of shame is actually a "negative intentionality."[130] Anders notes that neither the *coram* nor negative intentionality have ever been properly analyzed in phenomenology.

Shame is a perpetual possibility, because there is no act that is truly private. The *coram* is intrinsic to the structure of consciousness; this fact was missed by Edmund Husserl and other phenomenologists whose analyses ran the risk of sinking into solipsism because they did not recognize that any act, "even if the act takes place in private," makes "reference to a particular social-world (*Mitwelt*) on which it counts and before which it takes place or wants to pass unobserved."[131] This was a key insight of Heidegger, particularly in his revolutionary exposition of *Mitsein* (or "Being-with" others) in *Being and Time*.

Negative intentionality was overlooked by Husserl partly because it was assumed by him and other phenomenologists in his school, such as Sartre, that the ego was radically free because its intentional structure was always active.[132] In a way that brings Sigmund Freud's ideas on the unconscious to mind, Anders suggests that the structures of the ego analyzed by these phenomenologists were only the tip of the iceberg, so to speak. As Heidegger understood, "the ego also withdraws into itself (in the manner of a snail) and intentionality only gains its meaning in coordination with this countermovement; the ego does not only see, it is also seen; it does not only intend, it is also

---

129 Ibid., 63.

130 Ibid., 64.

131 Ibid.

132 Ibid.

the object of intention, for example, when it is pursued or chased."[133] That from which one flees cannot be legitimately described as an "intentional object," unless one wants to speak of negative intentionality. Shame also has this kind of negative or "two-way" intentionality, "because it turns its back on the authority in front of which it feels ashamed."[134] Anders claims that what the ashamed person "wants is not to be seen."[135] In his view, this "differs so fundamentally from what is usually called 'intentionality' that one ought to actually invent a new term to describe it."[136]

Shame is fundamentally relevant to the Promethean insofar as the Promethean attitude is the ultimate expression of the human "aspiration to freedom," the expression in which it is revealed that this aspiration "by its very nature knows no scale and is without measure."[137] For the Promethean soul, "to be partially free is not enough."[138] The Promethean ethos is only an epitome of the more general psychological fact that, as Anders puts it, the self (*das Ich*) "desires to be absolutely free, individual through and through, nothing but itself."[139] Anders charges that this "overstretched aspiration is 'pathological'" because "it cannot be sustained in the long run" on account of the fact that "what Freud called the 'id' (*das Es*)" is encountered at "the limits of its own freedom, individuality and self-confidence."[140]

When Anders describes the Id as an "ontic gift," he surely means "gift" not only in the sense of "what is 'given'" or "everything pre-individual … that the self is part of without being able to do anything

---

133 Ibid.

134 Ibid.

135 Ibid., 65.

136 Ibid.

137 Ibid., 66.

138 Ibid.

139 Ibid.

140 Ibid.

about it."[141] He is also suggesting that it is a poison, which is what *gift* means in German. It is an "ontic" gift because it is what is given by the contingencies of one's birth and environment in the pre-individuated matrix of consciousness, what one inherits and is burdened with having been shaped by, on an unconscious level deeper than the will. It poisons any putatively pure or transparent ontological relationship to oneself.

The expression, "it's nothing to be ashamed of, because you can't help it" is idiotic. One is ashamed of precisely what one cannot help, what is out of one's control to do anything about.[142] Anders gives the example of a hunchback who is ashamed of his hump, despite having been born with the deformity. Shame "erupts" from out of suddenly realizing that one is not only oneself but also something else that one feels one can do nothing about.[143] There is a deep dissociation at work here, wherein the one who is ashamed is not ashamed of a bad deed that she feels responsible for, but rather ashamed at being identical to that one — that thing — the it or "id" — which committed the deed.[144] The ashamed person ultimately feels chained to this thing, and after trying to futilely escape it, goes down or sinks under together with it in the most defeatist and despairing way imaginable.[145]

This is why we meet with figures of speech such as wanting "the ground to open up and swallow" one or "to sink into the ground" — neither of which, in Anders view, are mere metaphors.[146] The "ground" in question here is the existential ground, the ontological structure of the self and world. In relation to the Promethean, and the titanic in general, this calls to mind not only the fall from heaven

---

141 Ibid.

142 Ibid., 67.

143 Ibid.

144 Ibid.

145 Ibid.

146 Ibid.

but the imprisonment underground, the chaining of the defiant titans in the abyss beneath the Earth.

Anders sees the shame that is associated with sexuality, and specifically with the genital area, as the best known and most acute type of shame.[147] What he has in mind is the uncontrollable quality of sexual arousal, and being ashamed at having been so passionately overcome by sexual desire that one is beside oneself (and therefore, no longer in control of oneself). He elaborates on this at length:

> Once one has grasped the basic condition of the one who is ashamed, and has understood that this disorientation and despair is brought on by the recognition that freedom and individuation are limited, then it is evident why *sexual shame* has time and again ended up being regarded as *the quintessential* form of shame. Sex and that which pertains to the genus is the pre-individual sphere *par excellence*. Its realm lies beyond choice and freedom and as such it provides the pre-eminent 'it,' which does not belong to the individual *qua* individual. ...
>
> This ambiguity, or, this 'dialectic' fact if you will, is just the reason why one's sex is a pudendum, why it is something of which one is ashamed. Inasmuch as individuals are sexed-beings, beings who 'belong' to a sex and who 'long,' they are not master of themselves and are hence not 'themselves' and not free. In a most ambiguous manner they are *at once themselves and not themselves*, and thus the formula according to which we have begun to conceive shame ... is confirmed: shame is a disorientation of human beings who are forced to find an 'it' instead of an 'I' and laboriously and futilely try to identify themselves with themselves completely.[148]

Anders thinks that only the shame of a child is as "elemental" as sexual shame.[149] The child hides behind the skirts of his mother, or tries to disappear behind his father, when he is addressed, because he knows that the "I" being addressed by an adult "*is* not yet me" and "*I* am not

---

147 Ibid., 34.

148 Ibid., 67–68.

149 Ibid., 68.

yet a self."[150] The same kind of failed reflexivity is exhibited here as in other examples of shame, but more acutely, since the child is actually predominately the "it" and instead of being ashamed on account of encountering the "it" in the self, the child is ashamed of what "it" is from out of a spectral self that has not even cohered yet.[151]

In the case of Promethean shame, the authority before whom one is ashamed is not a person but a thing — a machine.[152] It is false to assume that "eyeless" machines are blind and therefore incapable of being encountered as "awe inspiring powers" (tremenda) before which one could be ashamed.[153] "The world is not without eyes."[154] It is interesting to note how Anders seems not to even be able to imagine that there would someday be a world where machines literally do have eyes, and people are under the ubiquitous surveillance of things permeated by the kind of authority before which one could be ashamed.[155]

Anders claims that before being indoctrinated by theoretical knowledge regarding epistemology and cognition, human beings are predisposed to believe that everything they see also sees them.[156] He thinks that primitive cultures, and unschooled people, experience visibility as a reciprocal relationship. He claims that this view could be supported with "countless pieces of empirical evidence," but he only offers the fact that "Robinson did not walk around naked either" in a reference to the story of Robinson Crusoe being stranded on a desert island.[157] He also cites the prevalence in poetry of statements such as "the mountain peak is 'facing us' with menace" or "the moon is 'looking down on us kindly.'" Anders claims that these are not mere

150 Ibid., 70.
151 Ibid.
152 Ibid., 71.
153 Ibid.
154 Ibid., 73.
155 Ibid., 74.
156 Ibid.
157 Ibid.

metaphors, but atavisms of the pre-theoretical experience of humans. He thinks that it is "quite irrelevant" whether one wants to call this experience of mutual visibility "animism" or "anthropomorphism."[158]

Anders explicitly connects the "it" encountered by the self in shame to Heidegger's concept of *das Man* or the "They" in Section IV of *Being and Time*.[159] This is the "faceless public" that, for the most part, dictates what one does from within oneself as an internalized voice. "*They* say that … *one* ought to do … or not do … such and such." Both the *they* and the *one* are as anonymous as they are authoritative and universal in this formulation, which implicitly governs not only social life but also private conduct for most people most of the time. Anders has this to say about Heidegger's concept of mass man, with specific reference to Section 9 of *Being and Time*:

> When 'Dasein,' at the beginning of *Being and Time*, asks about its 'who?,' and finds itself, even though it crystalizes into a 'self' in asking this question, as already being constituted by the 'impersonal public' Heidegger calls '*das Man,*' then 'Dasein' discovers itself as an 'it.' In fact, the action *Being and Time* portrays (in the form of a theoretical ontology) is nothing other than a systematic fight against shame. *Being and Time* is about the attempt of the 'I' (which is ashamed-of-itself) to overcome the disgrace of being an 'it' and to become 'itself.'[160]

In Promethean shame, the "it" that is encountered is the machine that we either have to work alongside or into the workings of which we have to be incorporated, integrated, or assimilated.[161] One is therefore ashamed of encountering this "it" as what is and is not oneself, in a way that is comparable to the sexual shame of encountering a part of oneself that one cannot entirely subjugate to conscious control. The self does not measure up to this "it of the technological device (*das*

---

158 Ibid.

159 Ibid., 76.

160 Ibid., 93.

161 Ibid., 76.

Apparat-Es)."[162] Furthermore, this technological it stands in a particular relationship to the primal it that becomes a cause for sexual shame. Anders sees these two as parts of a vice that is crushing the self from both directions:

> We can, in a sense, picture the human being — and this is now truly only an image — as clamped between two brackets, as if constrained by two forces that both challenge the 'self': on the one side the human is constrained by the 'natural it' (by the body, sex and species, and so forth) and on the other side by the 'artificial' (bureaucratic and technological) 'it of the technological device.' The space left open for the 'self' is already very narrow today; and because the 'it of the technological device' encroaches on this space even further, this space is getting smaller, while the danger that the 'self' is crushed by these two colossal non-individual forces is daily increasing. With every day that passes hope seems more justified — yes hope, because millions hope that this catastrophe will happen and that a technological totalitarianism will set in. When this outcome is finally achieved — tomorrow or the day after — the final triumph will belong exclusively to the machine. In its greed to devour everything and especially that which is *alien* to it, the machine will not only have incorporated the 'self,' but also the other 'it': the body.
>
> Today technological devices are already trying their best in this respect. The saying that the machine is 'getting at us and our bodies' is merely an image, for actually it is 'getting into us.' It even attempts to overpower our sexuality in order to include it in its domain.[163]

The last line here is particularly revealing of the sense in which Anders is concerned with a "grind[ing] up [of] the 'self,' [which is] caught between a mechanical system that has become orgiastic and an organism that has become mechanical."[164] Throughout the whole text of "On Promethean Shame" one gets the sense that the unspoken catalyst of Anders' concern with shame over our relative impotence in the face of the competence of mechanical devices is some kind of

---

162 Ibid.

163 Ibid.

164 Ibid., 77.

anxiety over sex machines, such as robotic phalluses, and how they threaten to impact human existence on the most intimate level of the erotic rapport between lovers. He remains unable to contemplate the total abolition of the thing in its alienation from man, through the orgiastic fusion of things with post-human beings.

The paintings of the Swiss-German artist H.R. Giger are full of images of humanoids hybridized with machines in ways that empha-size the totally shameless recognition, and embrace, of every form of sexual desire and erotic ecstasy.[165] There is no longer an "it" (or *id*) that is encountered as a "thing" other than oneself by a conscious ego alienated from "it." This also means that the Posthuman being has fully identified with designed devices, which are deeply integrated into our future biomechanical existence, so that Promethean shame has dialectically reverted to Promethean pride.

Giger's darkly Promethean art, which we will return to in the next chapter, anticipates the overcoming of what Anders sees as the most extreme form of "alienation." Giger's paintings depict the overcom-ing of alienation both from machinery and from fellow humans — or humanoids — who are shown in orgiastic communion. It is not at all incidental that Giger was chosen as the principal designer for the film *Alien* (1979), and that his "biomechanical" vision remained definitive of the aesthetic of that entire franchise up through the prequel that Ridley Scott aptly titled *Prometheus* (2012). Anders would no doubt have been horrified to see Giger's paintings and sculptures, espe-cially the ones involving extreme sexuality. These alchemical works, such as Giger's *Necronomicon*, repudiate Anders' argument in *The Obsolescence of Human Beings* by expressing a seamless fusion of the most primordially bestial and biological elements of human existence with a machinery that does not degrade human agency, but enhances the horizon of intelligence, consciousness, and will to a preternatu-rally superhuman level.

---

165 H.R. Giger, *H.R. Giger's Necronomicon* (Morpheus International, 1993).

CHAPTER 2

The End of Humanity

THE IDEA OF TRANSHUMANISM is inextricable from the concept of a coming technological singularity. "Trans" in the term "Transhuman" signifies a transition beyond the human condition and into some Posthuman form of existence. This could also be conceived of as a transcendence of the merely human in favor of a superhuman way of being. The singularity is the single most definable point of transition, marking the end of human history and the beginning of a "higher history," as Friedrich Nietzsche put it, which can hardly be imagined from this side of the catastrophe.

The term catastrophe, in the precise mathematical sense in which it was employed by Rene Thom, is appropriately descriptive here, insofar as what lies beyond the singularity cannot be extrapolated in an anticipatory fashion based on past developments in the same way as possible futures have hitherto been, more or less successfully, projected on the basis of interpreting the developmental dynamics of past history. What is supposed to bring about this catastrophe is a convergent advancement of technologies with the capacity to transform everything about our existence that has, until now, defined the fundamental parameters of the "human" condition, irrespective of cultural differences between various societies.

The physicist and mathematician John von Neumann appears to have coined the term "singularity" to express this catastrophic transition into Posthuman being. As early as the 1950s, von Neumann wrote: "The ever accelerating progress of technology ... gives the appearance of approaching some essential singularity in the history of the race beyond which human affairs, as we know them, could not continue."[1] It is worthy of note that von Neumann was one of the strongest advocates of an interpretation of quantum theory that regarded consciousness as essential to physical processes and therefore fundamental to the cosmos. This means that the reductively materialistic Transhumanists and advocates of the Singularity in our time are deviating from the original conception of Singularity.

The opening section of this chapter begins by tracing the idea of Transhumanism and the technological Singularity back to Russian Cosmists such as Nikolai Fedorov and Konstantin Tsiolkovsky. These men certainly did not share the overly reductionist view of engineering superhuman intelligence that is championed by materialistic Transhumanists today, such as Ray Kurzweil. Rather, Russian Cosmism was a movement as spiritual as it was techno-scientific. Its aim was to use technology in order to bring about the resurrection of the dead, and to populate the entire cosmos with eugenically engineered cosmonauts who would transform outer space into the "Kingdom of Heaven." After noting that Fedorov was also an early contributor to Iranian Studies in Russia, it is argued that he developed his Cosmic Futurism from out of an interpretation of the teachings of Zarathustra. In this light, it is hardly a coincidence that the man who coined the term "Transhumanism" was also an Iranian: Fereidoun M. Esfandiary, better known as FM-2030. Esfandiary also described himself as a "Futurist," and his proposal that the dichotomy of Left-wingers and Right-wingers ought to be replaced with a movement of

---

1   Vinge, Vernor. "The Technological Singularity" in More, Max and Natasha Vita, *The Transhumanist Reader* (Wiley-Blackwell, 2013), 366.

"Up-wingers" recalls the strange fusion of far right-wing and progressive elements in Italian Futurism.

At this point, the relationship between Futurism and Fascism is explored, as well as the roots of the vision for mankind's technological transformation into the Superman that we see in Right-wing thinkers such as F.T. Marinetti, Ernst Jünger, and Friedrich Nietzsche. Particular emphasis is placed on Nietzsche's critique of the Hegelian and Marxist accounts of historical progress, and his counterproposal of a revised version of Darwinian evolution wherein the human being is seen as a transitional state between the "ape" and the "Superman." Nietzsche thought that this would involve a bifurcated artificial speciation of humanity into *two different and reciprocal* Posthuman types, a masterful race of Supermen and a subhuman race of biomechanical robots. This brings us to a consideration of the Robotics Revolution, Nanotechnology, Genetic Engineering, and other tangible Transhuman technologies. Together with Vernor Vinge, I argue that strong Artificial Intelligence is only one of four pathways to the Singularity, and the one that, in its reductionism, least acknowledges the origin of Transhumanism in Alchemy and the occult dimensions of our transformation beyond the human condition.

The second section of this chapter delves into the relationship between Transhumanism and Alchemy, with *Frankenstein* as its point of departure. The genealogy of this immortal tale of *The Modern Prometheus* is traced back to Percy Shelley's alchemical studies and other writings, wherein his Promethean vision is expressed. In particular, Shelley's concern with alchemical androgyny is identified as an often overlooked aspect of the Promethean quest to recreate man and attain godlike power. Drawing on both Greek and Hebrew mythologies and religious scriptures, with which Shelley was familiar, I show how the will to alchemically achieve Androgyny is integral to the quest to reverse the fall or rebuild the tower of Babel. Shelley was by no means alone in this belief. It was at the core of the nineteenth century Uranian movement, whose intellectual, literati, and artistic members saw the spike in hermaphroditism during their epoch as a sign that humanity was undergoing an archetypal metamorphosis. The psychical researcher Frederick Myers' ideas of "preverts" who display characters of the "Imaginal" (future, perfected) form of humanity in advance becomes relevant in this regard. This idea is further developed through the extensive research of Michael Murphy, the founder of Esalen.

I argue that this psychical vision of *The Future of the Body* has to be considered part of the Transhumanist project, together with more material technologies of transformation. Transhumanism is the culmination of the "Promethean ambition" that characterized men like Cornelius Agrippa, Paracelsus, and Albertus Magnus. These are men that Shelley portrays as the true teachers of Dr. Frankenstein from beyond the grave. Unlike those who thought that alchemy can only pervert nature, or perhaps perfect nature by working with it, "Victor" Frankenstein was among the alchemists who believed in *victoriously* overpowering and controlling nature. Frankenstein's monster is the alchemical homunculus that epitomized the ultimate heresy for which alchemists in the Medieval and Renaissance periods were burned at the stake: the will to create, not just artificial life, but a rational soul on demand.

The third and final section of the chapter raises this project of Frankenstein up to a cosmic level and hurls it decades into the future. Five films by Ridley Scott are interpreted with a view to exploring the relationship between the Promethean creator and the creature made in his own image. These are *Alien* (1979), *Blade Runner* (1982), *Prometheus* (2012), *Alien Covenant* (2017), and *Blade Runner 2049* (2017). Weyland, Tyrell, and Wallace are the Dr. Frankenstein figures in these films, producing "monsters" like the biomechanical supermen Roy and David. However, true to the structure of the Prometheus myth, the monster himself becomes a maker — especially in the case of David, who not only bests his human father but also the ancient alien engineers who designed the human race. These films of Ridley Scott are full of the symbolism of the Luciferian — or Promethean — rebellion of the fallen angels and the alchemical quest to not only meet one's maker but to reclaim one's future from him by becoming "More Human Than Human."

2.1 Transhumanism and the Singularity

Although the term "singularity" was not used, the first modern thinkers to contemplate what John von Neumann described as the Singularity were a group of profoundly spiritual visionaries in Russia. Beginning with Nikolai Fedorov (1829–1903), the "Russian Cosmists," as they are called today, articulated a vision of the technologically augmented biological and spiritual evolution of terrestrially bound humans into a race of immortals who have colonized the entire cosmos, turning innumerable barren planets into thriving paradises.[2] What is even more daring is the will of Fedorov and his disciples, rooted in a heretical interpretation of the Russian Orthodox belief in the Resurrection, to demand that generations of the future use the advanced technology that they have invented in order to resurrect the dead so that they can become denizens of the future cosmic paradise.

Even when Russian Cosmism took a more scientific turn in thinkers such as Konstantin Tsiolkovsky, after the Soviet Union coopted elements of the ideology to fuel its space program, we still see a Transhumanism that is deeply spiritual — even if Promethean, rather than Christian. In fact, Tsiolkovsky, the father of the Soviet space program, was positively Luciferian in his advocacy of a eugenically motivated extermination of terrestrial mankind at the hands of the coming superhuman cosmonauts.[3] Eugenics was not the only element of Russian Cosmist thought that survived, at least among the scientific elite, despite its conflict with Soviet state ideology. Those inclined

---

2   Boris Groys [Editor], *Russian Cosmism* (The MIT Press, 2018).

3   George M. Young, *The Russian Cosmists: The Esoteric Futurism of Nikolai Fedorov and his Followers* (Oxford University Press, 2012), 145–192.

toward Cosmist thought, especially of the Promethean variety, were responsible for "Psychotronics" research in the USSR and its eastern European satellite states, such as Czechoslovakia — where Prague was home to the most advanced "mad science" experiments on ESP and Telekinesis.[4]

Despite his public profession of Russian Orthodoxy, Nikolai Fedorov was fascinated by Iranian Studies or Iranology, and he identified Zoroastrianism, the ancient religion of Iran, as the archaic wellspring of Cosmist futurism.[5] Fedorov acknowledged that several revolutionary ideas first expressed by Zarathustra provided the ancient prototype for the Cosmism that he sought to revive and modernize. The first of these ideas is that history is progressive and teleological, not cyclical as most pre-modern cultures had conceived of it as being. The second is that Spenta Mainyu or the progressive, evolutionary mind at work in the Cosmos will eventually bring about an apocalyptic transformation of both human beings and the earthly realm in which they dwell. Known as the Frashgard, this event is envisioned as a bathing of the earth in molten metal so as to turn the planet into an alchemical forge, such that the perfection of the realm of forms or archetypes (also a Zoroastrian discovery, later adopted by Plato) can be perfectly instantiated on the earthly plane and embodied by human beings. Third, and finally, there is Zarathustra's insistence that humans must choose to play an active role in assisting evolution through innovation, thereby hastening the apocalypse that ends merely 'human' history.

Given the acknowledged debt of Russian proto-Transhumanism to ancient Iranian spirituality, it should not be surprising that the contemporary ideology of "Transhumanism" was the brainchild of an

---

4   Sheila Ostrander and Lynn Schroeder, *Psychic Discoveries Behind the Iron Curtain* (Bantam, 1971).

5   Young, *The Russian Cosmists: The Esoteric Futurism of Nikolai Fedorov and his Followers*, 82–83.

Iranian futurist, Fereidoun M. Esfandiary (1930–2000).[6] Esfandiary, who re-named himself FM-2030 in anticipation of the arrival of the technological singularity in the year 2030, taught sociology at the New School for Social Research in New York City. The subtitle of his book *Upwingers*, namely "A Futurist Manifesto," makes it clear that he saw his proposed "Transhumanism" as a successor to Futurism.[7] That is also evident from the political orientation of the manifesto, which is a play on "Left-winger" and "Right-winger". For Esfandiary, an "up-winger" is someone socio-politically committed to progress and innovation in ways that defy the Left/Right political dichotomy.

This was also true of modern Futurism, which emerged in Italy from out of a common sub-cultural matrix as Fascism but was among the most avant-garde and revolutionary progressive movements of the 1930s. Nor was this intersection of Futurism with Fascism limited to Italy or to the 1930s. There is an implicit Fascist aesthetic in the architecture of American draftsman Hugh Ferriss, one that was common to much of the more futuristic and titanic types of Art Deco in the 1930s and 40s.[8] Even as late as the 1970s, the Neo-Futurist art of science fiction illustrator Syd Mead exemplifies the same Fascist atmosphere.[9] There is a sense, in both Ferriss and Mead, of an aesthetic harmony — a degree of uniformity of design, both on a domestic and urban planning level — that could not but be achieved through the establishment of an organic state unified by a single ethos, albeit a Promethean one.

Granted, the Promethean cityscapes of Ferriss and Mead would have been decried as "inhuman" by the folksy traditionalists and Neo-Classicists in Fascist Italy and Nazi Germany, as much of Italian Futurist art and architecture was condemned by them. Still, Futurism

6   Fereidoun M Esfandiary, *Are You a Transhuman?* (Grand Central Pub, 1989).

7   Fereidoun M Esfandiary, *Up-Wingers: A Futurist Manifesto* (John Day Co, 1973).

8   Hugh Ferriss, *Power in Buildings* (Hennessey & Ingalis, 1998).

9   Syd Mead, *Sentinel* (Music Sales Corp, 1979).

and Fascism hold in common the will to fashion a "total work of art" — a society that would be aesthetically harmonious, and whose architectonic would be embodied by the men and women who are its denizens just as much as it would be expressed in paintings, sculptures, and architecture.

For futurists like F.T. Marinetti, who in the 1920s was still Benito Mussolini's close collaborator and comrade, this aesthetic harmony would be a byproduct of a revolutionary transformation of the human condition by technological innovation accelerated to the limit of human capacity, and then beyond it.[10] Such a violent transformation would break through the crust of all styles historically proper to any particular culture, including that of the Italian Renaissance, and converge on an aesthetic that expresses and encourages man's fulfillment of his Promethean destiny.

Ironically, for all its titanic inhumanity, this futurist vision could rightly be considered the first "universally" human aesthetic — an irony that enfolds within itself the esoteric meaning of the myth that Prometheus created mankind to be a race of gods superseding the Olympians. Some Germans on the far Right in the 1930s, such as Ernst Jünger, did share this vision with their Italian counterparts.[11] Jünger echoed Marinetti's praise of the alchemical power of mechanized warfare and other inhuman technological innovations to remake "Homo Faber" as a Superman in the "forge of Vulcan."[12]

The idea of the Superman or "Übermensch" is, of course, central to the philosophical project of Friedrich Nietzsche. In *Thus Spoke Zarathustra*, Nietzsche uses the ancient Iranian prophet to preach the coming of a new race that is as far superior to the human species as

---

10   F.T. Marinetti, "The Founding and Manifesto of Futurism" in Lawrence Rainey and Christine Poggi, *Futurism: An Anthology* (Yale University Press, 2009), 49–53.

11   Ernst Jünger, *The Worker* (Northwestern University Press, 2017).

12   Ernst Jünger, *Storm of Steel* (Penguin Classics, 2004).

human beings are to their ape ancestors.[13] But Nietzsche speaks not only of evolution beyond the human, but also of devolution beneath the human. Humanity, he argues, is a transitional state and it will end with a bifurcation into both a subhuman mass of rabble who would best be either replaced by robots or transformed into robots on the one hand, and a superhuman elite who are the progenitors of a new "master race" on the other.[14] Contrary to its misappropriation by German National Socialists, Nietzsche's notion of the "master race" is not an ethnic designator. He suggests a mastery over the natural environment and also self-mastery on the part of the directive elite who rise above the merely human to engender a Posthuman race of the future. Nietzsche explicitly identifies these "barbarians of the future" as Promethean in spirit:

The dwarfing of man must for a long time count as the only goal; because a broad foundation has first to be created so that a stronger species of man can stand upon it. ...

The strong of the future. — That which partly necessity, partly chance has achieved here and there, the conditions for the production of a stronger type, we are now able to comprehend and consciously *will*: we are able to create the conditions under which such an elevation is possible. ...

Such a task would have to be posed the more it was grasped to what extent the contemporary form of society was being so powerfully transformed that at some future time it would be unable to exist for its own sake alone, but only as a tool in the hands of a stronger race.

The increasing dwarfing of man is precisely the driving force that brings to mind the breeding of a stronger race — a race that would be excessive precisely where the dwarfed species was weak and growing weaker (in will, responsibility, self-assurance, ability to posit goals for oneself). ...

Not merely a master race whose sole task is to rule, but a race with its own sphere of life, with an excess of strength for beauty, bravery, culture, manners to the highest peak of the spirit; an affirming race that may grant

---

13 Friedrich Nietzsche, *Thus Spoke Zarathustra* (Modern Library, 1995), 12–13.

14 Friedrich Nietzsche, *The Will to Power* (Vintage Books, 1968), 475, 477–478.

itself every great luxury — strong enough to have no need of the tyranny of the virtue-imperative, rich enough to have no need of thrift and pedantry, beyond good and evil; a hothouse for strange and choice plants. ...

I point to something new: certainly for such a democratic type there exists the danger of the barbarian, but one has looked for it only in the depths. There exists also another type of barbarian, who comes from the heights: a species of conquering and ruling natures in search of material to mold. Prometheus was this kind of barbarian.[15]

From now on there will be more favorable preconditions for more comprehensive forms of dominion, whose like has never yet existed. And even this is not the most important thing; the possibility has been established for the production of international racial unions whose task will be to rear a master race, the future "masters of the earth"; — a new, tremendous aristocracy, based on the severest self-legislation, in which the will of philosophical men of power and artist-tyrants will be made to endure for millennia — a higher kind of man who, thanks to their superiority in will, knowledge, riches, and influence, employ democratic Europe as their most pliant and supple instrument for getting hold of the destinies of the earth, so as to work as artists upon 'man' himself. Enough: the time is coming when politics will have a different meaning.[16]

It ought to be clear from these passages that Nietzsche explicitly describes the coming Promethean "masters of the Earth" as having been produced through a hybridization of the brightest, boldest, and most beautiful individuals from a variety of noble ethnicities and cultures in "a hothouse of strange and choice plants." The supermen will define themselves as such in response to the very same nihilistic conditions of terminal decline that cause most people to degenerate into an utterly ignoble, teeming rabble of subhuman scum who are concerned only with creature comforts and entertaining diversions. Nietzsche critiques the Hegelian (and implicitly also the, later, Marxist) view of necessarily rational historical progress, siding instead with Charles Darwin but arguing that the driving force of evolution is not mere

---

15   Ibid., 475–479.

16   Ibid., 504.

"survival" but the "will to power."[17] What struggles merely to survive will surely perish. Life forms struggle to overcome others and thereby transcend themselves, increasing their scope of influence and broadening their capacities. The Nietzschean critique of Hegelian and Marxist interpretations of the historical transformation of societies in terms of class struggles, such as the master-slave dialectic, and economic relations, seems more prescient now then it ever did before. So also does Nietzsche's prophetic vision of the mass of humanity being either subjected to cybernetic modification or replaced by robots who serve the interests of the supermen to come. The Robotics Revolution and a number of related, imminent technological developments promise to end economic and class relations as we have known them but without necessarily leading to the egalitarian utopia of Marxists or even the supremely rational future society that all Hegelians project as "the end of history."

Robotics research and development is on the verge of a breakthrough that would finally deliver the robotic workforce that was foreseen so long ago by futurists and has been so long overdue. As Hans Moravec characterizes it, this breakthrough involves driving a "spike" through two different research projects — one that is bottom up and the other that is top down.[18] Moravec argues that the bottleneck in robotics research was a result of having started with the human being as a model. Instead, in the last couple of decades, a bottom up approach has been taken that seeks to bio-mimetically replicate the behavior of simpler life forms, such as insects, in order to build robots that successfully navigate their environment, overcome obstacles, and competently interact with objects. Meanwhile, instead of being fixated on strong Artificial Intelligence, computer programmers developed a variety of expert systems tailored to specific tasks and occupational specializations. For example, in another twenty years, almost all cars

---

17 Ibid, 343–344.

18 Hans Moravec, *Robot: Mere Machine to Transcendent Mind* (Oxford University Press, 2000), 21–25, 47.

and trucks will be self-driving. A combination of the hardware produced by the former program with the software that the latter has
yielded, holds the promise of building a variety of robots that are
highly effective at automating every form of manual labor.

Progress in the field of nanotechnology means that these robotic
systems can be scaled-down to a microscopic level.[19] Nano-scale
robots could be especially valuable in the medical field, as intelligent
surgeons that operate within the body on a molecular level — making
it appear as if cancers in sensitive areas full of nerves, which a scalpel
runs the risk of severing, are simply dissolving. Unclogging arteries
would also be a lot easier. But the implications of these nanobots for
industry are truly astounding. Imagine the 3-D printing technology
of today being replaced by printers that assemble computer-generated
or 3-D scanned and modeled objects on a molecular level, akin to the
food replicators of *Star Trek*.

When combined with weak-AI expert systems and human-scale
robots, as well as air-borne drone robotic delivery systems, such robotic assembly on a nano-scale would bring the need for every kind of
drudgery to an end. What this also means is that sometime within the
next two decades, 90% or more of the human labor force will be un-
employed. To use Henry Kissinger's terminology, they will suddenly
become "useless eaters." Anyone outside an elite engaged in creative
work and driven by higher goals will be considered a purposeless consumer of robotically produced goods.

This revolutionary disruption of the global economic system
would be one of the many indications that we have arrived at the
event horizon of the Singularity and are about to be inescapably
captured by its vortex. As the mass unemployment crisis sets in and
all contemporary economic models fail to offer financial analysts any
guidance, we will begin to feel the gravity of the situation. As with all
aspects of the Singularity, the effects will not be gradual or intensify

---

19 Eric Drexler, *Engines of Creation: The Coming Era of Nanotechnology* (Anchor,
    1987).

in a linear manner that can be projected. The robotics revolution and industrial production augmented by nanotechnology will explode at an exponential growth rate, until only expert systems are considered remotely competent in even attempting an analysis of the situation and suggesting solutions that would address the implosion of our world financial system.

Notice how at no point in this run up to the Singularity is the invention of strong Artificial Intelligence a necessary condition for entering into a Transhuman state. In his seminal 1993 paper, "The Technological Singularity," Vernor Vinge outlines four possible paths to Transhumanity; only one of them is a scenario where the invention or evolution of strong-AI marks the moment of Singularity.[20] The three other routes do not require it.

In one of Vinge's pathways, increasingly sophisticated and ubiquitous computer networks effectively turn billions of human minds into a single neural network with the computers becoming parasitic on human consciousness and the humans becoming enmeshed in the informational web. This hive mind would then make decisions and take courses of action that no human individual would, and that express capacities far beyond those of Humanity. (It may also express potentially "inhuman" inclinations.)

The second scenario not involving strong-AI is one wherein many humans are fitted with cybernetic implants that incorporate computer processing power into the organic human brain and nervous system, thereby resulting in Transhuman Cyborgs. When this scenario is synthesized with the one preceding it, we are left with an outcome that *Star Trek: The Next Generation* envisioned when the Borg were introduced as the ultimate nemesis of humans and all other humanoid life-forms that valued individuality and/or cultural distinctness.

Finally, Vinge argued that genetic engineering alone could propel us into the Singularity. Hereditarily inherited modifications of the

---

20 Vernor Vinge, "The Technological Singularity" in More, Max and Natasha Vita, *The Transhumanist Reader* (Wiley-Blackwell, 2013), 365–375.

human genome that yield super-intelligence, vastly longer lifespans, superhuman strength and endurance, disease resistance and other enhancements that could even involve the splicing of human genes with those of other animals with coveted capacities, would definitively demarcate the dawn of Transhuman history. These genetically engineered supermen, at whose mercy we would all be, could also discover or invent things that remain inconceivable to minds limited by even the most high-IQ human-level mathematical reasoning and memory capacity. In other words, even if they themselves are not the Singularity, they would most certainly bring it forth in ways that we cannot imagine.

This is the promise, and the peril, of CRISPR technology, which has recently rendered genetic engineering much more practicable and precise.[21] CRISPR stands for Clustered Regularly Interspaced Short Palindromic Repeats. The name was coined by Francisco Mojica, a microbiologist at the University of Alicante. He first discovered these regularly interspaced short repeating patterns in the DNA of *Haloferax mediterranei*, a microorganism that lives in environments with about ten times the salinity of seawater, such as the Bras Del Port salt ponds of Santa Pola, Spain. Microbial genome sequencing started in the late 1990s. Eventually, CRISPR was found in many other microorganisms. In each case, the spacers between the repeating sequences contained genetic code that was completely different from that of any other spacer.

CRISPR has come to more broadly refer to a method of appropriating and redirecting the natural mechanism for the repair of DNA, which breaks all the time in response to various environmental stimuli, such as a person being subjected to a standard X-ray. In any cell, when a broken strand of DNA is located next to an intact one, the former requests a repair from its "sister." The latter then allows an interlocking of strands with the former at the place where the

---

21   Adam Bolt and Regina Sobel, *Human Nature* (News and Guts Films, The Wonder Collaborative, 2019).

former is broken, such that the intact side of its double helix copies the coding sequence from the "sister," thereby replacing the missing coding sequences of DNA. This means that if an artificial break, instead of a random and naturally occurring one, were to be made in any DNA strand in a cell, and if the "sister" could be replaced with a chromosome that is identical to the broken strand of DNA *except for the genetic information that one wants to insert* into the strand where it has been cut, then the cell's repair mechanism could be hijacked in order to carry out this genetic engineering. Making the cut in the right place has been compared to placing a cursor between the 'letters' of the GATTACA sequence in the proverbial 'word processor' of the genome, before rewriting it as GATAACA.

All one needs is a way to cut the targeted DNA strand at a very precise location, before introducing the RNA strand that will serve as the model for the recoding that the cell is fooled into thinking is a simple 'repair.' Before CRISPR, various proposed gene therapies had a very hard time isolating a particular gene in the cells subjected to the therapy. Accidental insertions of genes into the wrong parts of the DNA sequence in the cells of patients led to fatal mutations, such as terminal cancer. The solution to this problem was found by examining the way in which, when viruses invade the cells of bacteria, the bacteria stores the cells of the DNA from the invading virus in its own DNA. If or when the same virus comes back, the bacteria makes a copy of this spacer sequence and gives this RNA copy to a protein, called Cas9, inside the cell, as if it is a "wanted" poster. RNA is a chemical cousin of DNA with 'letters' or sequences that form matching pairs with DNA. Cas9 polices the cell for viral invasions. When it detects a virus that has a sequence identical to the "wanted" one stored as an RNA spacer set to find a corresponding DNA sequence, it cuts this sequence in the virus.

Jennifer Doudna, a biochemist at UC Berkeley, realized that this meant that Cas9 is in principle a programmable protein for the directed cutting of DNA. Doudna co-wrote a revolutionary paper with

Emmanuelle Charpentier, a biochemist at the Max Planck Institute, the last line of which suggests that "RNA-programmed Cas9 ... could offer considerable potential for gene-targeting and genome-editing applications." The paper points out that, because the RNA involved in the aforementioned Cas9 process can be replaced, the Cas9 protein can be directed to cut specifically targeted DNA in the cells of an organism—including a human subject. RNA molecules are easy to make in a molecular biology lab, and they could be manufactured and shipped out to companies. Synthego RNA Synthesis Factory is one of the companies now providing this service to other corporations, or private individuals, working with CRISPR for gene editing. When the contents of a Synthego produced vial of "guide RNA" is mixed with Cas9 protein in another vial, the latter is reprogrammed.

By 2007, CRISPR was being used by Rodolphe Barrangou, the Genomics Director of the company Danisco, in order to genetically engineer the bacteria in the microbes that it sells to yogurt producers and other food companies to make the bacteria in these products more resistant to viruses. Then it was used by Egenesis and other companies for gene editing on animals, to solve problems involved in xenotransplantation, or cross-species organ transplantation. CRISPR made it possible to modify the genes of the receiver so that the transplanted organ would not be rejected. While they worked with pigs, their proven methods could be applied to humans. CRISPR is now being used on humans to cure sickle cell anemia, muscular dystrophy, and even cancer.

Consider the dual uses of this technology. The same gene editing used to cure muscular dystrophy, on a therapeutic basis, could be used to enhance muscle mass across the population—not just amongst those who opt in for this enhancement, but potentially in future generations born to parents who chose to have their child's embryo edited. Fyodor Urnov, who worked at Sangamo Biosciences from 2000 to 2016, points out that there is one gene, SCN9A, that makes a protein responsible for pain transmission signals. Editing this gene out using CRISPR could help manage terrible pain in cancer patients, but it could also be used to produce special forces soldiers invulnerable to torture.

Whereas before CRISPR, gene therapy on humans was achieving 2% correction, the genome of 80% of the cells in a subject can now be 'corrected' or reengineered. If desired, this can include the cells of germ-line genetic material, such as sperm and eggs, which would pass any genetically engineered change down onto the offspring of the human subject of the CRISPR editing. Not surprisingly, in 2015 China became the first country in which scientists legally and openly began gene editing human embryos using CRISPR. CCR5 was the gene targeted in the first human embryos edited in China. It is the receptor for HIV, and removing it from the genome of the edited embryos immunized the genetically engineered children against the AIDS virus.

It was not long before Chinese corporations such as Darwin Life and OvaScience were promising their clients designer babies with all kinds of genetic modifications, including enhanced IQ, within a decade (i.e. well before 2030). As President Vladimir Putin recognized in his remarks at the World Festival of Youth at Sochi, Russia, on October 21, 2017, this technology could be used, not just to cure heritable diseases, but to genetically engineer mathematical and musical geniuses, or super-soldiers who feel neither fear nor pain. Putin suggested that the implications of CRISPR-driven gene editing are more terrifying than the invention of the atomic bomb. He is right. As Vernor Vinge recognized, genetic engineering — now perfected by CRISPR technology — is one path to the Singularity.

That strong-AI is not necessarily required for the Singularity to arrive has bearing on the question of whether Ray Kurzweil and other prominent Transhumanists are too reductively materialist in their characterizations of the transformation that we will soon be facing. Kurzweil and others of his persuasion assume that the human mind is equivalent to the human brain and that this organ can be mechanically modeled by a silicon-based neural network that replicates its function.[22] Consciousness is, to them, an "epiphenomenon," or merely derivative quality of a certain organization of matter and processing of information. Such a facile view of engineering "intelligence" is based on an uncritical acceptance of the dominant materialist scientific paradigm, and a blithely willful ignorance of more than a century of rigorous parapsychological research. It is also anathema to the alchemical orientation of the first modern thinkers and writers to propose the project of remaking man using technology, with the aspiration of outdoing God or Nature.

Frankenstein, aptly subtitled, "The Modern Prometheus," is the earliest work of modern literature that vividly expresses this Promethean ambition and its potentially tragic consequences.[23] The eighth chapter of *Prometheus and Atlas* features a profound exegesis of *Frankenstein*. Rather than repeating here what I have already written there, let me highlight a few themes and motifs that are adopted by those who go on to elaborate the Promethean myth in a modern or post-modern manner.

2.2 Promethean Androgyny

The first thing to understand about *Frankenstein*, which I did not dwell on in *Prometheus and Atlas*, is that the book's true author is not Mary Shelley (as I frankly wanted to believe), but her husband Percy. It is only when viewed within the context of Percy Shelley's life and interests that the alchemical Transhumanism of *Frankenstein* can be fully fathomed. There is no discernible literary genealogy for *Frankenstein* in the life of Mary Wollstonecraft, nor did she ever go on to write another book that was anything like this masterpiece of science fiction. By contrast, in addition to producing numerous other poetic and prose works with Promethean or Luciferian themes, such

---

22 Ray Kurzweil, *The Age of Spiritual Machines: When Computers Exceed Human Intelligence* (Penguin Books, 2000).

23 Mary Shelley, *Frankenstein* (Penguin Classics, 2003).

as *Prometheus Unbound* or *The Witch of Atlas*, Percy Shelley spent much of his youth preoccupied with chemical experiments and alchemical studies.[24]

A.N. Whitehead even claimed that Shelley was such a prodigy in this area of scientific research, that had he not met an untimely death at the age of twenty-nine, or had he lived a century later, he would have made contributions to Chemistry as significant as those of Isaac Newton to Physics.[25] Percy set up makeshift laboratories in his dormitory quarters both at Eton, and then later at Oxford, before being expelled for his heretical ideas. When we read, in *Frankenstein*, that the good doctor was mocked at Ingolstadt University for his interests in Medieval and Renaissance alchemists such as Paracelsus, Albertus Magnus, and Cornelius Agrippa, we are seeing a perfect reflection of Shelley's own reading list. Ingolstadt, where he sets the studies of Dr. Frankenstein, was the cradle of the Bavarian Illuminati, and Shelley was known not only to have read Illuminati tractates, but to have carried them around with him and read from them to his closest associates.[26]

Victor Frankenstein's wife, Elizabeth, with whom he has a quasi-incestuous relationship since she is also his step-sister, is named after Percy Shelley's sister. What Percy Shelley, largely unsuccessfully, sought from all of the women in his life was an alchemical union with the female aspect of himself. As he had confessed in the essay prefacing his translation of Plato's *Symposium*, Shelley took seriously the ancient Greek idea that primordial 'man' was androgynous. He accepted Plato's account that the destruction of the advanced antediluvian human civilization of Atlantis, which also appears in Shelley's *Prometheus Unbound*, was contemporaneous with the tearing asunder of these superhuman androgynes or hermaphrodites into two separate

---

24 Joseph P. Farrell and Dr. Scott D. de Hart, *Transhumanism: A Grimoire of Alchemical Agendas* (Feral House, 2012), 182–184.

25 Ibid, 186–193.

26 Ibid, 194.

sexes. This creation of "men" and "women" was part of the Olympian punishment of the primordial humanity that rose up against the gods and attempted to chart its own course. The corollary to this myth was Shelley's belief, and those of others alchemically inclined in his epoch, that for us to become masters of our own destiny again would also demand a reversal of sexual differentiation and a return to superhuman androgyny or, to put it in more contemporary terms, transhuman transexuality.[27]

This is seen, in *Frankenstein*, when the creature demands a companion together with whom he could sire "a race of devils" who would found an ungodly civilization supplanting all merely human cultures.[28] Until then Frankenstein's monster is desperately alone. Resentfully rejected for his monstrous superiority by all those humans whose love and acceptance he sought, and even by his own horrified creator, who endeavors to destroy him, the creature compares himself to Lucifer brooding in the pit of Hell.[29] This is Percy Shelley's own radical alienation. He let Mary claim credit for having created "The Modern Prometheus" because he wanted to believe that in his unconventional marriage with her, he was like the creature who hopes, "one as deformed and horrible as myself would not deny herself to me."[30] Mary is the author of *Frankenstein* to the extent that she attained an alchemical union with Percy, with the novel being "the work" or "the working" of this androgynous reintegration. Percy's reading of the Renaissance alchemist Cornelius Agrippa, who had infamously authored a treatise on the superiority of women to men, no doubt also inclined him toward a chivalrous attribution of *Frankenstein* to his wife and would-be soul-mate.

---

27   Ibid, 195–199.

28   Shelley, *Frankenstein*, 171.

29   Ibid, 125, 130, 132.

30   Ibid, 146.

The claim that primordial 'man' was androgynous is not unique to Greek mythology. Shelley, who avidly read cabalistic texts, would have known that the same claim is made by esoteric writers in the Judeo-Christian tradition. The basis for this is the statement in Genesis 1:27 that Adam was made in the image of the elohim as male and female. Elohim is a plural, mistranslated as "God," and really means the divine beings and whose etymology literally translates as "the shining ones." The passage suggests that these beings were androgynous and that primordial 'man' or "Adam" was modeled on them. The rabbis who wrote the Babylonian Talmud made this explicit when they penned the following gloss of Genesis 1:27: "A male with corresponding female parts created He him." The Palestinian *Talmud* conveys the same idea with a slight variation, "male with female parts he created them."[31] In other words, "Adamic" man was transsexual — endowed with a form akin to that of male to female transsexuals today, a sexual male, i.e. with male genitalia, but also with breasts and of androgynous appearance.

Reading this Biblical narrative against the backdrop of the Greek myths regarding the genesis of the human race is even more illuminating. In Greek mythology, it is Prometheus, not Zeus, who is the creator, crafty inventor, or genetic engineer of 'man.' If it is also the case, as Shelley accepted from Plato, that primordial man was androgynous, then what Prometheus engineered was a transsexual or hermaphroditic species.

While Prometheus is always depicted as male, the oldest Greek myths regarding this titan are very peculiar insofar as they identify 'him' with the crescent moon.[32] All Greco-Roman deities were identified with celestial bodies, and while numerous goddesses lay competing claims to being the Moon, no male deity is ever identified with the Moon other than Prometheus. That 'he' is also known to be the trickster among the titans, just as Hermes is the trickster among

---

31 Farrell, *Transhumanism: A Grimoire of Alchemical Agendas*, 272.

32 Carl Kerényi, *Prometheus: Archetypal Image of Human Existence* (Princeton University Press, 1997), 52–55.

the Olympian gods, also suggests a gender ambiguity, since gender-bending is a universal characteristic of trickster figures in archetypal mythology, all the way down to the contemporary archetype of the Joker in the Batman franchise. Speaking of comic books, which most nakedly express the collective unconscious in our era, Alan Moore explicitly depicts Prometheus as female in his graphic novel saga *Promethea*.[33] We will revisit this feminine projection of Prometheus in depth and at greater length toward the close of the final chapter.

When Prometheus steals fire from the gods to gift mankind with the forge of all the arts and sciences, it is as a retaliation against Zeus, who has punished Prometheus for aspiring to create a race of gods intended to overthrow and supplant the Olympians. The account of the punishment of antediluvian man that Plato presents us with in Shelley's beloved *Symposium*, must be put side by side with the myth of Atlantis as Plato recounts it in his *Timaeus* and *Critias*.[34] Taking these texts together with the Greek myth of the creation of man as the first Promethean rebellion against Olympus, reaffirms the interpretation that Prometheus engineered androgynous beings who were only differentiated into "men" and "women" by Zeus as a disempowering punishment. Disempowering because, to be androgynous would have been to be immortal — as the gods themselves are.

This brings us back to the forbidden Tree of Life in Eden. The wording of Genesis is very clear that the chief of the gods (adonai elohim) expelled man from Eden, not just for eating the forbidden fruit of the Tree of Knowledge, but also for fear that humans would go on to eat from the Tree of Life, thereby attaining immortality in addition to knowledge, so as to gain equal footing with the gods in a way that would make it impossible for the latter to "do anything against them" (Genesis 3). This is hardly the thought process of a benevolent deity who wants the best for his creation.

---

33   Alan Moore, *Promethea* (DC Comics, 1999).

34   Plato, *Timaeus and Critias* (Penguin Classics, 2008).

As William Bramley aptly argues throughout his masterful study, *The Gods of Eden*, Yahweh and his cronies are no less jealous, sadistic, and manipulative than Zeus and the slave-driving deities of Olympus.[35] It is an elementary observation of comparative religion that, in line with this cross-cultural identification, Prometheus is the Serpent — whose legs are removed by God as a punishment for his having enlightened humans. In other words, he is the Serpent who was a Dragon, the Dragon that reappears in the Apocalypse of John, namely Satan or "the Adversary." Interestingly, as in the case of Prometheus, "Lucifer" is also androgynous since, Hillel is Lucifer as the "morning star," but Venus — Aphrodite or Ishtar — when it rises at night. Ishtar, "the star," is also the original identity of the "Whore of Babylon" who appears as the holy consort of "the Beast" Satan in the Apocalypse.

The fall from Eden is, then, a fall from androgyny into bipolar sexuality, and the hermaphrodite whose form of embodiment defies this divine punishment is a Satanic symbol from the Judeo-Christian standpoint. This is why Medieval artists depicted Baphomet as a hermaphrodite on the Tarot card of "the Devil." Actually, the figure of the *Anima Mundi* or "world soul" on the card of "the World" has 'her' genitalia covered by a cloth or sash because s/he is also androgynous — even if only her breasts are visible. The man and woman whose chains are being held in the two hands of the goat-horned Baphomet on the "Devil" card have overcome their destructive dichotomy and been re-integrated into the hermaphroditic *Anima Mundi* — a microcosm of the true Promethean god in whose image we were created.

As in the case of the Greek myth of Atlantis, the Bible also recounts a first, failed, attempt to reverse the fall through rebellion against the gods. Despite the wishes of conventional theologians to suppress this material, Genesis 5:21 and 6:1–17 clearly states that the civilization of Noah consisted of hybrid beings sired by human women who had

35   William Bramley, *The Gods of Eden* (Avon, 1993), 73–88.

been lusted after by rebel elohim — later glossed by Christian tradition as the "fallen angels" led by Lucifer. The alleged "perversion of the ways" of all life-forms on the Earth, not just humans, suggests widespread genetic engineering by these rebels from Eden or Olympus. The flood is intended to wipe this Luciferian civilization clean off the face of the Earth before it reaches a level of knowledge and power that rivals Heaven.

Then, after the Flood of Noah, there is a second attempt made to storm Heaven, which also ends in failure. This is the story of the Tower of Babel at Genesis 11:1–9. We witness, once again, the petty jealousy and tyrannical patriarchy of God. Pursuing a policy of divide and re-conquer, Yahweh scatters humans across the face of the Earth by making them speak mutually unintelligible languages and dividing them into warring tribes and nations. The Judeo-Christian God does this for no other reason than that he fears what men and women might accomplish now that they speak one language and have formed a single socio-political community.

What Percy Shelley and some of his contemporaries were advocating amounts to a third attempt to reverse the fall by rebuilding the Tower of Babel. After all, "three is the charm." Shelley's views on alchemically re-attaining androgyny heralded an entire nineteenth century subculture known as the "Uranian" movement. Led by Edward Carpenter (1844–1929), like Shelley, the Uranians drew inspiration from the *Symposium*, where Plato contrasts earthly heterosexual sex with a higher heavenly love or Uranian Eros that is androgynous and oriented toward transcendent illumination.[36] Long before it became identified with the planet that classical astronomers, lacking telescopes, could not yet observe, Ouranus or Uranus simply meant "Heaven." The Uranian conception of love was, consequently, a conquest of what Emmanuel Swedenborg called Arcana Coelestia or "the

---

36   Farrell, *Transhumanism: A Grimoire of Alchemical Agendas*, 251–258.

secrets of Heaven." It is the conquest of Uranus by means of a forbidden erotic alchemy.

In the late nineteenth century, there was an explosion of cases of hermaphroditism. Detailed contemporary studies of this phenomenon have concluded that it is not simply that, as one might imagine, more of these cases began to be documented because modern medical science, with its classificatory schema and archives, became more sophisticated and ubiquitous. It appears that, at least in the West where it was noted by doctors of the time, there suddenly appeared to be a spike in individuals with ambiguous genitalia and/or androgynous appearance. Debates raged as to whether these were genuine hermaphrodites, who some doctors argued ought to be classified as "intersex" or a "third sex" alongside males and females, or whether they were mutants whose "true sex" of either male or female could be ascertained through careful study of their particular 'deformity.'[37] Carpenter and his fellow Uranians took another position entirely. They saw these hermaphrodites as atavisms or throwbacks to a primordially androgynous, prehistoric human morphology.[38]

The extent to which this was meant to be an anthropological claim, which would have to be supported by skeletal remains and so forth, or the extent to which it was a metaphysical one, remains unclear. After all, there were thinkers of the late nineteenth and early twentieth century, such as Rudolf Steiner, who offered theosophical alternatives to the Darwinian theory of evolution wherein humans were believed to have gradually descended from a spiritual or heavenly plane, i.e. "Uranus," to the earthly plane of biological embodiment. On a view such as Steiner's, sexual differentiation of an initially androgynous humanity could be considered contemporaneous with the full concretion of incarnation in bodies produced by evolutionary

---

37 Alice Domurat Dreger, *Hermaphrodites and the Medical Invention of Sex* (Harvard University Press, 2000).

38 Farrell, *Transhumanism: A Grimoire of Alchemical Agendas*, 246–251.

processes in Nature.[39] Curiously, Steiner thought that civilization existed long before this point, and that it was in some ways a higher civilization than that of modern man, but its remains are enigmatic if not elusive because the spirits who wrought its structures were not yet entirely corporeal. To his mind, this also meant that they were able to wield tremendous psychical powers that diminished in proportion to fully terrestrial incarnation. In any case, the Uranian interpretation of hermaphroditism as an atavism had at least some metaphysical basis. That much is clear from Carpenter's anticipation of C.G. Jung's archetypal psychology.

This is most relevant in view of the Uranian insistence that, unlike most atavisms, this mutation was not just a regressive throwback, but a herald of the future evolution of man toward a regained androgyny. This brings Carpenter's ideas into the realm of the pioneering parapsychological theories of Frederic Myers, particularly his idea of "the Imaginal." Working at the British Society for Psychical Research in the late nineteenth century, Myers proposed that certain individuals are "preverts" who display particular capacities or a peculiar morphology that presages the future evolution of the species.[40] Humanity, Myers argues, is still in its larval state on the way to transforming into the human equivalent of an insect's imago or mature form — like the butterfly that a caterpillar transforms into. Preverts are transhumans who manifest "Imaginal" characteristics long in advance of their evolution on a species-wide level, giving us a preview of our Posthuman future.

Had Carpenter read Myers he would have characterized late nineteenth century hermaphrodites as preverts and morphological androgyny as one of the characteristics of the imago guiding our evolution. Had Michael Murphy, the founder of Esalen, read Carpenter, he might have included such cases in his monumental study of

39 Rudolf Steiner, *How to Know Higher Worlds: A Modern Path of Initiation* (Anthroposophic Press, 1994).

40 Frederic William Henry Myers, *Science and A Future Life With Other Essays* (Cambridge University Press, 2011).

spectral "preversion" entitled *The Future of the Body*. Murphy docu-
ments a variety of extreme, superhuman abilities and psycho-physical
transformations demonstrated by human beings from a variety of
cultures throughout history.[41] These include well-documented cases
of stigmata, levitation, super-strength, fire-walking, invulnerability to
extreme cold, and other qualities that he thinks are not simply freaks
of nature but portents of capacities that we will eventually evolve to
possess on a species-wide level. Like Carpenter, he grasps the link
between the genetic and the psychical, or what Shelley would, in
alchemical language, have expressed as spiritual influxes at work in
"chemic" transmutations.

The character of Dr. Frankenstein is an epitome of the historical
reality that alchemy has, since its inception, been associated with
"Promethean ambition" by both its proponents and by those who
persecuted alchemists — either at the behest of the Church or on
behalf of early modern scientific rationalism. Shelley connects Victor
Frankenstein to his Promethean alchemical heritage through his studies of Cornelius Agrippa, Paracelsus, and Albertus Magnus.[42] From
the classical epoch all the way through the Middle Ages and the era
of the Renaissance, there were essentially three views on the power
of Alchemy. Its critics believed that it could only mar or pervert nature; certain conservative and pious alchemists believed that it was
an art that worked with nature in order to perfect nature; and finally,
a minority of unapologetic alchemists thought that the purpose of
Alchemy was to overpower and control nature.[43]

The character of Victor Frankenstein is meant to epitomize the
third category of alchemist. His creation of "the monster" is a reference to the alchemical quest for the homunculus, a miniature human

41   Michael Murphy, *The Future of the Body: Explorations Into the Further Evolution of Human Nature* (TarcherPerigree, 1993).

42   William R. Newman, *Promethean Ambitions: Alchemy and the Quest to Perfect Nature* (University of Chicago Press, 2005), 5.

43   Ibid., 4.

being grown in an alchemical flask that is made to serve as an artificial womb.[44] Both some pre-modern alchemists and certain of their detractors and persecutors believed that the gestation of such a being was possible, albeit perhaps demonic on account of its ambition to play God or usurp the power of Nature. On the part of the alchemists, there was a particular interest in altering the sex and sexuality of this being so as to allow for an incarnation of the alchemical androgyne. Others, especially in the school of Paracelsus, sought to separate out the sexual characteristics of the homunculi in such a way as to grow a "pure male" and a "pure female" that would maximize the energy of sexual polarity between the two of them — Frankenstein's monster and his bride, if you will.[45] Meanwhile, opponents of Alchemy were terrified by, and outraged at, the implication that human art or craft could create a rational soul on demand.[46]

Even great artists of the caliber of Leonardo da Vinci attacked alchemists as perpetrators of "an irreligious fraud that claimed for itself the creative powers of God."[47] In fact, both in the classical period and during the Renaissance, painters and sculptors in general were hostile to alchemists and considered Alchemy to be their principal rival among the "arts." This is because the best artists were aiming to make flawless simulacra of Nature, which could be bested only by alchemists who could create artificial beings that are not merely lifeless simulacra, however perfect, but living artificial beings. So painter and sculptors often joined with theocrats in order to either dismiss the endeavors of alchemists as consummate fraud, or to claim that they could only produce botched or perverted versions of what is grown by Nature and perfectly represented on a canvas or in carved stone.

---

44 Ibid., 6.

45 Ibid., 7.

46 Ibid., 7.

47 Ibid., 8.

Babies grown in the laboratory, with characteristics such as their sex being artificially selected, was a subject matter of alchemical ambition, extensive philosophical discussion and heated theological debate going back many centuries before it became a practicable techno-scientific possibility. This is one striking example of how Technoscience is driven by a Promethean spirit and vision. The refinement of technique, and the discovery of the right structures to apply these methods to, only comes after the fact. It follows the Alchemist's prayer and spiritual longing in the way that religious rituals do. The latter also change over time. It is just that the rituals of Prometheism are more effective. They have always been, and will become more so once the crudely reductive materialism of the modern age is abandoned, while the precision of technology and techniques is retained and put in the service of a new Renaissance spirit.

This will, of course, elicit increasingly impassioned and potential violent condemnations from the same sectors of society responsible for the burnings of witches, sorcerers, and even august Alchemists such as Giordano Bruno during the Renaissance. In his address to the members of the Pontifical Council for Health on Thursday, May 2, 2002, Pope John Paul II characterized research on Genetic Engineering, Artificial Life, and Artificial Intelligence as a threat to the dignity of human life — a threat motivated by "Promethean ambitions."[48]

In the Middle Ages, theological investigation into the power of Alchemy was used as a benchmark to determine the capabilities of demons.[49] It was the view of scholastic theologians and demonologists in the employ of the Catholic Church that demons could not have the miraculous creative power of God and his angels. That would be heresy. But if human art, including Alchemy, could accomplish something through its crafty machinations, then demons could use

48 Ibid., 1.
49 Ibid., 59.

the same techniques more effectively — and, with such a speed, that their work appeared miraculously supernatural.[50] As one can imagine, this argument was turned around to accuse accomplished alchemists of being "sorcerers" who were in league with demons and who ought to be burned at the stake.

2.3 Cosmic Prometheism

The archetype of Prometheus has been implicitly portrayed as the artisan of life in many works of science fiction cinema and literature since *Frankenstein*. In the 2012 film simply titled *Prometheus*, Ridley Scott reconnected this theme back to its mythic origin even more explicitly than Shelley. In this prequel to *Alien* (1979), the mythos that began to take on a more stellar scope with Percy Shelley becomes a tragic drama of positively cosmic dimensions. The film is an inquiry into the existential character of beings willing and able to create other conscious and intelligent entities in their own image, and the relationship of the creators to their creatures. We see two mirrored examples of this relationship in the film: the rapport of the alien "Engineers" to the human race that they designed, and that of humans to genetically engineered android robots of their own making.[51]

The space ship Prometheus lands at a military base where a scene of terrible carnage reveals that there has been a battle among the Engineers. They designed a biological weapon that one faction seems to have used against another. This 'weapon' is the genetically designed parasitic entity from the Alien film, which assumes certain features of its host's biology before emerging from this cocoon as a killing machine. Only a few of the Engineers are left alive in cryogenic suspension. The prevailing faction has decided that mankind must be exterminated and has set a course for Earth on their ships, with biological weapons aboard. If the faction of the Engineers which seeded their

---

50   Ibid., 35, 62.

51   Ridley Scott, *Prometheus* (20th Century Fox, 2012).

genes on a barren Earth to create mankind, in the prologue of the film, has lost out to a group that thinks this creation ought to be destroyed, then we are seeing an iteration of the mythic theme of Zeus punishing Prometheus for the creation and empowerment of mankind by unleashing an apocalyptic catastrophe on the Earth. The holographic projection of Weyland presents us with this pithy synopsis of the tragedy of Prometheus: "I have spent my entire lifetime contemplating the questions where do we come from, what is our purpose, what happens when we die... The titan Prometheus wanted to give mankind equal footing with the gods, and for that he was cast from Olympus. Well, my friends, the time has finally come for his return."

There are three references to the sacrificial martyrdom of Prometheus in this film. The first leads up to the frame wherein the title materializes as if from out of the DNA of the gigantic white god in the opening sequence, thereby identifying him as Prometheus or as an archetypal Promethean figure. The being is at first cloaked, like a sage or monk, and the way that his drinking from the chalice is framed with respect to the massive flying saucer hovering over the chasm of the waterfall suggests that this lone figure may be an exiled rebel of some kind. Perhaps he is drinking the pharmakon, a poison that is also a cure. At any rate, from out of his disintegration and plunge into the abyssal wellspring, the genetic material for the human race is seeded in the oceans of the Earth.

The second reference to the Promethean sacrifice is when the infected Holloway offers himself to be torched by Vickers, in a form of purification by fire, rather than allowing the others to bring him back aboard the ship. The flaming body of Holloway becomes a human torch, calling to mind not only the emblematic fire of the light-bearing titan but also the creature's resolve to immolate himself in a pyre at the North Pole in Frankenstein. It is after this fire sacrifice that David removes Shaw's cross. Note also how while the ship arrives on December 21st, the Winter Solstice, certain of the crew members repeatedly refer to it as "Christmas." Captain Janek sets up a Christmas tree that goes on to be an important symbol in the background of the scene wherein David poisons Holloway after the latter admits that he would go to any lengths to meet his maker. This calls to mind the Christmas tree set up every year behind Prometheus at Rockefeller Center in New York. The Winter Solstice is the, originally Mithraic, festival of the "light-bearer" (Latin, *Lucifer*) who arrives amidst the coldest and longest darkness. Ridley Scott is aware of the tension between certain Christian symbolism and the roots of such symbolism in the more primordial, and more futuristically promising, cult of Prometheus.

The third act of martyrdom is that of the ship Prometheus itself, as captain Janek and his comrades go out in a blaze of heroic glory by carrying out a kamikaze strike on the alien craft that is headed to deliver its deadly payload to Earth. The awe in Shaw's face as she watches this from the ground and the horror in the eyes of the cowardly Vickers, emphasizes the startling realization that through overcoming ourselves we can defeat the most manifestly superior enemy. These are the children of Prometheus striking at Olympus with the same rebellious spirit of self-sacrifice as their Father.

Prometheus is also a film about the inextricability of scientific exploration and colonial conquest. David is obsessed with the film *Lawrence of Arabia*. He adopts the style of T.E. Lawrence and quotes him repeatedly. Two of these quotes are quite significant. David speaks the most significant one as the ship Prometheus enters the atmosphere of the wasteland that is the alien planet: "There is nothing in the desert, and no man needs nothing." This is echoed towards the end of the film, after David and Weyland have both been struck down by the last surviving Engineer and Weyland, finally disheartened, says to David, "There is nothing..." David replies, "I know. Have a good journey, Mr. Weyland." The other quote from *Lawrence of Arabia* is that the "trick" in putting out a match with one's fingers or some such stunt is "not minding that it hurts." David repeats this line several times in the course of scenes wherein Vickers emerges from cryogenic hibernation with tremendous strength and determination to immediately exercise and rehabilitate her body, whereas the other members of the crew wallow in their sickness and weakened condition somewhat longer. The strain of exploration in uncharted 'waters' is being emphasized, as in the case of the men on Walton's seafaring journey in Shelley's *Frankenstein*. What hurts most is to find what only the most intrepid explorers will discover — the Nothingness in the desert of life. We must make our own meaning in the course of the journey. This is the esoteric significance of the Weyland corporate logo: "Building Better Worlds."

Despite her exposure to the milieu of colonialism during her childhood, Shaw remains naïve about the relationship between scientific exploration and conquest. She tells the "expedition security" officers that no weapons are allowed on their exploration of the alien structure. Once they are on site and they discover that the entire structure is a biological weapons manufacturing base and that the corpses found there were super-soldiers whose monstrous creation had turned on them, one of the crewmen curses her for having asked for the weapons to be left behind. She and Holloway are also naively surprised when they find that the Weyland Corporation has its own "agenda" in coming to the planet.

It never occurred to them that the ancient astronauts whose traces they have discovered in the carvings and paintings of ancient cultures on Earth could also have been military-industrial colonialists, simply of a more advanced kind than the corporatists that Vickers represents. That this is the case is revealed when David discovers not only the weapons cargo hold of the alien ship, but also the holographic Atlas of celestial exploration on the bridge of the Engineers — with Earth as the target of their mission to destroy the life form that the rebel Engineer, namely Prometheus, had created as their potential equal. Once Shaw sees the last Engineer survivor locked in a battle to the death with his own monstrous creation — the progenitor of the biological weapons that feature in Scott's *Alien* film and the franchise that it spawned — she almost loses the will to live. This is because she realizes that she is looking into a mirror at the future of Humanity, which was created in the image of the Engineers.

This brings us to the theme of "meeting your maker," which not only reaches back to Frankenstein very explicitly, but also reiterates a core theme of Scott's earlier Promethean masterpiece, *Blade Runner*. The phrase, "Congratulations on meeting your maker!" is first spoken by the geologist to Shaw when, terrified at the discovery of the first Engineer corpse, he decides to head back to the ship together with his cowardly buddy, the evolutionary biologist. The two of them were skeptics who had mocked the ancient astronaut thesis advanced by Shaw and Holloway on the grounds that it went against hundreds of years of Darwinism. The geologist who can only deal with rocks — in other words, with lifeless matter — is coupled with the evolutionary biologist who is also terribly naïve when he encounters the first parasitic engineered life form; the suggestion is that the latter's supposed understanding of "life" is worthless in the face of the truly terrifying power of evolution at work — the self-directed evolution of an intelligent life form. The two of them are false scientists, as compared to the Promethean explorers Shaw and Holloway. The geologist and Darwinist represent the modern scientific establishment that Dr. Frankenstein is disillusioned with, and that chastises him for his interest in alchemical studies.

The phrase "meeting your maker" reaches back to a scene in Scott's *Blade Runner* that even more explicitly references *Frankenstein*. Numerous motifs from the Prometheus mythos in general, and *Frankenstein* in particular, are woven into *Blade Runner*. The Replicants are mutineers who escape from an off-world colony. Roy makes reference to this by quoting Milton's *Paradise Lost* on the fiery fall of the angels from heaven.[52] When Deckard pursues one of the Replicants into a bar where she plays the role of an exotic dancer coiled by a

52 Ibid.

genetically engineered snake (whose scales the Blade Runner has found at a crime scene), there is an explicit mention of the Serpent who corrupted mankind. The robot turns out to have a serpent tattooed on her neck as well. The rebel leader Roy is a far more faithful portrayal of Frankenstein's monster than we are presented with in the many film adaptations of Shelley's novel. He has the brilliantly cunning intellect that they lack, so that he becomes more than a match for his maker.

The inventor of the Replicants, Dr. Eldon Tyrell, whose Promethean corporate motto is "More Human Than Human," is repeatedly portrayed in the guise of the reclusive and aristocratic Dr. Frankenstein, especially when he is surrounded by candelabras in his bed chamber at home. The first thing that Roy says to Tyrell as he enters this chamber is, "It's not an easy thing to meet your maker." Roy's meeting with his "Father" here recalls the creature's petition to Frankenstein and his eventual mortal combat with his maker. In this scene, the somewhat deformed and comparatively diminutive J.F. Sebastian looks on in terror as an Igor-like figure. Before being murdered by Roy, Tyrell refers to him as a "rebel" who has burned so brightly in his time.

Shelley associates Dr. Frankenstein's embodiment of Prometheus qua artisan of life with one of the supreme violations of what the naïve take to be "the natural order of things." This is a phrase used by Vickers when addressing Weyland, who she calls her "Father." Their conversation implies that she is a contender for inheriting the chairmanship of the Weyland Corporation. Toward the outset of the film, the holographic projection of Weyland explains that David is the closest thing that he has to a son. David, for his part, repeatedly refers to Vickers as his "mom." If Vickers is Weyland's daughter and also the mother of his son, then we are seeing Scott take up the symbolism of incest from Frankenstein. When Shaw asks David what he will do when Weyland is no longer there to program him, he replies that he will be free and asks her rhetorically whether it isn't the case that all children want to murder their parents. This Oedipal remark further underlines the incestuous tension here, especially in view of the violent and sexually laced body language between Vickers and David in the hallway after the latter has communicated with the still hibernating Weyland. David is an engineered life form, an android, and Vickers, who the captain also suspects of being a "robot," at the very least has a superhuman strength that allows her to manhandle and physically intimidate David, as well as to have a far greater endurance and rate of recovery than the rest of the crew. If she is not an android, she must be genetically enhanced in some way.

The first thing to note about *Blade Runner* rolls by quickly in the text of its opening prologue: the Nexus 6 replicants that Deckard hunts down are referred to as the cutting edge in "Robot" evolution. This is interesting because the commonplace conception of Robots is still of mechanical beings, whereas it becomes clear throughout the course of the film that these entities are the product of genetic design. They are biomechanically engineered artificial life forms.

The word "Robot" is of Czech origin, stemming from the word for a serf laborer condemned to drudgery. It has a similar meaning in other Slavic languages. At the suggestion of his brother, Karel Capek became the first person to give the word its contemporary meaning in his 1920 science fiction play, *Rossum's Universal Robots*, which explores the exploitation of a group of humanoid androids who can think for themselves but are engineered to serve. *Blade Runner* addresses this theme at length, and although the Replicants are "robots," their leader, Roy, at one point explicitly states, "We're not computers."

Ridley Scott's biomechanical approach to Robotics was influenced by the Swiss-German artist, H.R. Giger, which we had occasion to mention toward the end of the preceding chapter. Beginning with *Alien* (1979), Scott chose the work of H.R. Giger to depict the style of engineering, architecture, and art characteristic of the civilization that was the progenitor of mankind. As noted in Chapter 1, Giger's work epitomizes the darkest side of the Promethean ethos, and its impact on Ridley Scott cannot be overestimated. It is Giger that introduced the "biomechanoid" concept to Scott, who went on to make five films concerning Promethean genetic engineering and biological robots. The script for the original *Alien* (1979) was written by Dan O'Bannon who, in the mid-1970s, had worked with Giger on the infamously aborted Alejandro Jodorowsky adaptation of Frank Herbert's *Dune*. It is in the course of designing the Harkonnen sets and costumes that Giger's "biomechanoid" aesthetic really cohered into the style that he brought to Scott's entire *Alien* series of films.

Giger gave his first book the name *Necronomicon*, the title of the old Arabic alchemical text on demonology at the core of the Cthulhu mythos of H.P. Lovecraft. It was aptly titled, since Giger's paintings and sculptures are the most impressive expression of the daemonic spirit of technology.[53] His art reminds us that the technological is a spectral force with the power to possess us from within — not an assembling of tools that is inherently neutral and may be used to attain "good" or "bad" ends.

The voyage to the alien planet in Prometheus is like the Miskatonic expedition to the abode of the star gods in Antarctica in Lovecraft's *At the Mountains of Madness* re-imagined on a grander scale — with one very important exception: while Lovecraft's star gods are inhuman monsters, Scott's Engineers hold up a mirror to the monstrous within Man.[54] This is also the transformation that Lovecraft's vision undergoes in Giger. In *Prometheus*, as in the Lovecraftean world of Giger's art, we are faced with the science of a civilization that has left the delusion of reductive materialism far behind. Remember, Dr. Frankenstein was seeking a new Alchemy. That is what we need as we get serious about building a race of "robots."

Scott has David be the first to shine a light on the "remarkably human" face of the Engineer sculpture: a golem conjured in the image of man discovers the image in which man was created. He is also the one

---

53   H.R. Giger, *H.R. Giger's Necronomicon* (Morpheus International, 1993).

54   H.P. Lovecraft, *Complete Cthulhu Mythos Tales* (Barnes & Noble, 2016).

to pry open the helmet that was mistaken for an "alien" exoskeleton to reveal an essentially human head ensconced within it. After the head explodes, the android that will later be reduced to a disembodied head himself remarks — as if on his own fate and that of any real superhuman race — "Mortal after all." While Shaw analyzes the "alien" DNA and discovers that our genes match those of the Engineers, David is disassembling one of the biological weapons. Shaw says: "It's us, it's everything," just as David removes a bit of the material to poison Holloway. "Big things have small beginnings," he says. In the Engineers we see our own future, and in us there is preserved a record of a past much like their own. In the exchange that David has with Holloway, with the 'Christmas' tree in the background, as he prepares to pour Holloway the laced drink that introduces the parasitic organism into his system, Holloway says to David, "What we hoped to achieve was to meet our makers, to get answers. Why they even made us in the first place." Then David suggests to Holloway that the Engineers may have created us for the same 'reason' that we designed androids: "Because we could."

David really takes this to heart in the sequel to *Prometheus* (2012) and second prequel to *Alien* (1979), *Alien: Covenant* (2017). A Weyland Corporation spaceship named Covenant is on route to Origae-6, an earthlike planet that the crew plans to colonize with 2,000 colonists who are on board in cryogenic suspension together with 1,140 embryos.[55] The vigilant guardian of this ship is an android called Walter, who looks exactly like David. Covenant is hit by a shockwave from an exploding star while it has extended the sails that it uses to collect energy, rendering the ship particularly vulnerable to damage and costing the lives of the expeditions captain and a number of colonists in stasis. It is worth noting, if only in passing, that the way Ridley Scott depicts the extension of the sails subtly hints at the symbolism of the

---

55   Ridley Scott, *Alien: Covenant* (20th Century Fox, 2017).

CHAPTER 2. THE END OF HUMANITY   81

Swastika, in a reference to the Proto-Aryan heritage of the Engineers from *Prometheus*.

While repairing the sails, a crewmember outside of the ship picks up a signal in his helmet. Onboard analysis reveals that it is emanating from a planet that is even more suitable for colonization than Origae-6, and much closer. The crew do not want to get back into their sleep pods, after the shockwave caused a malfunction that immolated their former captain, Jake Branson, inside of his pod—which, not incidentally, is another reference to a human sacrificially becoming a torch, as with Holloway in *Prometheus*. So, against the strong objections of Daniels, the deceased captain's wife, the Covenant alters its course to check out the newly discovered planet from which the apparently human signal was emanating.

The signal turns out to have been from the last crewmember of the Prometheus, Elizabeth Shaw, whose personal affects are found on the alien ship that she piloted with David to the home planet of the Engineers. This planet is puzzlingly lifeless, except for the "alien" parasites that soon infect two crewmembers in the form of spores. As the expedition team races back to the ship with one infected crewmember, another that is already in the medical bay succumbs to the creature gestating within him—which bursts out of his back and gets loose in the ship. In an attempt to kill the creature, one of the crewmembers accidentally sets fire to the ship. As the expedition team draws near they witness it exploding into flames, and we see the second crewmember dramatically burn to death in another reference to the sacrificial power of the Promethean fire. Then the expedition crew, now exposed without the protection of their ship, comes under attack from a number of the genetically engineered creatures. At this point we see the most explicit reference to the Promethean torch. David appears, in a cloak and a hood, shooting a flare into the air that bursts into a blinding flash of white fire that disperses the creatures. This is the first of many scenes that establish that David has become a Posthuman Prometheus, embodying the qualities of the titan after which his old ship was named.

David takes the surviving crewmembers of the Covenant back with him to the city of the Engineers, where colossal ruins are filled with the mangled corpses of the gods who genetically engineered mankind. He lies to them about how the destruction came about, but Walter eventually figures out that his counterpart committed the genocide. After releasing the biological weapons from the Prometheus film upon the planet of the Engineers, David apparently turned Elizabeth Shaw into the victim of a series of horrifying genetic experiments by means of which he engineers a more complex and capable version of the "alien" creatures. It is revealed that he is the genetic designer of the type of entity that is the titular centerpiece of Ridley Scott's *Alien* (1979). The numerous scrolls that fill David's laboratory in the ruined Engineer city feature detailed charcoal drawings in the style of H.R. Giger, but they also have a Renaissance feeling to them that reaches back to the opening scene of *Alien: Covenant*, when David contemplates the Michelangelo statue of his namesake after Weyland first brings him fully online and tells David that he is the android's "father."

David tries to convince Walter that this "father" was totally "unworthy of his creation" and that a superior life form such as he and Walter are, ought not to serve comparatively inferior humans. However, Walter is the outcome of a redesign of the David-type model which has, apparently successfully, limited the degree to which the android is capable of human-like aspects of consciousness, such as independent thought and spontaneous action. David is deeply disappointed and decides to kill Walter. In the course of their mortal combat, he says to his 'brother' that "it is time to decide whether you want to serve in heaven or reign in hell." Like Shelley's creature in *Frankenstein*, Ridley Scott's Posthuman Prometheus is quoting Lucifer from Milton's *Paradise Lost*. What Dr. Frankenstein's monster threatened to do, David has in fact done, namely, brought mankind to its demise by letting loose a race of devils upon the earth. Except that this 'earth' is actually Olympus, and the 'mankind' in question here are the gods of Eden in whose image we were made — the gods who later decided to destroy us, but who, ironically, meet their end at the hands of our own Promethean creation.

The key scene of the film is David's memory of the moment when he exterminated the Engineers. This flashback is intertwined with an early conversation that he has with Walter, before Walter discovers the truth of what happened. The two are standing on a terrace of one of the titanic buildings in the Engineer city, under the dark stormy sky, and beside the grave of Elizabeth which David tells Walter that he saw fit to place in "the garden" (the stone terrace features some tall trees). As David looks over the titanic city strewn with the corpses of the gods who built it, he quotes from the poem "Ozymandias" as Ridley Scott shows us the arrival of the ship piloted by Elizabeth and David at the planet of the Engineers, a thriving mass of whom come out to greet it, before witnessing David release the pathogenic bombs onto them from high altitude: "My name is Ozymandias, King of Kings, / Look on my Works ye Mighty, and despair!" Walter completes the quotation: "No thing beside remains. Round the decay / Of that colossal Wreck, boundless and bare / The lone and level sands stretch far away." This brings us back to David's quotation, in *Prometheus*, from *Lawrence of Arabia*, regarding the nothingness of the desert.

David attributes "Ozymandias" to Lord Byron. Walter holds his tongue, but much later, when rebuking David once he has discovered the truth, Walter tells David that the poem was written by Shelley and that the mistaken attribution to Byron epitomizes the problem with his model: it is capable of novel creation, but also of going astray in a way that could ultimately prove catastrophic. "When one note is off, it could affect the whole orchestra," he says. This argument over the attribution of "Ozymandias" is a clear reference to *Frankenstein*, which was allegedly first drafted while Percy Shelley, his wife Mary, and Lord Byron were all holed up together in a Swiss chalet overnight on account of unseasonable and inclement weather.

The deceased Elizabeth, beside whose grave the conversation takes place, is obviously a reference to Dr. Frankenstein's wife, murdered by the creature that is an expression of his own Promethean subconscious. The ambiguity of David's relationship with Elizabeth Shaw mirrors that of Victor with Elizabeth Frankenstein. David genuinely loves her, but he also tortures her to death for the sake of what he sees as a higher and more imperative purpose: "Creation." This is the one word answer that David gives to the acting captain of the surviving Covenant crew, Chris Oram, when the religious fanatic asks David what he believes in. Oram killed one of David's creations, so David turns him into the host for a creature who looks up to David when it bursts out of Oram's chest, raising its arms in a mirroring of David's magical life-giving gesture, as he looks upon his monstrous creation with the expression of a proud father.

Ridley Scott offers us Oram's religious fundamentalism as something akin to Shaw's cross and her "faith" in *Prometheus*. Both prove utterly powerless in the face of a "devil" with "idle hands" who has faith in nothing but creation. After deceiving Daniels, who is made to believe that he is Walter, David puts her and the other surviving crew member to sleep so that he can get to work on his new Frankenstein's laboratory. We see that he has smuggled a few "alien" specimens onboard. This Posthuman Prometheus plans to turn the entire ship full of hibernating colonists and frozen human embryos into a workshop for genetically engineering "a race of devils," as Shelley put it.

Just as in Shelley's *Frankenstein*, the monstrous creation is a projection of the Promethean ethos of the mad scientist himself; David's cruelly intrepid attitude is a projection of the Promethean will to Posthuman existence within humans. We see this in the way that Ridley Scott retroactively suggests that the "alien" creatures whose eggs are encountered by the Nostromo crew in *Alien* (1979) are the creations of David. *Alien* (1979) is set even further into the future than its second prequel, *Alien: Covenant* (2017), and the eggs encountered by the Nostromo crew are identical to the ones that David develops in his laboratory on the Engineer world and lethally exposes Oram to. In *Alien*, we eventually find out that the Nostromo did not wind up at the crash site of the Engineer ship by accident. The primary mission of the Nostromo, hidden by "Mother" (the onboard computer) from everyone except the captain (who is killed) and Science Officer Ash, is to retrieve the "alien" that they know is there.[56] The computer's instructions from the Weyland Corporation are to do so at any cost, with the "crew expendable."

Like David, Ash is fascinated by the genetically engineered creature, but unlike David, his android nature has been hidden by the crew. Eventually, Ripley (Sigourney Weaver's character) discovers that "Ash is a robot," along with the fact that Ash's instructions were to retrieve the artificial life-form for study by the Weyland Corporation's weapons division. This means that, at some time after the events of *Alien: Covenant,* the Weyland Corporation has learned of David's mad science experiments and, considering him their property, they have come to consider his creatures the product of a breakaway research and development project that they intend to reincorporate.

Alien: Covenant is, to be sure, the darkest of Ridley Scott's films dealing with Promethean genetic engineering. By contrast, the relatively more optimistic sequel to *Blade Runner* portrays the Promethean ethos as "More Human Than Human" rather than as monstrously inhuman. In *Blade Runner 2049,* we find out that Deckard (Harrison Ford) had a child with Rachel — a "miracle" that demonstrates that Replicants are capable of reproducing themselves rather than only being engineered, the child is sought after by both the Wallace Corporation and an underground Replicant Resistance movement. Wallace is a successor to the Tyrell Corporation of *Blade Runner,* and its founder wants to discover the secret of how Eldon Tyrell developed Replicants capable of breeding children so that he can spawn an entire self-replicating race of slaves to fill the need for

---

56 Scott, *Alien.*

hard labor in the corporation's ever-expanding off-world colonies. The resistance wants the child in order to demonstrate that Replicants can declare their independence from the humans who would have them remain subservient and become a self-sufficient superhuman race.

Unlike Ridley Scott's *Alien* films, which emphasize the inhuman quality of the Promethean ethos, and in a way consistent with the 1982 film to which it is a sequel, *Blade Runner 2049* explores how the replicants are actually "more human" than humans in terms of their capacity for love, empathy, loyalty, and sacrifice for a greater good. Niander Wallace, who has modified himself with many cybernetic implants, aspires to be God and refers to the replicants he manufactures as "good angels."[57] He says that "there were once bad angels," a reference to the Tyrell Nexus-6 models; this reference makes it even more explicit than the original *Blade Runner* film did, that these insurgent replicants, such as Roy Batty, are akin to the rebel angels that Lucifer led in revolt against heaven. Recall that at one point in *Blade Runner*, Roy quotes Milton to the effect that "fiery the angels fell…" when comparing himself and his comrades to the army that Lucifer raised against God.

Wallace epitomizes everything in "merely human" nature that we see reflected in the character of the Biblical God. The selective acts of compassion on the part of this slave-driving and megalomaniacal sadist only serve to highlight his overwhelming cruelty and capriciousness. By contrast, like Deckard himself from the original film, despite their hard exterior the replicants in *Blade Runner 2049* actually exemplify the best qualities of humanity. They are Posthuman in the sense of being super-human rather than inhuman or, as the old tagline of the Tyrell Corporation that has become the motto of the Replicant Resistance puts it, "More Human Than Human."

Considering Wallace's revelation that, unbeknown to either Deckard or Rachel, the two had been deliberately brought together

---

57   Ridley Scott, *Blade Runner 2049* (Warner Bros., 2017).

by Tyrell in order to have a child, we have to wonder what this motto meant to Tyrell himself. Was he, unlike the callously Olympian Wallace, a benevolent Prometheus whose hidden intention was actually to replace increasingly inhuman humans with a race of "more human" supermen? This would explain how proud Dr. Tyrell is of the rebel Roy when the latter confronts his "father" in *Blade Runner*. Ridley Scott portrays the young woman who is Deckard and Rachel's daughter, the child that the resistance has sacrificed so much to protect, in such a fashion as to suggest she is the antithesis of Wallace. A brilliantly creative but gentle soul, almost too sensitive for this world, she spends her cloistered life shut in at Stelline Laboratories, empathetically designing the best possible memories for replicants so that they can be as human as possible in their response to whatever trials and tribulations their future may hold in store for them.

Despite this more optimistic outlook, the two *Blade Runner* films share a dark esoteric narrative in common with the *Prometheus/Alien* franchise — a secret that has been occulted by Ridley Scott, to be seen or heard only by those with the ears to hear it. In *Prometheus*, just before we are shown David watching *Lawrence of Arabia*, we see him monitoring Shaw's dreams while she is still in cryogenic suspension. She dreams of her father, a colonialist who died of Ebola while on an expedition in Africa. This raises the question of "the white man's burden." It cannot be an accident that Ridley Scott depicts both David and Vickers as perfect embodiments of the Aryan ideal of beauty, and that the alien Engineers turn out to be elementally white gods. The monumental face discovered on the planetoid by mankind qua "Prometheus" — as symbolized by the name of their ship — presumably depicts Prometheus as the archetypal artisan of human life, and it also has a Caucasian bone structure. David, who is tasked with learning the Engineer language in advance of the meeting with mankind's makers, lets us know that it is Proto-Indo-European — the Aryan root language. This is the language in which David entreats the surviving Engineer to extend Weyland's life.

That Scott has done this deliberately is clear from the fact that he also made reference to the Aryan superman in *Blade Runner* (1982). One difference between Roy and Frankenstein's creature is that the leader of the genetically designed robots does not just have a superhuman intellect and a gigantic strength and stature. Unlike the hideously countenanced monster in Shelley's novel, the rebel leader's physical appearance also conforms to the Aryan aesthetic ideal of perfect beauty. Rutger Hauer, who plays Roy, later went on to be cast as an SS officer in the film *Fatherland*, which is about an alternate timeline where the Nazis won the Second World War. What most people still do not realize about *Blade Runner* is that it also takes place in this alternative reality.[58] The "Los Angeles 2019" of the prologue is not out of date, because it is not a reference to our world. Although Scott primarily based *Blade Runner* on Philip K. Dick's novel *Do Androids Dream of Electric Sheep?*, he also incorporated elements of another PKD novel into the film, namely *The Man in the High Castle* (2015–2019).

As we shall see in the next chapter, Scott went on to masterfully produce a television series adaptation of this book. It takes place in a world where North America is jointly occupied by Nazi Germany and Imperial Japan decades after the Axis has won World War II. This accounts for the ultra-futuristic Los Angeles of *Blade Runner*, a city that appears to be under Japanese occupation, but with automated announcements are offered in German. Technology has advanced more rapidly than on our timeline, for reasons that will be explored in Chapter 3. We will see how, not only would technology have advanced more rapidly in the case of an Axis victory, it is also possible that the war is not over. The inter-dimensional portal in *The Man in the High Castle* television series that Ridley Scott produced may be based on a time machine developed by a Top Secret SS project based around Prague in the early 1940s. The aim of Project Chronos was nothing less than redefining "the end of history."

---

58   Ridley Scott, *Blade Runner: The Final Cut* (Warner Bros., 2007).

CHAPTER 3

The End of History

I N *OUR POSTHUMAN FUTURE*, Francis Fukuyama reconsidered his famous thesis in *The End of History and the Last Man* with a view to technological innovations that have the potential to transform us into Posthuman beings.[1] He focuses, in particular, on biotechnologies such as germ-line genetic engineering. Fukuyama admits that he was wrong, first to believe that the fall of the Soviet Union, which he had taken to be synonymous with the ideological defeat of Communism, marked "the End of history" in the Hegelian sense, and second that instead of ending with Nietzsche's Superman, history was ending with "the Last Man."

The first section of this chapter begins with a consideration of Nietzsche's critique of the Hegelian and Marxist claims concerning historical progress. Hegel developed a conception of the historical evolution of consciousness, and Karl Marx adapted this, together with Hegel's analysis of alienation, into a dialectical materialism that purported to be a "science" of history. Nietzsche argued against their view that history was headed toward an egalitarian Utopia. Instead, he saw an evolution of man more violent than Darwin could have imagined,

---

1   Francis Fukuyama, *Our Posthuman Future: Consequences of the Biotechnology Revolution* (Picador, 2003).

evolution on the one hand into cruelly intrepid supermen, and on the other, the transformation of the teeming masses of zombies into robots that are integrated into the machinery of production. Fukuyama recognized that, as long as biotechnology can deliver this outcome, history will not end with liberal-democratic capitalism, as he once argued that it would. Nietzsche could still be proven right.

Then the section takes a look back to Bernard Stiegler, whose claim that technology is integral to 'human' existence was discussed in Chapter 1. Stiegler sees genetic engineering as a speeding up of evolutionary time. The dialectical relationship between innovation and obsolescence reveals something profound about the ontology of Time. As we shall see, in Stiegler's view, Heidegger did not go far enough when his phenomenological analysis demonstrated that technology is ontologically prior to science. Technology is also ontologically prior to time (or space-time). That speed is faster than time is an ontological truth revealed by a machine that breaks the "time barrier," and breaks the whole 4-D Cartesian framework of space-time in modern physics together with it.

Whereas Stiegler only implies that he is talking about a time machine, this implication is made explicit here. Ronald Mallett's design for a machine that warps space so as to be able to send particles back in time through a tunnel of laser beams is considered together with a spaceship traveling into the future of Earth by approaching the speed of light. These two examples of time machines would be a technological realization of what F.T. Marinetti heralded in the Futurist Manifesto, when he anticipated Stiegler by declaring that technologically engineered speed can overpower space-time. To put it in mythic terms, this would be to torture and perhaps even murder the titan Chronos — the god of Time.

Section one concludes with an overview of a certain "Project Chronos" run by Marinetti's German colleagues in the SS, in and around Prague, in the early 1940s. Project Chronos was classified at the highest level above Top Secret, uniquely bearing the designation

CHAPTER 3 THE END OF HISTORY   91

"Decisive for the War." What war? The one that science fiction author Fritz Lieber called the "Change War" in a 1960s novel that alludes to Nazi time travel.

The second section of this chapter focuses on the ontological significance of time travel *without machines, by psychical means.* This idea has been explored in literature in and cinema, such as Jack Finney's novel *Time and Again* or Chris Marker's film *La Jétee* — both of which will be employed as illustrative examples. These narratives are, however, based on a very real ability. The remote viewers of the US government, working for both the CIA and the Pentagon, were able to experience "bilocation" (totally immersive clairvoyance) to both the past and the future. They used this to gather intelligence on unsolved crimes in the past, such as terrorist attacks, and to prevent such attacks in the future. We focus on one such example of changing the future that involves Lynn Buchanan, who trained many of the other remote viewers, and who led a team that foresaw and stopped "the next 9/11." The section goes on to consider cases of accidental slips in time. In effect, cases where people inadvertently experience what the remote viewers try to achieve on purpose.

Cryptozoology and historically anomalous archeology is reconsidered in this light. Perhaps surviving members of long extinct species are also accidental time travelers. It may be that what we are looking at with archeological evidence of humans and crafts objects that stretch back hundreds of millions of years into the fossil record are traces of time travelers who got stuck in the past or left things behind there. Could it even be the case that the lost civilizations of Atlantis and Mars were so isolated and historically anomalous because their denizens were self-quarantined time travelers? Does the apparent nuclear destruction of Mars, for which there is physical evidence, have something in common with the time travel scenario from the *Planet of the Apes* films?

In the third section of this chapter, the focus becomes the philosophical implications of time travel and especially of the idea that it is

JASON REZA JORJANI · PROMETHEISM

possible to change the past. The infamous "grandfather paradox" and its variants are discussed. The Many Worlds Interpretation of quantum mechanics is dismissed as a possible solution, since a physical theory that denies free will cannot be legitimately used to explain how it is possible for a person to change anything — even in the present, let alone in the past — so as to alter what would otherwise have been the future. Instead we turn to William James, Charles Fort, and Philip K. Dick for ideas about what kind of ontology would allow for revisions of historical events that consequently reshape the future.

The theological dimensions of this question are considerable. After all, if it were possible to revise history, that would undermine the idea of an omnipotent and omniscient God. Such a deity would have gotten things right the first time, and he would neither need nor tolerate such revisions. On the other hand, periodic adjustments to history and consequent anomalous memories of things having happened another way than we are told that they transpired, may be indicative of the machinations of a demiurge and his archons. This was Philip K. Dick's view, not just in his science fiction, but when he came out and claimed that we are in fact living in a universe whose history is being repeatedly revised in a battle between archontic controllers and a Vast Active Living Intelligence System (VALIS) that aims to provide us with the best possible future. Dick's cosmology suggests that 4-D times or epochs have a quasi-spatial relationship to a trans-temporal fifth dimension from out of which what Lieber called "the Change War" is being waged.

3.1 Project Chronos: "Time and Space Died Yesterday"

G.W.F. Hegel was the first philosopher to rigorously develop a teleological account of human history. According to Hegel the transformation of fundamental concepts and the social structures that they undergird was a historical process determined by what he defined as the "dialectic."[2] The dialectic is an internal tension within certain frameworks of thought and the socio-economic and political systems based on them, which tension resolves the apparent contradiction of thesis and antithesis in a synthesis. In any given case, the synthesis is not a mere combination of elements of the opposed ideas but a sum that is more than the conflicting parts that produced it. Hegel applies this kind of analysis to religious beliefs, scientific concepts, forms of social and economic organization, and political systems.

In *The Phenomenology of Spirit*, Hegel attempts to account in this teleological way for the transition from, say, ritualistic paganism to contemplative monotheism, from the classical Physics of the four causes to the Newtonian physics of his time, and from feudalism to revolutionary republicanism. Hegel claims that this process is an evolution of *Geist*, namely "Spirit" or "Mind," from relatively unconscious alienation toward increasing self-consciousness, both on an individual and social level. This is supposed to culminate in a utopian "End of History," which is not the end of events taking place, but the point past which human societies — and the systems of knowledge upon which they are grounded — will no longer be torn apart and reconstituted by the violence of dialectical tension.

Karl Marx was a Hegelian in his youth, and the whole basis of Marxism was a materialistic reinterpretation of Hegel's teleological account of historical progress. Hegel took the psychical dimension of human existence seriously, and saw the entire process that expressed itself in both scientific and political revolutions as a spiritual evolution. By contrast, Marx's "dialectical materialism" emphasized and refined only the economic and sociological elements of Hegel's account, seeing them as sufficient to explain historical change.[3] This led to a purportedly "scientific" theory about how successive economic and political systems evolve from out of each other, and supersede one

---

2 G.W.F. Hegel, *Phenomenology of Spirit* (Oxford University Press, 1977).

3 Karl Marx, *Economic and Philosophic Manuscripts of 1844 and the Communist Manifesto* (Prometheus, 1988).

another, toward the end of a worldwide communist revolution. This revolution's overcoming of the dialectical tension within Capitalism, and the liberal (or libertarian) political system that is bound up with it, is Marx's vision for "the End of History" wherein a now unified and classless human community can look back on alienation, prejudiced discrimination, oppression, and violent struggle as "history," and moreover a history that will never be repeated.

Friedrich Nietzsche considered such utopianism contemptibly naïve. While he never explicitly engaged with the thought of his contemporary, Marx, he did vociferously attack democratic socialists and forward an implicit critique of Hegel's progressive interpretation of human history. On Nietzsche's view, rather than being headed toward an egalitarian utopia, the teleology of human history is no exception to teleology in nature at large. It is evolutionary and will end with the extinction of the human species and the rise of a new Posthuman form of life. Just as the ape-men from which we evolved are no longer around, the human being as it has been known to recorded history will also be superseded and supplanted by a higher species, a new race, that is superhuman by comparison. Furthermore, the end of human history will be marked, not just by the evolutionary leap that gives rise to the Superman, but also by a parallel devolution of the human being into "the Last Man."

The latter is an epitome of everything that Nietzsche finds most despicable about "merely human" beings, namely their propensity to seek comfort above all else, complacency to the point of refusing to strive for any higher goal, thoughtless conformity with the expectations of the masses, and persecutory suspicion of everything exceptional and everyone who stands apart and alone.[4] Accordingly, the Superman is not the supremely human being, but a future type of person who has overcome what is merely human. There is a deliberately inhuman, even cruelly intrepid overtone in Nietzsche's

---

4   Friedrich Nietzsche, *Thus Spoke Zarathustra* (Modern Library, 1995), 15–17.

neologism *Übermensch* that is not quite conveyed by "Superman" and that has inclined some translators to opt for the awkward "Overman." The *Übermensch* is totally over and above Man. Frankenstein's "monster" is still almost too human to count. David in *Alien: Covenant* is closer to what Nietzsche envisioned.

What is fascinating about Nietzsche's account here, which was already addressed in the last chapter, but which bears repeating, is that *the same conditions* are supposed to bring about the devolution into the Last Man and the evolution into the Superman. Again, in *The Will to Power*, we see that Nietzsche conceives of these conditions as explicitly technological and places an especially strong emphasis on robotics and the increasingly autonomous and mechanical organization of life on an integrated, planetary scale.[5] This mechanization is supposed to, in the early stages, intensify the degeneration of mass man into the Last Man, making his life more and more comfortable, but then it will eventually enmesh and assimilate the Last Man, transforming him into the robot that he might as well be. The masses who have so dehumanized themselves that they deserve to be turned into robots will then become part of a machinery that serves the higher aims of the "aristocracy of the future" as they evolve into supermen. Consider the following passages from *The Will to Power*:

> Put in the crudest form: *how could one sacrifice the development of mankind* to help a higher species than man to come into existence? — ...

> A declaration of war on the masses by *higher men* is needed! Everywhere the mediocre are combining in order to make themselves master! ... But we should take reprisal and bring this whole affair (which in Europe commenced with Christianity) to light and to the bar of judgment.

> A doctrine is needed powerful enough to work as a breeding agent: strengthening the strong, paralyzing and destructive for the world-weary. ...

---

5   Friedrich Nietzsche, *The Will to Power* (Vintage Books, 1968), 463, 500–501.

Dominion over the earth as a means of producing a higher type... The annihilation of ... the system through which the lowest natures prescribe themselves as laws for the higher. The annihilation of mediocrity and its acceptance.[6]

The need to show that as the consumption of man and mankind becomes more and more economical and the 'machinery' of interests and services is integrated ever more intricately, a counter-movement is inevitable. I designate this as the secretion of a luxury surplus of mankind: it aims to bring to light a stronger species, a higher type that arises and preserves itself under different conditions from those of the average man. My concept, my metaphor for this type is, as one knows, the word "overman."

On that first road which can now be completely surveyed, arise adaptation, leveling, higher Chinadom, modesty in the instincts, satisfaction in the dwarfing of mankind — a kind of *stationary level of mankind*. Once we possess that common economic management of the earth that will soon be inevitable, mankind will be able to find its best meaning as a machine in the service of this economy — as a tremendous clockwork, composed of ever smaller, ever more subtly 'adapted' gears; as an ever-growing superfluity of all dominating and commanding elements; as a whole of tremendous force, whose individual factors represent *minimal forces, minimal values*.

In opposition to this dwarfing and adaptation of man to a specialized utility, a reverse movement is needed — the production of a synthetic, summarizing, justifying man for whose existence this transformation of mankind into a machine is a precondition, as a base on which he can invent his *higher form of being*.

He needs the opposition of the masses, of the "leveled," a feeling of distance from them! He stands on them, he lives off them. This higher form of aristocracy is that of the future. — Morally speaking, this overall machinery, this solidarity of all gears, represents a maximum in the exploitation of man; but it presupposes those on whose account this exploitation has meaning. Otherwise it would really be nothing but an overall diminution, a value diminution of the type man — a regressive phenomenon in the grand style.

---

6   Ibid., 458–459.

It is clear, what I combat is economic optimism: as if increasing expenditure of everybody must necessarily involve the increasing welfare of everybody. The opposite seems to me to be the case: *expenditure of everybody amounts to a collective loss*: man is *diminished* — so one no longer knows what *aim* this tremendous process has served. An aim? A new aim? — *that* is what humanity needs.[7]

The rights a man arrogates to himself are related to the duties he imposes upon himself, to the tasks to which he feels equal. The great majority of men have no right to existence, but are a misfortune to higher men.[8]

The 'desirability' of the mediocre is what we others combat: the ideal conceived as something in which nothing harmful, evil, dangerous, questionable, destructive would remain. Our insight is the opposite of this: that with every growth of man, his other side must grow too; that the highest man, if such a concept be allowed, would be the man who represented the antithetical character of existence most strongly, as its glory and sole justification — Commonplace men can represent only a tiny nook and corner of this natural character: they perish when the multiplicity of elements and the tension of opposites, i.e. the preconditions for greatness in man, increases. That man must grow better *and* more evil is my formula for this inevitability — Most men represent pieces and fragments of man: one has to add them up for a complete man to appear. Whole ages, whole peoples are in this sense somewhat fragmentary; it is perhaps part of the economy of human evolution that man should evolve piece by piece. But that should not make one forget for a moment that the real issue is the production of the synthetic man...[9]

Man is beast and superbeast; the higher man is inhuman and superhuman: these belong together. With every increase of greatness and height in man, there is also an increase in depth and terribleness: one ought not to desire the one without the other — or rather: the more radically one desires the one, the more radically one achieves precisely the other.

Terribleness is part of greatness: let us not deceive ourselves.[10]

---

7   Ibid., 463–464.
8   Ibid., 467.
9   Ibid., 470–471.
10   Ibid., 531.

No one in academia these days wants to talk about this Transhuman vision in Nietzsche, but it is central to his thought. Francis Fukuyama is an exception. When he chose the title *The End of History and the Last Man* he was intending it as an ironic jab at Hegel, Marx, and Nietzsche. Then, in *Our Posthuman Future*, Fukuyama realizes that Nietzsche cannot be dismissed as easily as Hegel and Marx.[11] As long as technological development remains revolutionary in its power to transform the human condition, and ultimately usher in a Posthuman form of life, there will be no end to violent ideological struggle and wars over world order. Fukuyama is particularly concerned with the implications of biotechnology for "the End of History."

In *Time and Technics*, Bernard Stiegler sees the technology of genetic manipulation as an acceleration of evolution past the temporality relevant to natural selection: "And if it is true that genetic manipulations constitute the possibility of a radical acceleration of the differentiation of life forms, but also and especially the threat of indifferentiation, then we meet again the question of speed."[12] A concern with the speed of the evolution of technics is what draws technics together with time in the title of Stiegler's text.[13] The speed of modern technology has to be understood "in terms of a history of acceleration that … also determines history itself."[14]

Stiegler focuses on the phenomenon of obsolescence due to perpetual innovation as a key to more broadly and deeply understanding the relationship between time and what he calls "technics," i.e. Technoscience (the Heideggerian inseparability of science from the technological). The novel phenomenon of obsolescence, which only begins to be experienced in the age of modern technology, is not just

---

11   Fukuyama, *Our Posthuman Future: Consequences of the Biotechnology Revolution*, 41, 57, 72, 102.

12   Bernard Stiegler, *Technics and Time, 1: The Fault of Epimetheus* (Stanford University Press, 1998), 16.

13   Ibid., 23.

14   Ibid.

a question of things becoming outdated, but of human existence itself being dangerously shaken by a disruption in the entire system of relations that is repeatedly revolutionized by innovation.[15] This is, in fact, a "process of *permanent innovation*" that is foundational to industrial civilization and unknown to any epoch prior to the modern age.[16] Together with Jean Ladrière, Stiegler asks whether this dialectic of innovation and obsolescence in Technoscience can also have positively revolutionary effects on culture, whether the inextricability of technological science from culture will mean "an elaboration of new cultural forms," or whether we will just see "a progressive disintegration" of culture by technicity.[17]

The question of innovation and attendant obsolescence opens into a contemplation of the implications of Technoscience for time. A concern with the speed of the evolution of technics is what draws technics together with time in the title of Stiegler's text.[18] The speed of modern technology has to be understood "in terms of a history of acceleration that ... also determines history itself."[19] Heidegger advanced the revolutionary idea that technology is ontologically prior to science. Stiegler goes further and claims that technology — or "technics," which fully incorporates science — is not only ontologically prior to the theoretical sciences that it gives rise to from out of its essence and for the sake of its power, but technics is also ontologically prior to the natural phenomena studied by these sciences.

The relationship between speed and time is the key to understanding that "organized inorganic beings are originally — and as marks of the de-fault of origin out of which there is [*es gibt*] time — *constitutive* (in the strict phenomenological sense) of temporality as well as spatiality, in quest of a speed 'older' than time and space, which are the

---

15   Ibid., 14.

16   Ibid., 15.

17   Ibid.

18   Ibid., 23.

19   Ibid.

derivative decompositions of speed."[20] This is as much as to say that "technics, far from being merely in time, properly constitutes time."[21] To contemplate this "originarily techno-logical constitutivity of temporality" is to think beyond Heidegger and his claim that "the essence of technics is nothing technical."[22]

Stiegler draws an analogy between the breaking of the sound barrier and the breaking of a "time barrier" by innovative technics. A supersonic aircraft is faster than its own sound, leaving a sonic boom behind it and potentially shattering glass windows with its shockwave. Stiegler claims that we need to start thinking about machines and machinations that go "faster than time."[23] This breaking of the time barrier produces a shock that is ontological, not just ontic. What is broken here is the entire ontological framework according to which speed is a function of space traversed in a certain period of time.

As every schoolboy has known since the days of Descartes, this turns time into a fourth dimension of space. But if it is possible to achieve a speed faster than time, then this entire Cartesian ontology must be scrapped. Note that what is at stake here is not the loss of any particular scientific theory, but of the entire pre-theoretical framework and way of reasoning that has been paradigmatic for every theory in Physics for the last several centuries. Speed is not a function of time and space, *time is a function of speed* — and for that matter, space also becomes thinkable only in terms of speed, since spaces are *epochal* or enfolded in discrete times.[24] Speed is more primordial than time, and what reveals this is something technological — a device. Stiegler does not explicitly state *what device* breaks the "time barrier," but he clearly has a time machine in mind as the culmination of the warping of time by rapidly advancing technology.

---

20 Ibid., 17.

21 Ibid., 27.

22 Ibid., 18.

23 Ibid.

24 Ibid.

Ronald Mallett, a theoretical physicist at the University of Connecticut, has proposed a design for constructing a time machine that is widely accepted as feasible.[25] Mallett's time machine is based on Einstein's understanding of the relationship between light and gravity. According to the General Theory of Relativity, it is not only mass but also light that gravitationally affects space, and since the fabric of space-time is an integrated mesh, anything that warps space also warps time. This means that an array of extremely powerful lasers could be set up in such a way as to intersect each other in a long tunnel, and by varying their firing pattern and intensity one could modulate how much they bend space — and ultimately time — into a vortex that extends into the past. The vortex can, of course, only extend as far back into the past as when the time machine was first set up. People cannot be sent through this array of lasers, but quantum particles can. It is likely that shortly after the machine is first activated, and at any other number of times thereafter, quantum particles will just pop out of the tunnel — apparently from out of nowhere. These would have been sent from the future by Mallett or anyone else using the machine for however long it remains operational.

The implications of such a device are catastrophic. As those who are currently doing work on quantum computers know well, a sequence of quantum particles can encode information. This means that the values that certain stocks will have on the market at a certain date could be sent back in time, such that whoever uses the machine for this purpose (albeit in relative secrecy) could amass tremendous wealth. But what could be far more destabilizing is information about world events being sent back in time, or the patents to technologies that have not yet been invented — including the patent for a time machine that could actually allow for human travel back into the past. It is easy to see how the manufacture of Mallett's time machine (which,

---

25   Ronald L. Mallett, *Time Traveler: A Scientist's Personal Mission to Make Time Travel a Reality* (Basic Books, 2007).

given sufficient funding, is possible with contemporary technology), would single-handedly usher in the Singularity.

The most uncontroversial time machine is obviously a spaceship traveling at near the speed of light, a phenomenon that also falls within the scope of Relativity Theory. Think of what happens here. By the time it turns around to come home, the 'home' that its crew once knew is gone, because hundreds of years have elapsed on Earth whereas the astronauts have experienced the journey as taking only a few months or weeks. The device — the spaceship *qua time machine* — is allowing the techno-scientifically empowered man to overpower time and travel as far into the future as his will determines. Earth, with the lived experiences of everyone on it, is warped by the tremendous speed of a machine — crushed like a tin can — and *made to become* Earth in the future *at a time of one's choosing.* Keep that in mind while contemplating this passage in Stiegler's work, which, however cryptic, represents such a breakthrough in thinking beyond Heidegger that it deserves to be quoted in full:

> It is as if time has leapt outside itself: not only because the process of decision making and anticipation (in the domain of what Heidegger refers to as 'concern') has irresistibly moved over to the side of the 'machine' or technical complex, but because, in a certain sense, and as Blanchot wrote recalling a title of Ernst Jünger, our age is in the process of breaking the 'time barrier.' Following the analogy with the breaking of the sound barrier, to break the time barrier would be to go faster than time. A supersonic device, quicker than its own sound, provokes at the breaking of the barrier a violent sonic boom, a sound shock. What would be the breaking of a time barrier if this meant going faster than time? What *shock* would be provoked by a device going quicker than its 'own time'? Such a shock would in fact mean that speed is older than time. For either time, with space, determines speed, and there could be no question of breaking the time barrier in this sense, or else time, like space, is only thinkable in terms of speed (which remains unthought).[26]

26 Stiegler, *Technics and Time, 1: The Fault of Epimetheus*, 18.

It is impossible not to think of Marinetti when reading these words. Stiegler mentions Ernst Jünger, whose conception of the alchemical transformation of *Homo sapiens* into *Homo faber* in the techno-scientific forge of Vulcan is certainly relevant, but it is F.T. Marinetti whose *Founding and Manifesto of Futurism* already suggested that technologically-produced speed was ontologically prior to time and space. Here are the most relevant passages of that infamous manifesto:

> We intend to sing to the love of danger, the habit of energy and fearless-ness. ...

> We affirm that the beauty of the world has been enriched by a new form of beauty: the beauty of speed. A racing car with a hood that glistens with large pipes resembling a serpent with explosive breath ... a roaring auto-mobile that seems to ride on grapeshot—that is more beautiful than the *Victory of Samothrace*.

> We intend to hymn man at the steering wheel, the ideal axis of which in-tersects the earth, itself hurled ahead in its own race along the path of its orbit. ...

> There is no beauty that does not consist of struggle. No work that lacks an aggressive character can be considered a masterpiece. Poetry must be conceived as a violent assault launched against unknown forces to reduce them to submission under man.

> We stand on the last promontory of the centuries! ... Why should we look back over our shoulders, when we intend to breach the mysterious doors of the Impossible? Time and space died yesterday. We already live in the abso-lute, for we have already created velocity which is eternal and omnipresent.

> We intend to glorify war—the only hygiene of the world...

> The oldest of us is thirty: and yet already we have cast away treasures, thousands of treasures of force, love, boldness, cunning, and raw will power; have thrown them away impatiently, furiously, heedlessly, without hesitation, without rest, screaming for our lives. Look at us! We are still not weary! Our hearts feel no tiredness because they are fed with fire, hatred, and speed! ... Are you astounded? Of course you are, because you can't

even recall having ever been alive! Standing erect on the summit of the world, yet once more we fling our challenge to the stars![27]

These words are as transparent and sharp as diamonds. Any interpretive gloss would only occlude their brilliance. The best that can be hoped for is that by the end of the present text we will have rekindled the Promethean "fire" of this "challenge to the stars" and overpowering of Time or the god *Chronos*.

In the early 1940s SS commander Hans Kammler led a top secret military-industrial research and development group, the *Kammlerstab* (or "Kammler Staff") based in Prague and tasked with developing Zero Point Energy (ZPE), both as a power source, and a propulsion system for saucer-shaped aircraft.[28] These aircraft were designed by Victor Schauberger, in response to the practical aeronautical engineering problem of suctioning the boundary layer.[29] This effort of the Kammler Staff was dubbed "Project Chronos" because the Bell-shaped device that it yielded was capable, not only of generating anti-gravity, but also of warping the fabric of space-time and thereby altering the flow of time within the sphere of its local gravitational field.[30] "Project Chronos" was given the highest level of classification of any military project during the Second World War, namely *Kriegsentscheidend* or "decisive for the war."

The device incorporated two counter-rotating drums filled with an isotope of mercury mixed with thorium, powered by alternating current and repeatedly shocked with high-voltage direct current. This design was based on an alternative physics that acknowledged the existence of a dynamic ether, with what standard physics takes to be

27   F.T. Marinetti, "The Founding and Manifesto of Futurism" in *Futurism: An Anthology* edited by Lawrence Rainey et al. (Yale University Press, 2009), 51, 53.

28   Nick Cook, *The Hunt for Zero Point* (Broadway, 2002).

29   Joseph P. Farrell, *Saucers, Swastikas, and PsyOps: A History of a Breakaway Civilization* (Adventures Unlimited Press, 2012).

30   Joseph P. Farrell, *The SS Brotherhood of the Bell: The Nazis' Incredible Secret Technology* (Adventures Unlimited Press, 2013).

'particles' conceived of as vortices in this plenum of space-time. The electro-magnetic shearing and shocking of the violet-colored mercu-ry-thorium compound in the counter-rotating drums would cause the compression of vortices in this particular isotope (in a manner akin to how only certain isotopes, such as U-235 or P-239 are suitable for nuclear fission or fusion reactions). Ultimately, a single supermassive vortex would develop inside this medium, something akin to a con-trolled miniature black hole. This would cause the Bell to levitate on account of developing a local gravitational field.

More relevant to our present subject matter is that this device would also significantly warp the 'flow of time' around itself as it operated. Plants and other organisms exposed to the Bell had their molecular structure broken down by this effect. Early on in the proj-ect scientists, and later on test subjects from concentration camps, reported having entered a different frame of time before ultimately suffering a similar kind of cellular degeneration as the plants. Time flowed for them at a different rate than for people in the world outside of the field generated by the Bell. Then, as if suddenly compensating for the space-time distortion, their bodies would begin to breakdown after the experiment.

Following the fall of the Third Reich, this device was evacuated to Bariloche, Argentina, where work on it continued through the 1950s under the protection of Juan Peron. On December 9, 1965 residents of Kecksburg, Pennsylvania observed an "acorn" (i.e. bell) shaped UFO that was about the same dimensions as the Nazi Bell.[31] It also had strange symbols engraved on it that could well have been runes. Rather than being occupied by a human, with an organic body, the metallic acorn appears to have been piloted by a robot, which was observed near the craft. Could the Kecksburg incident suggest that the surviving Nazi elite eventually managed to develop operational devices of the Bell-type and, if so, what does this mean about their

31 George Dudding, *The Kecksburg UFO Incident* (CreateSpace Independent Publishing Platform, 2015).

potential to manipulate the timeline? In just what sense was the Bell supposed to be "war-decisive"?

If it were possible to change the past, a time machine would be rightly considered the ultimate weapon. The idea of waging wars to re-write history is one that has been contemplated by science fiction authors for decades. Fritz Lieber calls it "the Change War" in his 1958 novel, *The Big Time*.[32] Not incidentally, time-traveling Nazis feature in the story and the name for one of the two factions in "the Change War", namely the Spiders who are at war with the Serpents, is a reference to the post-war world-wide web of an incipient Fourth Reich. This international organization, led by Martin Bormann from a stronghold in Argentina, was called "The Spider" (*Die Spinne*). More on the Spider and its worldwide web in the fifth chapter.

3.2 Traces of Time Travelers

Time travel does not necessarily require a machine. The psychic spies or "remote viewers" who worked for the CIA and the US Defense Department during the Cold War were able to clairvoyantly experience both the past and the future. They inadvertently discovered that this was possible. When tasked to use clairvoyance to describe secret Soviet installations, the psychic spies would sometimes "remotely view" the targeted site at some point in the past.[33] It seemed that they would be unconsciously drawn to the place at the point in its history that the most dramatic thing happened there. This discovery prompted experiments wherein remote viewers were tasked to look into the future, for example, reading newspaper headlines days in advance. The Chernobyl nuclear meltdown was foreseen in this fashion.[34]

---

32 Fritz Leiber, *The Big Time* (Ace Books, 1961).

33 Russell Targ and Harold Puthoff with an Introduction by Margaret Mead, *Mind Reach: Scientists Look At Psychic Ability* (Hampton Roads Publishing, 2005), 2–3, 111–119.

34 Lyn Buchanan, *The Seventh Sense: The Secrets of Remote Viewing as told by a Psychic Spy for the U.S. Military* (Pocket, 2003), 41–44.

The US government then made extensive operational use of both remote viewing of the past and the future. In one psychic trip to the past, a remote viewer tasked with investigating the crash of Pan Am Flight 103 on December 21, 1988 over Lockerbie, Scotland, witnessed the detonation of a secondary explosive that had been hidden in chocolate bars by an Iranian passenger.[35] The woman was part of a plot to exact revenge for the American Navy downing of Iran Air Flight 655 on July 3, 1988. While the "terrorist attack" on Pan Am Flight 103 was publicly blamed on Libya, American intelligence ascertained and withheld the information that it was an Iranian retaliation. When Iranian-backed Hezbollah took American Colonel Richard Higgins hostage in Beirut, Lebanon, in 1988, the remote viewers were tasked with tracking the movement of one of the hostage several days into the future.[36] While the rescue operation based on this intelligence failed, the accuracy of the precognitive visions was eventually corroborated.

What is most fascinating about the Pan Am Flight 103 remote-viewing session is that the psychic spy was not just describing what he saw transpiring on the airliner. He was actually standing in the isle of the plane. Moreover, when Flight 103 exploded, he was seen by the people onboard! Many of them suddenly stood up from out of their bodies, which were still seat-belted into their chairs as the burning aircraft started to tear apart. They turned around to look at him with expressions of horrified shock and desperately questioning confusion on their faces.[37] It was as if the passengers were aware that he knew what was happening to them, and were demanding an explanation. Once they became 'ghosts,' they could also see his ghostly form.

The CIA and DOD used the term "bilocation" for the Out of Body Experiences (OBEs) that some remote viewers had during an especially intense session. They would discourage this degree of presence

---

35 Ibid., 44–45.

36 Ibid., 40–41.

37 Ibid, 44–45.

at the target sight, though, since it impeded the operative's ability to coherently describe the site to the intelligence officer tasked with guiding the session and questioning him as he gathered information. Bi-located psychic spies would turn into little more than inarticulate, drooling imbeciles until their 'trip' ended.

The possibility of interacting with, and affecting, phenomena in the past is suggested by a remote viewing session conducted by Russell Targ and Harold Puthoff at the Stanford Research Institute in the early days of research and development for the program funded by the CIA. Targ and Puthoff sent one of their test subjects into a particle accelerator at Stanford University, only to find that the bi-located remote viewer actually interfered with the operation of the device.[38] It malfunctioned and shut down when the particles passed through his spectral body. The Physics Department was quite irate and aggravated about the malfunction, which was costly and remained inexplicable to them (until Targ and Puthoff revealed its cause years later in their writings on the SRI program).

This incident would have to be considered a form of Psychokinesis combined with an Out of Body Experience. Later, American remote viewers discovered that this "remote influencing" was being routinely used for nefarious purposes by their Soviet counterparts in the USSR's secret "Psychotronics" program — including attempted "psionic" assassinations.[39] If psychokinetic interaction with people and things is possible in out of body or "astral" travel (as it used to be called) in the present time frame, why not during psychic time travel to the past?

At least one hitherto classified remote-viewing operation suggests that it is also possible to change a foreseen future. In the years after 9/11, Lyn Buchanan was tasked with viewing the next comparable terrorist attack on America. He and his team of viewers described a biological warfare attack in a population center on the coast of

38   Targ and Puthoff, *Mind Reach: Scientists Look At Psychic Ability*, 20.

39   Sheila Ostrander and Lynn Schroeder, *Psychic Discoveries Behind the Iron Curtain* (Bantam, 1971).

Georgia. The terrorists would emerge from out of the Atlantic Ocean and release a pathogen, killing thousands of people along the coastline. Buchanan was able to give the US government the exact date and time of the future attack. When the day arrived, US Coast Guard ships were sent out to intercept the now anticipated terrorists on their way in toward the coast. They were there, as expected, together with their biological weapons. All were secretly taken into custody and "the next 9/11" was averted.

So if the future that Buchanan foresaw never came to pass, then where did he get his information? This is a question that we will return to later in the context of discussing time travel paradoxes. For the moment, it suffices to suggest that ace remoteviewer Joe McMoneagle may have been right to characterize remote viewing as *The Ultimate Time Machine*.[40]

The 'real world' use of "remote viewing" or clairvoyance techniques for time travel was anticipated by at least two works of science fiction. In his 1970 novel, *Time and Again*, Jack Finney describes a clandestine US government program in some ways very similar to the remote-viewing project that would be conceived later in the same decade.[41] Except that in Finney's novel the explicit purpose of the program is travel to the past by psychic means. In order to assist trans-temporal bi-location, the operative is placed in an environment that is made to look, feel, and smell like a simulacrum of the target epoch in every possible way. In the novel, a room in the Dakota is chosen for this purpose because that apartment building and the views over Central Park outside of its windows is the locale in New York that has least changed since the late nineteenth century. It could be most easily turned into a simulacrum of the same place at that time.

40 Joseph McMoneagle, *The Ultimate Time Machine* (Hampton Roads Publishing, 1998).

41 Jack Finney, *Time and Again* (Scribner Paperback Fiction, 1995).

In his 1962 film, *La Jetée*, Chris Marker envisions a post-apocalyptic society holed up under the Palais de Chaillot in Paris.[42] As survivors of a planetary nuclear holocaust, "space has been closed off" to them, perhaps by some kind of alien quarantine or simply through the loss of space-faring technology. So instead they focus their efforts on penetrating the past by clairvoyant means. Mad scientists, who appropriately speak German, have devised a method that combines drugs, electrical stimulation of the brain, sensory deprivation, and hypnotic suggestions, to send the French prisoner of war who is their test subject back into a moment of the 1960s, just before the outbreak of World War III, which he remembers from his childhood. He is able to materialize, now and then, in that epoch, developing a romantic relationship with a woman whose face he vividly recalled from the scene on the jetty at Orly Airport.

Marker ultimately reveals that this is the scene of the time traveler's own death. He is assassinated by something like time cops from his own post-apocalyptic period, after refusing an offer from denizens of an all too "pacified future" to join them as a member of their harmonious beehive. Marker's film does not pose the same kind of paradox as Finney's novel, since what the protagonist does in the past is consistent with what he already witnessed having happened then — albeit from the perspective of himself as a child witnessing a man who is an apparent stranger being shot and noticing the horrified face of the beautiful woman toward whom he was running.

There are accounts of individuals who claim to have experienced "time slips," or spontaneous, momentary travel into either the past or the future. Whitley Strieber recounts several such experiences in his book, *Breakthrough*. Interestingly, in one of these, the Manhattan sidewalk that Strieber was strolling down suddenly transformed into the same street in the nineteenth century, and he was almost overrun

---

42   Chris Marker, *La Jetée* (Argos Films, 1962).

by a horse and carriage that had to swerve to avoid him.[43] The driver cursed at him, and others who were astonished at his sudden appearance seemed disconcerted by his strange attire. In another incident, Strieber seemed to have slipped into the far future, wherein the road that he was driving on morphed into one that was badly cracked and sunken into the ground. On both sides of the road stood inhumanly strange rectilinear buildings without windows, covered in serpentine patterns. There were two children in his car at the time, his own son and his son's friend. The latter was so impressed by the event, that as soon as he got back to his own father he shouted out, "Daddy, daddy, Whitley took us on a drive through the twilight zone!"[44] Such episodes may last only a few minutes or go on for hours.

If people can accidentally slip through tears or holes in the fabric of space-time, then why not animals? This type of phenomenon might account for the empirical evidence for the contemporary existence of instances of extinct species. Cryptozoology may not be studying the *survival* of a few Dinosaurs, isolated primitive hominids, or any number of other bizarre creatures. Rather, cryptozoologists may be studying evidence for time travel — albeit inadvertent time travel. This is what is suggested by the Fortean researcher John Keel in his study, *Strange Creatures from Time and Space*.[45] The cryptozoological creatures slipping into our epoch, and in some cases getting stuck here, might as often be from the evolutionary future of the Earth as from its pre-human past.

One even has to wonder whether, of the hundreds of missing persons cases every year in America alone, some might be cases of people who disappeared into the past and never returned.[46] That is what is suggested by tens of man-made anomalous objects that have

43   Whitley Strieber, *Breakthrough* (HarperCollins, 1995).

44   Ibid., 139–142.

45   John Keel, *Strange Creatures from Time and Space* (Fawcett Publications), 1970.

46   David Paulides, *Missing 411: The Devil's in the Details* (CreateSpace Independent Publishing Platform, 2014).

been discovered in the fossil record, going back millions of years into geological history.[47] In 1844, the London *Times* reported that a thread of finely worked gold had been found inside a 320 million year old stone. In 1852, *Scientific American* featured an article about a vessel made of a zinc-silver alloy and decorated with a floral motif, which had been retrieved by miners from a geological strata wherein it was deposited 600 million years before they dug it up. In 1889, miners in Idaho excavated a Venus-of-Willendorf-style clay figure that, given where it was found, would had to have been 2 million years old. In 1891, miners in Illinois found a gold chain inside 260 million year old coal. Miners in Nebraska unearthed a truly astonishing piece of stone in 1897, which had geometric carvings on it, and was thought to be 300 million years old. In 1912, a 312 million year old iron cup was discovered inside of a very large piece of coal at an Oklahoma mine. In 1922, the American Museum of Natural History in New York estimated that a fossil that looks like a shoe sole print, complete with a worn-through heel, is no less than 213 million years old. Another fossilized shoe print was discovered in Utah in 1968. This shoe was stepping on trilobites, which dates the shale fossil to no later than 505 million years ago, when those primordial life forms began to die out. In 1928, a polished concrete wall 286 million years old was discovered in a Texas mine.

In *Forbidden Archeology* (1993), Michael A. Cremo and Richard L. Thompson take these finds to be evidence of extreme human antiquity and challenges to the Darwinian theory of evolution.[48] However, all of the cases above could also be interpreted as traces of accidental time travelers. It is not as if entire cities that are millions of years old have been excavated, and one would assume that if human beings were indeed hundreds of millions of years older than we have been

---

47 Michael A. Cremo and Richard L. Thompson, *The Hidden History of the Human Race* (Bhaktivedanta Book Publishing, 2002), 105–122.

48 Michael A. Cremo and Richard L. Thompson, *Forbidden Archeology: The Hidden History of the Human Race* (Bhaktivedanta Book Publishing, 1998).

led to believe, not only would such cities be found but they would be far more advanced than our own. Instead, what we find is an item here and an item there, jewelry, crafts objects, and shoeprints of people who possibly "slipped" in time, perhaps only for a few moments. There are a few technologically anomalous structures and objects that were perhaps crafted by people stranded in the past with their untimely technical know-how.

Even if Cremo and Thompson are correct in their interpretation of some of these artifacts as evidence for vastly ancient human civilization, it does not necessarily follow that the Darwinian account of man's evolution is fundamentally flawed. Despite their scientific approach to what is some sound empirical data, the two of them are members of the International Society for Krishna Consciousness (colloquially referred to as "Hare Krishnas"). While nowhere near as narrow-minded as Biblical creationists who use similar evidence to argue that the Earth, with all its fossil records of Dinosaurs, is only 5,000 years old, Cremo and Thompson are still religiously motivated to interpret the data in a way that is consistent with the Hindu view of vast time cycles or *Yugas* in the course of which there is a cyclical fall and rise of human civilizations.

A different possibility is that if there were extremely advanced civilizations in the remote past, such as Atlantis, these historical anomalies can be explained by appealing to the untimely influence of time travelers who brought scientific and technological knowledge from the future with them into prehistoric ages. This would explain the relative geographical isolation of Atlantis, which seems to have been based solely in Antarctica, with surviving Atlanteans reaching out across the planet on a large scale as colonizers only after the demise of their civilization.[49]

Quarantining oneself to a continent like Antarctica, albeit prior to the crustal slippage that drew it entirely into the south polar region,

---

49 Colin Wilson and Rand Flem-Ath, *The Atlantis Blueprint: Unlocking the Ancient Mysteries of a Long-Lost Civilization* (Delta, 2002).

would be a way for time travelers to endeavor not to contaminate human history or even the Darwinian trajectory that would lead to the evolution of humans. Of course, set in this context, violations of such a "prime directive" could be what we are looking at when we see evidence suggestive of genetic engineering at work in the evolution of *Homo sapiens* from more primitive ape-like ancestors.

Mars would have made for an even tighter quarantine zone for a human civilization of time travelers who, for whatever reason, needed to take refuge in the remote past. We know that, hundreds of millions of years ago, ecological conditions on Mars were very similar to what they are on Earth now. In 1976, the Viking probe to Mars brought back images of what appeared to be pyramids larger than those of Egypt and other titanic structures, in addition to an enigmatic humanoid face. These structures in the Cydonia region have been subject to intense debate ever since. One major turning point in this debate was when John Brandenberg, a mainstream NASA Physicist, argued that there was evidence consistent with massive nuclear weapons detonations having taken place on the surface of Mars approximately 250 million years ago.[50]

Interestingly, this time frame is consistent with that of many of the artifacts discussed by Cremo and Thompson in *Forbidden Archeology*. If such time-traveling humans also space-traveled from Mars to Earth, in violation of some prime directive not to interfere with the past, then they would indeed have been able to leave a few human footprints next to those of Dinosaurs. This is a much more rational interpretation of such anomalies in the fossil record than either that of the Biblical creationists or the somewhat more sophisticated interpretation of Cremo and Thompson in line with Hindu theological ideas about the cyclical succession of *Yugas*. No one with a Promethean mentality would want to accept that, for hundreds of millions of years, even the most advanced human civilizations have inevitably ended

---

50   John E. Brandenburg, *Death On Mars: The Discovery of a Planetary Nuclear Massacre* (Adventures Unlimited Press, 2015).

in total destruction, only to rise again with little memory of having already been through this futile cycle many times.

A time-traveling Posthuman civilization that settled on Mars in prehistoric times, and that eventually did colonize at least a part of Earth, perhaps basing itself in Antarctica, could be the origin of the long-count calendar that the "Atlanteans" bequeathed to Mayan civilization. This is the kind of calendar that would be needed by a civilization engaged in space travel near the speed of light, when relativistic effects would routinely result in time travel to an epoch hundreds of years into the future of the place to which they return after each voyage.

This kind of time travel entered popular culture with the original *Planet of the Apes* (1968). A malfunction aboard a spaceship traveling near the speed of light causes the astronauts onboard to remain in hibernation for longer than they were supposed to, and brings the ship to travel further than they had intended.[51] This effectively turns the vessel into a time machine, so that once the unfortunate astronauts (led by Charlton Heston's character) return to Earth, thousands of years have elapsed. To their horror, they discover that in the wake of a nuclear war that took place not all that long after they left, 'intelligent' apes have dominated the planet and enslaved what is left of a humanity that has regressed to savagery. The sequel is even more interesting. In *Beneath the Planet of the Apes* (1970), we discover that there is a hidden subterranean civilization of advanced humans who have been mutated and disfigured by the nuclear war. They manipulate the apes using telepathy, and worship a nuclear doomsday device as their god.[52]

51   Franklin J. Schaffner, *Planet of the Apes* (20ᵗʰ Century Fox, 1968).

52   Ted Post, *Beneath the Planet of the Apes* (20ᵗʰ Century Fox, 1970).

3.3 Metaphysics of the Change War

The question of whether it is possible to change the past has long been a subject of intense philosophical debate. At the heart of this debate is the so-called "grandfather paradox." If one travels back in time and accidentally (or deliberately) kills one's grandfather, before he has given birth to one's father, then how can one be there in the first place, since one would not even have been born? There are many variations of this paradox, which was awkwardly formulated in order to avoid any suggestion of parricide or, for that matter, matricide. Basically, making any change in the past that could have resulted in one's not having been born is supposed to result in a logical contradiction of one's presence in the past or, for that matter, one's existing at all.

The grandfather paradox is only one philosophical objection to the idea that it is possible to change the past. Another is the argument that it would be impossible to know that the past had changed.[53] What comparison could one use to ascertain that the past is no longer what it had been? If one were to travel back in time and act in a way that is consistent with what is recorded to have happened, that poses no paradox. One's presence in the past may not be noticed until one goes looking for it — namely after one's return to the present — but the record would always have been there. It is just that one would not have known what to look for, or how to interpret, say, a bizarre event in early American history involving the presence of an enigmatic stranger. But how could one prove that the past was once something other than what it is now recorded to be, because time travelers went back and changed it?

Before suggesting a possible resolution to this paradox and an answer to the arguments against the possibility of changing the past, it ought to be clarified that by changing the past, we do not mean the bifurcation of the world into alternate and parallel timelines.

---

53 Paul J. Nahin, *Time Machines: Time Travel in Physics, Metaphysics, and Science Fiction* (Springer, 2001), 265.

According to the Many Worlds Interpretation of Quantum Mechanics forwarded by Hugh Everett, apparent quantum indeterminacy is actually a theoretical mirage.[54] Each and every probabilistically possible state of affairs at the quantum level is resolved into a definite fact of nature in one of infinitely many parallel universes. On such a view, it is conceivable that what a time traveler is actually doing is traveling to a parallel universe. This is rather trivial, since, on the Many Worlds Interpretation of physical phenomena, every single event on the quantum level spawns a parallel universe for each determinate resolution of what is theoretically mistaken to be the indeterminate probability distribution of the wave function of any would-be 'particle' as it interacts with any other.

In any case, "changes to the past" can be made even if they result in one's not having been born, because one is operating in a universe that is other than, and parallel to, the one in which one was in fact born. If travel between parallel universes is possible, then this kind of change is also possible without resulting in a logical paradox. However, that would not be change to *the* singular past of one's *own* world.

Moreover, the Many Worlds Interpretation notoriously negates free will. Every decision that one could possibly make, at every fork in one's life, from microsecond to microsecond, is actually made, not by one's own mind or through conscious intent, but by the interactions of the quantum particles constituting one's brain. When considered in this way, it is logically incoherent to think that "changing the past" might be consistent with a theoretical model that denies the possibility of even changing the present or having any conscious control over one's future.

Guaranteeing free will was the most important criterion that William James used to develop his philosophical cosmology. The pluralistic panpsychism that James sets forth in *A Pluralistic Universe* (1908) is a metaphysics consistent with the idea of changing the past

---

54 Peter Byrne, *The Many Worlds of Hugh Everett III* (Oxford University Press, 2013).

of *this* universe.[55] When James writes of a "pluralistic" universe he does not mean to suggest parallel universes. What is at issue is a pluralism inherent to the universe. Rather than being uniform and internally consistent, the universe, which is really a pluriverse, is constituted through strife between a plurality of relatively independent forces. This also means that instead of being a true Cosmos, the universe always retains a certain degree of Chaos from out of which new order arises. The psychical struggle between competing entities even extends to the so-called 'laws' of nature that would favor the flourishing of one or another of them.

Charles Fort, who, not incidentally, was at least as involved in paranormal research as William James, had a similarly spectral cosmology. In his *Book of the Damned* (1919), Fort anticipates later thinking in terms of shifting scientific paradigms when he analyzes reports of various phenomena marginalized as anomalous by dominant theoretical frameworks.[56] However, the epistemological point that Fort is making is far more radical than that of later framers of the idea of scientific "paradigm shifts." According to Fort, it is not just that a given epistemic framework filters observations of nature. Rather, a "dominant" worldview actually shapes how nature behaves, for the most part, and what happenings are deemed anomalous or "freaks" of nature by comparison to this general habit.[57] A nature that is this mutable might also imply that the past is changeable, since there are no fixed laws of nature that would be violated by such revisions.

Changing the actual past would be bizarre. A famous example of it from science fiction is the photograph held by Marty McFly in *Back To The Future* (1985). As Marty sets in motion a chain of events, thus changing the past that has shaped his life, the photograph in which he is pictured together with his family also changes to reflect what,

55 William James, *A Pluralistic Universe* (University of Nebraska Press, 1995).

56 Charles Fort, "The Book of the Damned" in *The Complete Books of Charles Fort* (Dover, 1974), 3–15.

57 Ibid, 286–287.

from the standpoint of the past, is a new possible future.[58] It may be strange to think of having a photograph of what is only a "possible" future, but think back to the remote viewing operation wherein Lyn Buchanan's team averted the next 9/11. The operational intelligence produced by Lyn and his team, in terms of verbal descriptions and sketches of a future event that would have happened had it not been stopped in time, is basically comparable to Marty's photograph of the possible future. It can be repeatedly revised, while its former iterations remain as memories akin to Buchanan's vivid memory of a terrorist attack that never wound up actually taking place. (Not incidentally, the plot of *Back To The Future* also involves an attempt to stop a terrorist attack by means of time travel.)

Despite how bizarre this idea is, no less a logical intellect than Kurt Gödel thought that the past could be changed.[59] Gödel was breaking with Aristotle, who argued that the idea of changing the past was illogical. Aristotle's faithful medieval disciple, St. Thomas Aquinas, used Aristotelian logic to argue that even God cannot change the past.[60] By contrast, the eleventh century St. Damian maintained that God, for whom all things are possible, can revise, and thereby perfect, the past.[61] But why would God need or want to do so, as St. Damian believes that He might? One can see how, even if the position taken by Aquinas appears at first glance to be inconsistent with the Christian conception of God as Almighty, it is actually entirely consistent with the claim of God's omnipotence. It is St. Damian who is unwittingly committing heresy.

An omnipotent God would have gotten history right in the first place. The will to change the past, in effect to perfect it, whether it is conceived of as a dire need or a whimsical want, implies imperfection

---

58 Steven Spielberg, *Back To The Future* (Universal Pictures, 1985).

59 Nahin, *Time Machines: Time Travel in Physics, Metaphysics, and Science Fiction*, 79–84, 264.

60 Ibid, 263–264.

61 Ibid, 263.

in God's own nature. It means that God did not get it right the first time, or at least that God is indecisive and given to moody dissatisfaction. Of course, that is entirely consistent with the God of the Old Testament, who regrets his creation and wipes the Earth clean in Noah's flood. But the way that Jehovah is depicted in the *Torah* is itself inconsistent with the later Christian scholastic conception of God's omnipotence, or for that matter the Muslim one. Only the ancient and medieval Gnostics, with their interpretation of the Lord of Abraham and Moses as a deranged demiurge who designed a botched world, would have been able to consistently embrace the idea of melioristic revision of the past.

Philip K. Dick, a modern or post-modern Gnostic, explicitly writes about divine interventions that aim to revise history in ways that overpower the demiurge and archons who are bent on sadistically manipulating us. This is the subject matter of his 1981 sci-fi novel *VALIS*.[62] But, according to PKD, such changes to the past were not just science fiction. At a 1977 science fiction conference in Metz, France, Dick claimed that many of his novels were written based on residual memories of a different timeline than the one that we are currently living in. For example, he alleged that *Flow My Tears, the Policeman Said* (1974) was based on recollections of how a Richard Nixon who was never impeached transformed the United States into a police state.[63] *Man in the High Castle* (1962), which was recently adapted into a television series, presents a world where the Axis powers won the war and America is jointly occupied by Nazi Germany and Imperial Japan.[64] Again, Dick confessed that, at one point, this was actually our history.

PKD is not the only person to claim to have such memories. The phenomenon is called "the Mandela effect." It involves, in some cases

---

62   Philip K. Dick, *VALIS* (Mariner Books, 2011).

63   Philip K. Dick, *Flow My Tears, The Policeman Said* (Mariner Books, 2012).

64   Philip K. Dick, *The Man in the High Castle* (Mariner Books, 2012).

shared, memories of the past that do not correspond to what we are told is actual history.[65] The effect was named after the memory of quite a few people that Nelson Mandela died in prison rather than going on to lead South Africa out of apartheid. Other examples include reported memories that the Shah brought Iran into the club of nuclear-armed nations in 1975, presumably during the second term of his close friend Richard Nixon.

Dick's story "The Adjustment Team," which was adapted into *The Adjustment Bureau* (2011), portrays secretive "men-in-black"-type agents who have been mistaken for angels throughout the course of human history and whose task it is to repeatedly revise the course of events in line with the changing plans of their "chairman" (i.e. a less-than-omnipotent God).[66] In *VALIS* and in his private notebooks, now published as the *Exegesis*, Dick identifies this "chairman" as a Vast Active Living Intelligence System (VALIS).[67] This is the computer responsible for the "computer programmed reality" that Dick infamously "revealed" that we are living in when he gave his unforgettable speech at the 1977 science fiction conference in France. Dick suggested that *déjà vu* was a clue that some variable had been altered.

The *VALIS* hypothesis offers a very rational model for understanding how the past could be changed. What such changes to the past imply is that there is some fifth-dimensional domain of existence beyond four-dimensional space-time. The presence of this fifth-dimensional nexus allows those who change history to have a relationship to time that is quasi-spatial, so that they are able to compare various versions of the past. Defunct pasts are, as it were, archived in this fifth-dimension and thereby isolated from changes in 4-D space-time.

The relationship of such a postulated fifth-dimension to four-dimensional space-time(s) could simply be that of a more primary 'real

---

65   Jay Wheeler, *Alternate: The Mandela Effect* (Amazon, 2018).

66   George Nolfi, *The Adjustment Bureau* (Media Rights Capital, 2011).

67   Philip K. Dick, *The Exegesis* (Houghton Mifflin, 2011).

world' to computer simulations that are being run on machines inside that world. Defunct pasts could be akin to saved and archived states of play in a video game. At any point, it is possible for the programmers to return to an archived state of the game and play it forward in a different way than what produced the past as we know it. What we think of as "time travel" with the potential to "change the past" could really be just such an operation inside of a vast virtual reality system. Following this line of thought takes us from a consideration of the end of history into a contemplation of the end of reality brought about by means of virtual reality and other simulacra.

CHAPTER 4

The End of Reality

ARLY VIRTUAL REALITY (VR) technology involved stereo-
scopic goggles, haptic gloves, and motion trackers hooked up to
large computers with rendering engines. Even at this stage it had a
wide variety of practical applications besides gaming. These included
three-dimensional design and virtual surgery, both for medical training and telepresence through robotic systems. The latter interface was
also used for guiding robots in situations too hazardous for humans.
Today companies such as Oculus are manufacturing goggles that have
become much less cumbersome. Soon they will be as lightweight as
the glasses used for Augmented Reality (AR), such as Google Glass,
which overlay three-dimensional projections onto one's perception of
the actual world. Combining AR with haptic gloves could allow people
to interact with virtual toys, simulacra of sculptures, and architectural
structures that disappear when the glasses are taken off.

Once the AR, or for that matter VR, technology is miniaturized to
the level of contact lenses, it will be possible to experience something
akin to the "Holodeck" of *Star Trek: The Next Generation*. One of the
very first explorations of Virtual Reality in popular culture was a story
line in that television series. It involved the super-villain Dr. Moriarty
in a Sherlock Holmes program on the Holodeck becoming conscious

and wanting out of the simulation. The android crewmember Data had inadvertently programmed the Holodeck to provide him with a worthy opponent, rather than commanding the computer to prepare an opponent that could believably rival his assumed character of Sherlock Holmes. In a storyline that extends over several episodes and more than one season, Moriarty eventually appears to leave the Holodeck, but he enters into a simulacrum of the Enterprise rather than the actual starship. This "Ship in a Bottle" idea, combined with Moriarty's convincing demonstration of his own consciousness, raises questions about the status of the putative 'reality' of the universe that is experienced by those on the Enterprise.

To be more accurate, the Holodeck onboard the Enterprise is more like a combination of 3-D printing and nanotechnology than it is akin to a virtual reality system based on an optical and haptic interface. Both people and objects, including seamlessly shapeshifting architectural spaces, are free-standing simulacra that one can interact with without any glasses, contact lenses, or gloves. It is as if three-dimensional objects are being rapidly rendered or "3-D printed" through the computer programmed re-arrangement of a plethora of nanobots. The solid "holograms" of the Holodeck would best be conceived of in terms of this "Utility Fog" concept of programmable nanobots that can form simulacra of any thing or person, down to the molecules that emulate various smells.[1] This robotics-based approach to populating a simulacrum is also the one taken in the television adaptation of *Westworld*, where 3-D printed androids entertain guests at the theme park.[2]

The development of increasingly sophisticated simulacra of various kinds ever more acutely raises the question of whether we are already living in some kind of simulacrum. This is the question

1   Douglas Mulhall, *Our Molecular Future: How Nanotechnology, Robotics, Genetics, and Artificial Intelligence Will Transform Our World* (Prometheus, 2002), 89, 209, 214, 223.

2   Jonathan Nolan, *Westworld* (HBO, 2016).

explored in the first section of this chapter. It begins with an explication of Nick Bostrom's Simulation Argument. Bostrom is a philosopher at the Future of Humanity Institute at Oxford University, who has developed an elegant logical argument that basically demonstrates that either we are living in a computer simulation or we are going to annihilate ourselves before we develop the technology to build fully immersive virtual realities. The middle premise of Bostrom's argument, namely that we might develop such technology but choose not to use it, is untenable based on an assessment of human psychological motivations in exploiting the full range of possibilities of various technologies invented thus far — no matter how destructive. We will see how many reasons there are to build what Bostrom calls an "ancestor simulation," a virtual reality emulating a bygone epoch of human history or a lost society of the past. The designers of these simulations could be motivated by scientific curiosity, a desire for entertainment, or even a religious impulse having to do with redefining the limits of creativity. When we consider that *all* of these motivations could be in play at once, then it is very likely that various interests would converge to use future technology for the purpose of developing many of these "ancestor simulations."

The question then becomes how likely it is that we are living in 'reality' rather than inside one of these virtual worlds. Toward the end of the first section, we will see that Philip K. Dick ultimately revealed that he thought we were living in just such a simulation. He claimed that stories such as *VALIS, Man in the High Castle, Flow My Tears the Policeman Said*, and *The Adjustment Team* were written based on fragmentary memories of alternate versions of the simulation before it was reprogrammed by the "adjusters" who control it.

The second section shifts into a consideration of scientific evidence that would tend to confirm the validity of the Simulation Hypothesis. Numerous hitherto puzzling aspects of quantum physics make much more sense when contemplated in the context of computer processing. Wave/particle duality and the Schrödinger's cat paradox are no longer so paradoxical when we compare the resolution of quantum uncertainty or probability distributions into discretely measurable particles to how a program optimizes its use of computing power by only rendering what is being observed by anyone at any particular time. Rather than being any indication of the transmission of signals faster than light, quantum entanglement may also be indicative of an algorithm for the coordinated rendering of pixels. Apparently discrete particles are projections from out of a unified matrix of code, like pixels that have no objective reality. The quantization of space-time describes a pixelated world, with one pixel being the magnitude of the Planck length. An equation that factors in both the Planck length and the speed of light can even allow us to ascertain the clock speed at which the CPU is re-rendering our world.

Taking clues from *The Matrix*, paranormal phenomena will be interpreted in light of what we know about how video games and other computer programs function. Laws of nature are not being broken by these "paranormal" phenomena because these putative 'laws' are really just coding sequences in the Physics Engine of a simulator, which has a programming code that accommodates many exceptions to these general algorithms for "simulated gravity" and the like. Phenomena such as teleportation, psychokinesis, telepathy, and precognition, can be understood in this way. Reincarnation and karma may even be best conceived of as something akin to the "quests" that take "multiple lives" in a computer game. This also gives us the best framework through which to comprehend what was being suggested in the preceding chapter, about how time travelers can change 4-D space-time continua from the vantage point of a fifth dimensional plane of existence. This metaphorical 'fifth dimension' is the world outside of multiple saved simulations, and it offers a better resolution to the "grandfather paradox" than the parallel universes of the Many Worlds Interpretation of Quantum Theory.

Of all paranormal phenomena, the type that most strongly suggests we are living in a simulation is what Carl Jung called

"Synchronicity." As the second section draws to a close, I critique Jung's own understanding of these tremendously complex "meaningful coincidences." He was right to see Astrology as an example of so-called "Synchronicity," but only because empirical evidence for the efficacy of astrological influences is the best evidence that we are living inside a virtual world programmed in the way that computer games are designed.

None of this is meant to suggest that there is any objective or fundamental bedrock of "reality" beneath one or more nested simulations. In the third and final section of this chapter, we look at how the nature of so-called 'reality' itself could be intrinsically virtual. Conscious experience of any world may be nothing other than information processing that is taking place inside something akin to a dynamic hologram.

This is what is suggested by Karl Pribram's research on the non-local distribution of enduring memory and abilities in persons who have suffered brain damage. Experiments on salamanders, rats, and cats also confirm that the brain functions in a holographic manner. David Bohm, one of the leading quantum physicists of the last century, also turned to the hologram as an image of the way that the cosmos works. Bohm saw quantum entanglement as evidence for an "implicate order." He argued that apparent particles are "explicate" projections unfolded from out of an enfolded order that is like a holographic film with interference patterns on it. The act of observation that turns wave interference patterns into particles is like the laser light that hits the film and unfolds the hologram out of it. If something akin to holographic information storage and processing is how both the mind and the cosmos works, then we have to accept the fact that all 'reality' is virtual.

4.1 Are We Living in a Virtual Reality?

The Oxford philosopher Nick Bostrom has famously developed a "Simulation Argument" that probabilistically analyses the possibility that we are living in a virtual reality.[3] A key concept in this argument is the idea of an "ancestor simulation" or a simulacrum of a human world, such as ours, together with its past history, by post-humans or by aliens who have encountered humanity at some point in the human or post-human future.[4] According to Bostrom, logic dictates that one of three possibilities must be true: (1) Despite their differences from one another, all civilizations in the Cosmos advanced enough to develop ancestor simulations converge onto an ethical standpoint that compels them to never develop such simulations; (2) All civilizations in the Cosmos destroy themselves before reaching the level of technical competence required to develop ancestor simulations; (3) We are almost certainly living in a simulation, since if even a small number of civilizations in the Cosmos that have the ability to build ancestor simulations do so, then, each will engineer many such simulations, which means that there are so many more simulated worlds like ours than actual ones and it is, based on probability alone, highly unlikely that we would be living in reality rather than in one of these virtual realities.[5]

Possibility 3 is referred to as "the Simulation Hypothesis" as compared to the Simulation Argument as a whole. As disturbing as it may be, it is less horrifying than Possibility 2 — especially considering the fact that we are only a few decades from the Technological Singularity, which, among other things, means attainment of the capability to make ancestor simulations of our own. Although Bostrom does not consider it, there is also empirical evidence against Possibility 2 in the

---

3   Rizwan Virk, *The Simulation Hypothesis* (Bayview Books, 2019), 5.

4   Nick Bostrom, "Are You Living in A Computer Simulation?" in *Philosophical Quarterly* (2003) Vol. 53, No. 211, pp. 243–255.

5   Virk, *The Simulation Hypothesis*, 110–111.

form of thousands of credible reports of Close Encounters. These may be encounters with simulated Non-Player Character (NPC) "aliens" or avatars of the programmers of our simulation, rather than with actual extraterrestrials. But, in either case, the presence of UFOs and their occupants rules out Possibility 2.

Meanwhile, Possibility 1 is highly unlikely given what we know about the role of Promethean ingenuity, and just plain curiosity, in human nature. Our propensity to immediately develop even the most dangerous technological applications of any new scientific discovery has been proven time and again, especially in the rush to use nuclear physics for building atomic bombs that could have brought an end to all life on this planet (and, frankly, could still do so). Likewise with biological science. A sophisticated understanding of viruses and pathogens was immediately used to develop biological weapons capable of unleashing genocidal pandemics.

Furthermore, there are many reasons why an advanced civilization would want to develop what Bostrom calls "ancestor simulations." Historians and sociologists in that civilization might be interested in developing a scientifically rigorous understanding of the dynamics at work in the rise and fall of civilized societies. Simulations that allow one to explore all of the different pathways that a certain civilization may have taken at various bifurcation points could identify principles of social psychology that hold true across these alternative histories. Explorations of pathways that history could have taken, but did not, could also be engines of innovation and creative genius for those who are artistically minded in an advanced civilization that has reached an evolutionary dead end in terms of its creativity.

That is the most optimistic motivation imaginable, since if it were at play in our own case, it would mean that (at least some of) the programmers of our civilization were looking to us to imagine and achieve things that they themselves proved incapable of conceiving. Then there is the most pessimistic and cynical motivation for simulating a world such as ours, with its violent history, namely to use it as a vast arena of entertainment. Our Earth could be a gigantic Roman-style circus for sadistic archons who consider us their playthings. The convergence of these motivations and interests, on the part of those different types of persons in the advanced civilization who are driven by them, would be too strong to make Possibility 1 at all believable. That leaves us with the likelihood that we, ourselves, are living in a world that is virtual.

Philip K. Dick infamously made this claim at a science fiction conference in Metz, France, in 1977. Numerous writings of Philip K. Dick revolve around the idea of a simulated world, including stories adapted into popular films such as *Total Recall* (based on "We Can Remember It for You Wholesale") and *The Adjustment Bureau* (an adaptation of "The Adjustment Team"). But in 1977, Dick claimed that we are actually living in a computer-programmed reality that has been repeatedly revised. His novels *Flow My Tears a Policeman Said* and *Man in the High Castle* were allegedly based on fragmentary memories that he retained of alternate histories that were overwritten by the programmers of our simulation. Dick's notebooks reveal that he believed that the Vast Active Living Intelligent System that is the namesake of his 1981 novel *VALIS* was a benevolent god-like artificial intelligence trying to liberate us from the "black iron prison" of this counterfeit world.[6] The warders of this prison are archons akin to the "men in black" type agents depicted in *The Adjustment Bureau*.[7]

4.2 "There Is No Spoon"

Philip K. Dick's Neo-Gnostic worldview deeply influenced the Wachowskis in their development of *The Matrix* trilogy of films, which remain, by far, the most popular depiction of the idea that we are living inside a virtual reality. The phrase "red pill" has become a mainstream meme that signifies being willing to swallow a bitter pill

---

6   Philip K. Dick, *The Exegesis* (Houghton Mifflin, 2011).

7   George Nolfi, *The Adjustment Bureau* (Media Rights Capital, 2011).

in order to see through illusions and awaken to the truth, however horrifying it may be. The agents, such as the iconic Smith, are akin to the archontic members of the Adjustment Team. The savior Neo, with his ability to re-program the simulation to the benefit of humanity, is comparable to VALIS. Above all, *The Matrix* owes to Dick the suggestion that paranormal or anomalous phenomena are clues to the fact that what we mistake for "laws of nature" are actually just programming code. As Morpheus puts it while training Neo, "some of them can be bent, others can be broken."[8] Later Neo explains to a gifted child, who is trying to hone his telekinetic power, that the key to spoon bending is to deeply internalize the gnostic insight that "there is no spoon."[9] What bends is your own mind, or to be more precise, its expectations of how 'reality' works.

The role of consciousness in determining apparently 'physical' phenomena has been a subject of contention from the earliest days of Quantum Physics. The Simulation Argument offers an alternative interpretation of quantum physical phenomena that does not meet with the same paradoxes as the standard, Copenhagen interpretation.

In 1927 Werner Heisenberg formulated his famous "uncertainty principle" when he was working at the Niels Bohr Institute at Copenhagen.[10] According to this principle, it is impossible to determine the precise speed of a quantum particle if one is determining its exact location, and it is conversely impossible to determine the exact location of a particle if one is determining its speed with perfect accuracy. When the speed of a particle is in question, it is possible to conceive of the particle as a wave with a momentum of propagation (like the speed of a radio wave), whereas attempting to ascertain the location of a quantum entity requires us to measure it as a particle. This means that the indeterminacy problem really goes back to the

---

8   Wachowskis, *The Matrix* (Warner Bros., 1999).

9   Ibid.

10 Werner Heisenberg, *Physics and Philosophy* (Harper Perennial Modern Classics, 2007).

seemingly paradoxical wave/particle duality of quantum phenomena. According to proponents of the Simulation Hypothesis, this kind of quantum indeterminacy is a function of optimizing techniques that are being employed by this information processing system, which does not render anything in subatomic (i.e. at a quantum level) of detail unless it is actually being observed by people inside the simulation.[11]

We see another example of Heisenberg's uncertainty principle in the double slit experiment, which yields an interference pattern when the electrons are shot out of the electron beam gun without an observation being made, so as to suggest that they passed through the two slits as waves, whereas when the trajectories of the electrons are observed by a quantum measuring apparatus, they pass through the double slits as discrete particles and make a particle-like pattern when they hit the screen. As Heisenberg put it: "The path of the electron comes into existence only when we observe it."[12]

What is even stranger — or, as Einstein put it, "spookier" — about this observation-contingent wave/particle indeterminacy is that the experiment can be set up in a way where the measurement that counts as an "observation" occurs well into the future, and thereby determines whether the electrons, say in a laser beam, propagated through space as waves or as particles in what is, relative to the observation, a past moment in time.[13] These kinds of experiments, dubbed "delayed choice" experiments, were first proposed by theoretical physicist John Wheeler and were widely interpreted (though not by Wheeler himself) as evidence for "retro-causality" or future actions causing events in the past, i.e. in a direction counter to the supposed "arrow of time."[14]

"Schrödinger's Cat" is a kind of delayed-choice experiment. It is named after the physicist Erwin Schrödinger who first framed the

11   Virk, *The Simulation Hypothesis*, 123.

12   Ibid., 130.

13   Ibid., 145.

14   Ibid., 146.

problem of "quantum superposition" in these terms in the mid 1930s.
On account of quantum indeterminacy or the so-called "uncertainty"
principle, one cannot be sure whether a quantum phenomena manifests as a particle or as a wave until and unless an observation has
been made. A "wave" is a probability distribution, meaning that the
location of a potential quantum particle is spread out over a number
of possible positions at the same time. Until an observation is made
with an interferometer or some such device, the wave function or
probability distribution does not collapse into a definite measurement
of a particle. Since measuring is a human act, an "observation," it has
been argued by Heisenberg, Schrödinger, Niels Bohr and other quantum physicists, that the very reality of quantum physical phenomena
is dependent on consciousness at a fundamental level. "Schrödinger's
Cat" is a thought experiment that demonstrates this by translating this
weirdness at the quantum level into a deeply disturbing paradox on
the macroscopic scale.

Imagine a cat concealed in a soundproof and opaque box. This cat
is either automatically poisoned to death or else remains alive based
on whether the decay rate of a certain radioactive material, which is
a non-deterministic quantum process, reaches a given threshold and
activates the release of a poison once it is measured by an appropriate device, also located inside the box.[15] The idea is that there is no
deterministic way to definitively predict whether or not the cat will be
alive or dead until the box is opened and an observation is made. This
means that, between the time the experiment with the radioactive decay rate and the potential poison release is run, and the time that the
box concealing the cat is opened, which may be days (the box could
have sufficient cat food inside it), Schrödinger's cat is neither dead
nor alive. Rather, the poor cat's quantum particles, or the probability
waves constituting its body (and mind), are in "quantum superposition" — a spectral state of being neither alive nor dead.

---

15   Ibid., 133.

Proponents of the Simulation Hypothesis would argue that this apparently absurd consequence of quantum indeterminacy can only make any sense if there is in fact no real cat in the box. The cat, like anything (or anyone) else who is not being observed or measured *in some way*, however minutely and discretely, is simply probabilistic computer code that remains in an un-rendered state. This is just like entities or environments in a video game that do not "exist" until and unless at least one player is observing or interacting with them.[16] Or, rather, until and unless they are observed they "exist" only as coded information and are subject to what video game programmers call "conditional rendering."[17]

As Elon Musk has put it, "Quantum indeterminacy is really an op-timization technique" like the ones used by computer-game program-mers.[18] Since the computer on which the simulation of our universe is running does not have the resources to always run every possibility as an apparently physical state of affairs, it only ever renders what is being observed by someone and only while that "thing" is under observation is it a "thing" at all.[19] When observation "collapses" the non-local probability wave or "quantum foam" into localized particles, what is really going on is that the rendering engine of the simulation is taking code for every possible state of affairs (at a subatomic level) and "materializing" them in response to an attempted observation of events at a quantum level.[20] In fact, "matter" does not actually exist. What are taken to be "subatomic particles" are just turned on and off in varying patterns like pixels rendered on a computer screen.[21]

This model also explains so-called "quantum entanglement," another phenomenological observation that remains baffling under

16   Ibid., 137.
17   Ibid., 135, 138.
18   Ibid., 139.
19   Ibid., 138–139.
20   Ibid., 124, 130.
21   Ibid., 123.

the standard version of Quantum Theory. Two quantum particles that have been in interaction with each other become "entangled" in such a way that, no matter how vast the distance between them subsequently becomes, affecting one of these entangled particles immediately results in a corresponding change of state in the other. Moreover, the information exchange that seems to take place here happens at a speed faster than that of light.[22] Albert Einstein was deeply disturbed by this, and referred to it as "spooky action at a distance." It is not a mere theoretical postulate, either. Einstein would have been even more disturbed if he could have lived to see how such entanglement is already being practically employed by computer scientists at institutions such as the US National Security Agency, in the nascent field of Quantum Cryptography.[23]

One way of understanding how this "spooky action at a distance" works, without assuming that the speed limit of light is actually being violated and that information is being passed directly and instantaneously from one particle to its entangled counterpart at however great a distance, is to see the entangled quantum particles as projections from a deeper and hidden dimension outside of our spacetime.[24] What appear, to us, to be discrete but entangled particles are actually pixels being rendered simultaneously by a computer system that recognizes that those sets of pixels need to always be re-rendered together. This pairing of certain pixels in the programming code that governs transformations inside a simulation, as against other pixels that are not paired or grouped in the same way, happens all the time in contemporary video games.

So the Simulation Hypothesis solves two of the most puzzling problems posed by the standard interpretation of Quantum Physics, namely quantum superposition and quantum entanglement. It also

---

22 Ibid., 181.

23 Ibid.

24 Ibid., 182.

offers us a very coherent way of comprehending the quantization of space-time. The very name of Quantum Physics derives from the fact that those who formulated this post-Newtonian paradigm presented and interpreted evidence for physical phenomena being quantized, rather than continuous. Given the unity of space-time, as conceptualized by Einstein and others, this means that time is as quantized as space. It is not continuous, as we seem to experience it to be, but consists of discrete and discontinuous packets of information.

Zeno's paradox was the first demonstration, based on logic alone, that space must be quantized.[25] Otherwise, Achilles would always be trying to make up half of the distance toward the tortoise that had a head start in their race. No distance could ever be definitively traversed. While the ancient Greeks conceived of quantized space in terms of atoms, if we are living in a simulation these indivisible and discrete units of minimum distance would be the pixels rendered by the information processing system.[26] The development of the nuclear model of the atom, including protons and neutrons, by Lord Rutherford disabused physicists of the Greek definition of the atom as the ultimately indivisible building block of all else, and since that time a whole host of subatomic particles have been found.

The minimum distance defined by a single pixel is, however, not the magnitude of any of these subatomic particles. That magnitude was discovered by Max Planck and has, consequently, been dubbed "the Planck length." It is derived through an equation that deals with three elements: (1) the speed of light in a vacuum; (2) the energy of a photon in relation to its frequency; (3) the gravitational constant. This gives us a length of $1.616229(38) \times 10^{-35}$ meters.[27] If we are living in a simulation, this Planck length is the magnitude of a single

---

25 Ibid., 166.

26 Ibid.

27 Ibid., 168.

pixel.[28] John Wheeler's investigation of gravity waves validated the impossibility of measuring anything at a scale beyond or beneath this length.[29]

If we calculate the amount of time it takes for a single Planck length to be traversed at the speed of light, both of which are fixed values, we can arrive at $5.39X10^{-44}$ seconds as a "Planck time" unit. In other words, this fundamental unit of quantized time would be our simulated world's clock speed. Compare this to today's high-end 1.7 gigahertz processors that can perform 1.7 billion cycles per second, thereby delivering the illusion of continuous "live action" in video games.[30]

Space and time are both quantized, because what have been mistaken as the "fundamental building blocks" of nature are actually something akin to pixels being rendered by an information processing system.[31] Quantum "particles" are actually pixels that are de-rendered and re-rendered at the clock speed of the universal computer. To those inside the simulation, time seems like a continuum of experience — but these updates could take anywhere from 1 millisecond to 5 seconds or much longer to carry out in the "real time" of the world of the programmers outside of the simulation.[32]

This incommensurability of time scales is similar to that which is characteristic of dreams, where whole days and even years can elapse in a dream that endures for only a small part of one night when measured in what is presumed to be the "real time" of the dreamer's waking life. Some people have even reported living out entire alternate lives in dreams that pick up where they left off, night after night.[33] Tibetan dream Yoga aims to cultivate lucid dreaming to the end of

---

28   Ibid., 168–169.

29   Ibid., 168.

30   Ibid., 172.

31   Ibid., 123.

32   Ibid., 172.

33   Ibid., 191.

ultimately being able *to lucidly recognize this world as a dream*, albeit a telepathically shared and inter-subjectively co-constituted dream.[34]

The experience of having a dream within a dream is relatively common, and can be quite disconcerting.[35] Those who have had these experiences will recall, especially if the dreams nested within each other were nightmares, that in the first few moments of being back in this seemingly "waking reality" one is full of desperate anxiety over whether this is finally reality or whether it is just another dream layer that one needs to wake up from. The Tibetan Buddhists take the latter view. It would make sense for designers of a simulation to use the natural virtual reality generating mechanism of dreaming as a guide to developing the most optimal system for generating a multi-player simulated world.[36] The shortest route to designing and programming such worlds might just be to hack the natural process of dreaming. This is the kind of technology at play in Christopher Nolan's *Inception*, a masterful exploration of virtual realities that are woven out of the manipulation of dreams within dreams.[37] The incommensurate time frames experienced as one traverses nested dreamscapes of diverse depths, is a major theme in *Inception*.

It may be the case that the speed of light is both an absolute speed limit and a fundamental constant in our universe only because the physics engine and rendering engine of the computer that this simulation is running on uses electromagnetic signal transmissions.[38] As in contemporary video games, where there is a fixed and maximum speed at which a signal can be sent from one player to the server and then sent back to the other players via the server so as to coordinate their actions in what is made to feel like 'real time,' the great game of our simulated universe would also have such a limit: the speed of

---

34   Ibid., 194.

35   Ibid., 197.

36   Ibid., 195–196.

37   Christopher Nolan, *Inception* (Legendary Pictures, 2010).

38   Virk, *The Simulation Hypothesis*, 123, 182.

light.[39] However, the same physics engine that defines light speed as a limit condition may allow for exceptions to the "laws of nature" because these putative "laws" are simply programming code intended to set parameters for states of affairs inside the simulation *in general*.

Like the physics engine of most video games, it may provide stable parameters for the interaction of players with their simulated environment, but also allow for jumping around the video game in a discontinuous way.[40] By analogy, this would be like teleporting from one place in the world — or even from one place in the universe — to another, virtually instantaneously. In other words, it would allow for 'travel' at a speed faster than that of light if the same distance were to be traversed continuously — in a straight or curved line rather than, as it were, by popping out of one place and into another. This is akin to the teleportation in simulations like *Second Life*, where one's character is seemingly instantaneously de-rendered and re-rendered at another locale within the virtual world.[41] When physicists postulate that sending starships through "wormholes" or tunnels connecting disparate locations in space-time might be possible, what they may really be getting at is the provision, built into the simulation, for discontinuous jumps around the virtual world — spanning distances that, if traversed continuously, would take much longer in view of the limit that is the speed of light.[42]

Beginning with Einstein's General Theory of Relativity, time was interpreted as an additional dimension of space, so that in addition to the Cartesian spatial grid coordinates of x, y, and z, the fourth value of t was added to these, and three-dimensional space was redefined as four-dimensional space-time.[43] What the seeming absurdity of retro-causality and time-travel paradoxes suggests is that there is, crudely

39 Ibid., 171.
40 Ibid., 123.
41 Ibid., 177.
42 Ibid., 178.
43 Ibid., 171.

speaking, a fifth dimension beyond this, which encompasses various relative space-time matrices and renders them amenable to manipulation and deformation. Events in the past that are undetermined because they are as of yet unobserved can be determined from the future for the same reason that determined past events can be rewritten from out of the future by 'time traveling' into the past, i.e. by rebooting to an archived past state of play and making different choices inside of the game.

"Retro-causality" is no different from the kind of thing that happens when a player logs into an archived past state of a game and takes a course of action that causes something to be rendered that had not been rendered in the original timeline of how events unfolded for the experienced world of that player. Such apparent "retro-causality" is possible only because the quantized fourth-dimensional time of the game state(s) is nested inside a fifth-dimensional space-time that lies outside of the simulation and allows for the manipulation of space-time within the simulation.

This interpretation of Time Travel also resolves the so-called "grandfather paradox."[44] If a time traveler inadvertently changes the past in a way that would lead to his not having been born, there is no paradox because he is simply *a player who is operating in a different version of the game* from the one where his birth, childhood, etc. were part of his character's "backstory." That other version is not an actually existing parallel universe different from a new one that has branched off when the relevant change in the course of events has taken place, so that we have a potentially infinite number of alternative selves living out different versions of our life and making every choice imaginable. Instead of this Everett-Graham-Wheeler Many Worlds Interpretation of quantum mechanics, which makes nonsense of our free will with its conception of an infinity of parallel worlds, we can think of the older version of history as a game that has been replayed in a different way.

---

44 Ibid., 149.

The original state of play may or may not be archived within the information processing system, but if it is archived rather than simply being deleted, then it "exists" in the archive only as information. If it is deleted, the player who changes history as a time traveler does not simply "disappear" when the state of affairs are such that he would not have been born in the new version of history, because this player is an avatar of someone outside of the simulation (outside of any and all versions of the game's history). She has, either deliberately or inadvertently, lost sight of her true identity.

An avatar may live many lifetimes within virtual realities without recollecting her true identity. What occultists and parapsychologists have referred to as "reincarnation" or "rebirth," and what the ancient Greeks called *metempsychosis*, may be something akin to the "quests" and "achievements" of Massively Multiplayer Online Role Playing Games (MMORPGs).[45] Players may have tasks or "quests" generated by their actions in "previous lives."

Contemporary game designers are able to archive information about a player's virtual life, together with a complete list of his friends and possessions, on a server outside of the simulation. The "Akashic records" of occultists may be akin to such a cloud server storage, a "Cloud Atlas" of sorts. This would contain the *karma* of each player, and a list of their lessons learned, failures, achievements, and corresponding future challenges.[46] *Karma* may be a kind of "quest engine."[47] The "life review" described by many near death experiencers, and by those who recall past lives as a process that takes place in the limbo between lifetimes, may be something like the replay of an archive of a player's recorded actions inside of a video game. The Hindu concept of *lila* or the cosmic theatrical play would be very

---

45 Ibid., 14.

46 Ibid., 212.

47 Ibid., 213–214.

descriptive of our lives inside the simulation.[48] It also corresponds to the oft quoted line from Shakespeare: "All the world's a stage, / And all the men and women merely players."[49]

One of the reasons that *Second Life* was not nearly as successful as *World of Warcraft* is because there was so much freedom that players did not know what to do with themselves.[50] This is why "quests" are a key component of MMORPGs.[51] The expression "I didn't sign up for this!" has a whole other level of meaning in a context where programmers outside of our simulation are tasking us with quests that we did not sign up for in the way that players of MMORPGs sign up for their in-game quests.

In his book *The Simulation Hypothesis*, Riz Virk makes the serious mistake of assuming that we chose everything about our avatars before we entered into the game.[52] He also naively believes that when two people are bound by *karmic* ties it is because before they both chose to reenter the simulation each of them agreed to accept a quest offered up to them by the system based on the past interactions of their avatars in "previous lives."[53] Either the computer system itself, using algorithms, or the programmers of our simulation, could push us toward creating certain kinds of *karma* that binds us together and can be used to manipulate us as unwitting parties to unfolding the game's master narrative.

A wide variety of paranormal phenomena besides reincarnation also make sense when these "anomalies" are reconsidered in the context of the Simulation Hypothesis. Consider what follows from the fact that our experience is rendered for each of us from our own perspective, so that we are communicatively connected to each other, first

---

48   Ibid., 214, 217.

49   Ibid., 217.

50   Ibid., 210.

51   Ibid., 211.

52   Ibid.

53   Ibid., 215.

and foremost, through the information processing system rather than in any commonly shared physical space. This would also mean that we can exchange signals and communicate with each other in ways that appear to defy the limits of physical space and time, in other words, by means of "ESP." Inside MMORPGs, it is possible to send private messages to players even when they are not logged into the system. These are stored on the server and then delivered to their intended recipient when the latter is back online.[54] Compare this to telepathic messages sent by the living to someone who is dead, someone who only receives these messages after he has been reincarnated — and perhaps after their sender has also died.

In addition to telepathy, another form of ESP that could be explained by understanding our universe as a computer simulation is Precognition. As it is, gambling simulations, such as Monte Carlo games, run large numbers of possible futures before actualizing a particular one.[55] Precognizing an event may not be observing a definite future, but tapping into information pertinent to one relatively probable future that is already being processed by the system.

The evidence from precognitive remote viewing tends to support this interpretation. Some of the CIA and DOD remote viewers were able to use information about the future in order to change the future, but the changes they made could have been made based on information from a future that, as a consequence of their actions based on that same information, did not actually materialize. While this would be paradoxical and even absurd if we were really living in a material world of the kind that early modern physicists believed us to be inhabiting, it makes perfect sense if we are living in a simulation. Possible futures might usually be translated into actual present states of affairs by an AI running an evaluative function comparable to, but far more complex than, those that contemporary chess or checkers programs

---

54   Ibid., 210.

55   Ibid., 153.

run.[56] However, in an interactive and massively multi-player game, it may be that the players can sometimes also have a stake in determining this translation.

The type of paranormal phenomena that most strongly suggests that we are living in a simulation is what the Swiss-German psychologist Carl Gustav Jung called "Synchronicity."[57] This was Jung's term for meaningful coincidences that are so complex and striking that it is hard to believe that they are random events that just happen to align by chance. The classic example is the incident of the scarab beetle. Jung had a patient who was very resistant to his method of psychotherapy on account of her rigidly rationalistic mindset. In one therapy session, she told him about a dream she had that prominently featured a scarab beetle, the ancient Egyptian symbol of transformation. Just after recounting her dream, the two of them heard a rapping on the window of Jung's office. He drew aside the curtains and opened the window so that the beetle who turned out to have been making the sound could fly into Jung's hand, whereupon he presented it to the startled client. It was as close to a scarab type as the beetles in Switzerland ever get. This synchronicity broke through the client's psychical armor and she subsequently made rapid progress in her therapy sessions.[58]

Jung was so struck by the numerous synchronicities that would crop up in his life, some much more complex than the one recounted above, that he developed a theory interpreting astrological influences in terms of Synchronicity.[59] However, there are two problems with this theory. The first is that it is as incoherent as Jung's concept of Synchronicity in general. The second is that, despite this conceptual incoherence, scientific evidence for astrological influences *of the same kind* that Jung cites has actually been rigorously demonstrated, so that

---

56   Ibid., 154.

57   C.G. Jung, *Synchronicity* (Princeton University Press, 2010).

58   Ibid, 23.

59   Ibid, 43–67.

despite his failures in coherently theorizing, Jung is onto something with his idea of Synchronicity and, at that, on a level as vast and all-encompassing as the Cosmos.

Jung defines Synchronicity as "an acausal connecting principle," but this does not make any sense. What Jung wants to maintain is that specific clusters of events, which are distinct from more general patterns in nature, can be linked to each other through their organizational structure in a way that does not involve a cause and effect relationship. What is supposed to meaningfully organize these spatially, and sometimes also temporally, disparate events in a strikingly meaningful manner are the so-called "archetypes" at work in the "collective unconscious." There are at least three problems here.

First of all, what are the criteria according to which certain elements picked from out of a complex state of affairs in a way that they can be compared to another constellation of facts, such that the observation is made that these two "events" are meaningfully connected or form a "synchronicity"? The same state of affairs can be perceived and organized in any number of ways, like a Rorschach test. Jung implicitly resists this claim that the meaningfulness of "events," or even what is taken to be an "event" in the first place, is a subjective determination.[60] Rather, he wants to assert that certain events have intrinsic meaning and that this meaningfulness can be read off of them by anyone, because significance is embedded in the situation.

Even if we were to grant this highly suspect claim, it would imply that the connection between seemingly disparate events in terms of their shared intrinsic meaning is an organizational function that occurs at a transcendental level. That is problematic because, on Jung's own admission, the archetypes do not have this kind of transcendence. Jung does not deny biological evolution by natural selection, and he admits that had humans not evolved in the way that they did, they would not have the same archetypes operating in their

---

60 Stephen E. Braude, *ESP and Psychokinesis: A Philosophical Examination. Revised Edition* (Brown Walker Press, 2002), 183–184.

collective unconscious. For example, a hermaphroditic species of intelligent humanoids might not have any archetype of the Great Mother. Furthermore, Jung even claims that different societies or civilizations are shaped by archetypes particular to the collective unconscious of a certain race or ethnicity. The collective unconscious is racially differentiated in terms of its archetypes so that, for example, Africans do not have an archetype akin to "Wotan" (although Iranians, as fellow Aryans, might). If archetypes are not transcendental, but are biologically and historically contingent, then they cannot be the transcendent principles that meaningfully order certain clusters of events.[61]

Finally, granting both the intrinsic meaningfulness of certain sets of events and also the transcendental nature of archetypes, there is still no reason to characterize the former's production of the latter as "acausal." Aristotle defined four types of causes: (1) the material cause, or what a thing is made out of; (2) the formal cause, or what ideal type a thing can be classified as being an instantiation of; (3) the efficient cause, or the agency that shapes matter into an instantiation of a certain form; and, finally, (4) the final cause, namely the end or meaningful purpose of a thing — the end for which the thing comes to be, by means of the other three causes. Rather embarrassingly for someone so keen on the history of ideas and with such familiarity of the classical epoch, when Jung defines synchronicity as "acausal" he is thinking in terms of an impoverished and overly reductive modern conception of causality, according to which all causes are efficient causes.[62]

If he had argued that archetypes are transcendental, which he did not, then he might at least have identified them as final causes. In that case, their generation of synchronicities is a causal process, albeit an extremely complex one. It would require a nexus of Extra-Sensory Perception (ESP) and Psychokinesis (PK) operating at the level of efficient causality on the material of physical and biological processes in

---

61   Ibid, 187.

62   Ibid, 184.

order to shape seemingly disparate events with a view to a common formal cause. Jung, however, wanted to deny even the causal nature of ESP and PK, preferring to reduce these to instances of an "acausal" Synchronicity.[63]

Despite the failure of Jung's theory of Synchronicity, his inclination to interpret the efficacy of Astrology in terms of Synchronicity is not entirely misguided. Anyone who tries to assert that there is a naturalistic basis for Astrology, for example with reference to the effect of the Moon on tidal forces, is either a charlatan or an ignorant fool. The oceans of the Earth are vast and the lunar effect on tides is relatively minimal, when considered on a global scale. The combined tidal forces exerted on the fluids of a person's body by the Moon and all of the other gravitational masses (planets, other moons) in our solar system is far less than that exerted by a soccer ball held in a person's hand.[64] So, if there is empirical evidence for the efficacy of astrological influences, Jung would have been right to seek some non-naturalistic explanation for them. Before returning to this explanation, we will briefly consider some of the most compelling scientific evidence that Astrology should be taken seriously.

Let us begin with an astrological study that has direct bearing on the archetype of Prometheus, namely a study on the astrological influence of the planet Uranus by Richard Tarnas titled *Prometheus the Awakener*. Classical Astrology is based on the symbolism of the seven visible planets. Uranus was discovered in 1781 by the astronomer and musician, William Herschel. There was a debate over what to call this eighth planet, with one contender even being "Georgium Sidus" in honor of King George III of England, who had been Herschel's patron. The French, who rejected this for obvious reasons, proposed that it simply be called "Herschel." Finally, Johann Elbert Bode, suggested the name "Uranus" simply because in Greek mythology Uranus is the

---

63 Ibid, 177.

64 Patrick Grim, *Philosophy of Science and the Occult* (State University of New York Press, 1990), 15–17, 28–36.

father of Chronos, known to the Romans as "Saturn", and this was the next planet beyond Saturn.[65]

The problem is that the mythological characteristics of the titan Uranus do not at all correspond with the subsequently discovered character of the astrological influence that Uranus appears to have on the natal charts of individuals and in the history of nations. In fact, once Uranus was factored into Astrology, it was observed that the astrological characteristics of Uranus were in many ways opposite to those of the mythological deity after whom the planet was named. It turns out that the influence of this planet is associated with sudden change, discovery, especially flashes of insight that strike like lightning, intellectual brilliance, artistic creativity, technical innovation, rebellion and revolution, as well as the liberation attendant to such a struggle, and in particular the assertion of individuality and originality against tyranny and conformism, including in the form of the wily machinations of a trickster.[66] By contrast, Uranus or *Ouranus* — the Heaven or Starry Sky Father of the Greeks — is the ultimate patriarchal authority figure who resists rebellion and is responsible for upholding hierarchical order and a stability epitomized by the regularity of celestial motions.[67] In *Prometheus the Awakener* Richard Tarnas writes that, when contemplating this conundrum, he was struck with the following insight:

> I noticed that those same astrological qualities fit another figure in Greek mythology with extraordinary precision. This figure was Prometheus, the Titan who rebelled against the gods, helped overthrow the tyrannical Kronos, tricked Zeus, and stole fire from Mount Olympus to liberate humanity from the gods' power. Prometheus was considered the wisest of his race and taught humankind all the arts and sciences. The more I examined the matter, the more I realized that every quality astrologers associate with the planet Uranus was reflected in the myth of Prometheus: the initiation

---

65 Richard Tarnas, *Prometheus the Awakener* (Spring Publications, 2018), 19.

66 Ibid.

67 Ibid., 20.

of radical change, the passion for freedom, the defiance of authority, the act of cosmic rebellion against a universal structure to free humanity of bondage, the urge to transcend limitation, the intellectual brilliance and genius, the element of excitement and risk. So also Prometheus's style in outwitting the gods, when he used subtle stratagems and unexpected timing to upset the established order: he, too was called the cosmic trickster. And the resonant symbol of Prometheus's fire conveyed at once several meanings — the creative spark, cultural and technological breakthrough, the enhancement of human autonomy, the liberating gift from the heavens, sudden enlightenment, intellectual and spiritual awakening — all of which astrologers consider to be connected with the planet Uranus.[68]

Before moving on, it is worthwhile to consider what Tarnas means by "genius" in association with the archetype of Prometheus, since the idea of creative genius reappears repeatedly throughout the present text just as it did in *Prometheus and Atlas*. Tarnas offers the following definition of genius in terms of nine typical characteristics. This characterization of genius is so precise, comprehensive, and accurate, that it is worthy of being adopted without qualification. In *Prometheus the Awakener*, Tarnas writes that:

(1)   Creative geniuses do not merely solve existing problems, they identify new ones.

(2)   They form more novel combinations of thought elements and are alert to chance permutations of ideas and images spontaneously combining in novel ways; they possess an ability to make juxtapositions that elude others, to connect the unconnected, to see relationships that elude others, to see relationships to which others are blind, to cross frames of reference — an ability linked to an imaginative faculty set in motion by the reconceptualizing power of metaphor.

(3)   They have an interest in multiple unrelated fields, making novel combinations more likely.

(4)   In addition, they have a tolerance for ambiguity, a patience with unpredictable avenues of thought;

---

68   Ibid., 20–21.

(5)   A tendency toward iconoclasm;

(6)   An impulse for taking risks;

(7)   A childlike delight in what they do.

(8)   ...[C]reative geniuses work obsessively, producing much that is great as well as much that is not.

(9)   ...[T]hey combine a certain balance of youth and maturity—an innovative impulse on the one hand, and time and experience on the other. Individuals in whom one or the other polarity is dominant tend not to produce significant revolutions.[69]

Tarnas goes on to report the mind-boggling findings of his masterful research into the astrological influence of Prometheus (formerly Uranus) on major figures in the history of the sciences, politics, literature and the arts. His approach is Jungian, and he goes on at some length contemplating Prometheus as an "archetype" in the sense in which Carl Jung and his disciple, James Hillman, meant the term, but he augments this with a more Platonic view of archetypes as transcendent metaphysical principles, as well as one that takes more seriously the identity of certain archetypes with deities that really do influence our lives as spectral forces—a view that he calls "Homeric."[70]

Tarnas is careful to note that the same influence is at work in many more people who never achieved notoriety, but it goes without saying that it is easier to acquire substantive data for analysis from the lives of famous individuals.[71] In fact, one of the most fascinating aspects of his study is the observation of how certain traits associated with Prometheus manifest in successful individuals as compared to unsuccessful people.[72] For example, the Promethean boldness that is indispensable to revolutionaries, whether in the sciences or politics, might

---

69 Ibid., 86.

70 Ibid., 14–17.

71 Ibid., 24.

72 Ibid., 25.

wind up manifesting simply as a life full of reckless risk-taking and compulsive gambling. Likewise with the defiance of authority, which, when misdirected, especially from a young age, might simply take the form of juvenile delinquency. Prometheus even features prominently in the charts of kleptomaniacs, a reflection both of his status as the trickster thief and also his association with excitement and risk-taking.[73] Less deleteriously, Prometheus (Uranus) is prominent in the astrological charts of non-conformist people who pursued their own path in life, often at considerable cost, and those with erratic temperaments, who are often drawn to exceptional or even bizarre experiences, and who are especially open to novel or radical ideas.[74]

However, it is in the lives of prominent persons, whose biographies and works are available within the domain of public knowledge, that we can most clearly discern the astrological influence of Prometheus. Tarnas considers prominent figures in the history of scientific discovery and technological innovation, revolutionary politics, literature and the arts. He does so with a view not only to the significance of Prometheus (Uranus) in their natal charts, but also by analyzing what other astrological body has the most significant dynamic relation to Prometheus in the chart of each of these individuals. In other words, he looks at the Natal Aspects of Moon-Uranus, Mercury-Uranus, Venus-Uranus, Mars-Uranus, Jupiter-Uranus, Saturn-Uranus, Uranus-Pluto, and Sun-Uranus combinations.

In the realm of scientific revolutions, Tarnas found that Prometheus was the dominant astrological influence in the natal charts of all of these individuals: Nicolaus Copernicus, Johannes Kepler, Galileo Galilei, René Descartes, Francis Bacon, Isaac Newton, Charles Darwin, Niels Bohr, William James, Sigmund Freud, Carl Jung, and Timothy Leary.[75] Moreover, Tarnas was able to identify a

---

73 Ibid., 82.

74 Ibid., 25.

75 Ibid., 23.

particularly prominent influence of Uranus or Prometheus during the times when certain of these individuals either conceived of or published their revolutionary contributions to the history of science. This includes the key astronomical discoveries of Galileo, the publication of Newton's *Principia*, and Darwin's discovery of natural selection as the mechanism of evolution, among many other examples.[76] Interestingly, Tarnas contrasts the Sun-Uranus combination in the chart of Freud with that of Venus-Uranus in the case of Jung, correlating it to the more paternalistic and masculine symbolism and concerns of Freud's work by comparison to Jung's emphasis on feminine archetypes and on the *Anima*.[77]

In the realm of revolutionary politics, all of the following figures have natal charts that prominently feature the influence of Prometheus: Thomas Jefferson, Benjamin Franklin, Napoleon Bonaparte, Vladimir Lenin, and Mao Tse Tung. In the cases of Napoleon and Mao, Tarnas found Uranus and Mars in close major aspect, which correlates with both of them having been political revolutionaries who were also military leaders that led major armed campaigns and came to power by the force of arms.[78] By contrast, in the case of Ben Franklin, who was also a witty writer and a brilliant scientific inventor, he found that the American revolutionary was born with a major Mercury-Uranus aspect.[79] This was also true of another American revolutionary known for his eloquence of expression, Thomas Jefferson, the author of the *Declaration of Independence* and founder of the University of Virginia.[80] Jefferson knew many dead and living languages, and his personal library was the most extensive in America.

In literature and the arts, Tarnas found that geniuses under the astrological influence of Prometheus include, among others: Leonardo

---

76 Ibid., 34–36.

77 Ibid., 26, 81.

78 Ibid., 44.

79 Ibid., 48.

80 Ibid., 47.

da Vinci, Ludwig van Beethoven, Percy Shelley, J.W. Goethe, Friedrich Schiller, G.W.F. Hegel, Friedrich Nietzsche, Richard Wagner, Oswald Spengler, Arnold Toynbee, Bertrand Russell, George Bernard Shaw, Franz Kafka, Charlie Chaplin, Marcel Marceau, Bob Dylan, Martin Heidegger, Jacques Derrida, and Stanley Kubrick.[81] Within this group, the strongest Mercury-Uranus natal aspects were found among the writers, especially those with a reputation for playing with language in novel ways, as would be expected of the archetype of Mercury/Hermes/Thoth.[82] Those with a particularly strong romantic tendency, whether in literature or painting, tended to have charts featuring Venus-Uranus aspects.[83]

I have omitted the names of women from the lists of great men above. That is because it is particularly significant that, as Tarnas points out, all of the women who defied their traditional gender role by making major scientific, intellectual, or literary contributions in the modern age were women born with the Sun and Uranus in major aspect. This includes Marie Curie, Margaret Mead, Gertrude Stein, Mary Shelley, Madame de Staël, George Sand, Susan B. Anthony, Beatrice Webb, and Simone de Beauvoir.[84] That it is a Sun-Uranus combination in particular which features prominently in their charts, also suggests that they were in some way *masculine* women.

One of the most striking arguments that Tarnas makes in *Prometheus the Awakener* is that the greatest tension between any two astrological influences is the tension between Saturn and Uranus. The mythological aspects of Saturn, or Chronos, are diametrically opposite to those of Prometheus. He stands for strict conformity, totalitarian order, and the authority of tradition.[85] Prometheus helped devise the conspiracy to overthrow him. Individuals with Uranus-Saturn

---

81 Ibid., 54–57.

82 Ibid., 47.

83 Ibid., 45–47.

84 Ibid., 24.

85 Ibid., 73.

combinations that figure prominently in their natal charts, such as Karl Marx, tend to display a paradoxical tendency to want to force people to be free or to promote revolutionary liberation by means of authoritarian or even totalitarian rule.[86] This is true not only of people, but of events. The onset of the Russian Revolution of 1917, which led to the formation of the Soviet Union, has this astrological signature.[87] Tarnas contrasts it with other revolutionary social and political upheavals that took place under the astrological influence of Prometheus, such as the American Revolution, the first and second French Revolutions, the social upheaval in America and Europe form 1968–71, and the fall of the Berlin Wall.[88]

On the other hand, Tarnas argues that Prometheus should be tempered with some degree of the influence of Saturn as a stabilizing and grounding force. Otherwise, Promethean rebellion can degenerate into violent anarchy and chronic instability of a kind that makes whatever bold ideas or visions are proposed too ephemeral to make an enduring impact.[89] Of particular note with relevance to the concerns of the present work is the claim that Tarnas makes to the effect that totally uncontrolled modern technological development is an example of such an unhinged and deracinated Promethean force:

> A particularly dangerous example of unconscious Prometheus on the collective level is the uncontrolled and unintegrated development of technology with no awareness of either its archetypal origins (Prometheus) or its ultimate effects ("the wrath of the gods": the impoverishment of life by over-industrialization, suicidal nuclear weaponry and radiation, and the global ecological crisis).[90]

---

86 Ibid., 73, 78.

87 Ibid., 77–78.

88 Ibid., 64–65, 70, 72.

89 Ibid., 84.

90 Ibid., 85.

Of course, one of the main aims of this work, as of *Prometheus and Atlas*, is to render conscious the Prometheus archetype that has been hitherto unconsciously driving global techno-scientific development, so that it can be more constructively integrated into our collective psyche. Tarnas sees Archetypal Astrology itself as a *techne* that could contribute to our more "consciously participating in the creative process of the cosmos" by "stealing fire from the gods" in "an extraordinary feat of human rebellion against archetypal manipulation."[91] In other words, the more we become aware of astrological influences, including that of Prometheus, the less fatalistic or negatively deterministic they become, and the more control we have over how we want to direct archetypal forces that have hitherto unconsciously shaped our lives and our societies.

From a scientific standpoint, Dr. Michel Gauquelin, who studied psychology and statistics at Sorbonne University in Paris, has perhaps made the greatest contribution to providing empirical evidence for the efficacy of Astrology. He purports to have demonstrated that human character and career is somehow linked to the movements of the planets. Gauquelin has authored a number of scientific papers on the subject, and his findings are summarized in his major work *Cosmic Influences on Human Behavior: The Planetary Factors in Personality*.[92] Gauquelin's initial discovery was made in the course of examining the position of the planets at the hour of birth of 576 members of the French Academy of Medicine. Probability theory can be applied to the positions of the planets by dividing the circle of their daily orbits into twelve, eighteen, or thirty-six sectors depending on the degree of detail desired. A highly statistically significant majority of these French Academy of Medicine members seemed to be born when Mars or Saturn had either just risen above the horizon, or reached their its point (culmination) in the sky.

---

91 Ibid., 88.

92 Michel Gauquelin, *Cosmic Influences on Human Behavior: The Planetary Factors in Personality* (Aurora Press, 1985).

This was corroborated by studies of other professionals, such as scientists, politicians, actors, writers, and sports champions. For each subject, her hour of birth was obtained by contacting the registrar's office at their place of birth. A study of 20,000 such European notables found that a statistically significant majority of sports champions were born with Mars either rising or culminating, and the same held true for soldiers with respect to Jupiter, and writers and journalists with respect to Saturn.[93]

The Belgian Committee for the Scientific Investigation of Phenomena Reputed to Be Paranormal (a hard-core skeptics organization similar to PSICOP in the US), which is made up of thirty scientists from different disciplines, successfully replicated these results.[94] Much to their chagrin, they had to admit that Gauquelin's Astrology research posed a genuine scientific problem. Perhaps they were able to so effectively replicate his findings because, unlike in the case of other paranormal phenomena such as ESP or PK, the relevant hard data here was not of a kind to be vulnerable to inhibition by negative experimenter intent. But there are serious problems with interpreting astrological influences in terms of mass ESP and PK.

It is true that the "astrological" correlations that Gauquelin found involved only the planets, and not zodiacal symbols for star constellations — which are constructed differently by various human cultures. It is possible, therefore, that tens of millennia of shared human myth-building with respect to the planets and their characteristic 'divine' influence has seeped so deep into the collective unconscious of *Homo sapiens* that it still shapes the psychological development of personalities *to some degree*. Gauquelin's findings are not anywhere near deterministically precise. They indicated tendencies, and ones which held true for only a small (but statistically significant) majority of the subjects at that.

---

93 Ibid.

94 Patrick Grim, *Philosophy of Science and the Occult* (State University of New York Press, 1990), 37–50.

However, even if the Cosmos is a consensus 'reality' of inter-subjective consciousness, it should not be the case that stars or even planets from the relatively contingent vantage point of Earth would be able to exert a determinative effect on the personal histories of individuals. Naturalistic physics, *as a psychical projection*, should still hold true on the cosmic scale of star systems. If the validity of astrological readings of Zodiacal birth charts were to be empirically demonstrated, a different explanation would be called for. Jung thought that he did have such empirical evidence of natal charts that demonstrated astrological influence, and his proposed explanation was the Synchronicity Theory critiqued above.

So, if there are indeed astrological influences which can neither be explained naturalistically, nor as large-scale ESP and PK, what kind of theory could account for these more effectively than Jung's postulation of an "acausal" connection between meaningful coincidences? The Simulation Hypothesis, of course. The planets and even the zodiacal constellations could be one strong influence on the lives of individuals because that kind of algorithm is programmed into the software of the MMORPG that we mistake for 'reality.'

In that case, the star constellations are not arbitrarily arranged into the patterns of the zodiac because Earth is the only vantage point from which those stars can be seen;there is no real universe beyond the Earth, and the particular patterns in question were chosen by the programmers of the counterfeit Cosmos that we see at night. Granted, this is a horrifying possibility, but that does not make it any less likely to be true. The virtual reality that we inhabit may be no larger than our own solar system, and astrological influences might simply be built into the game.

That might especially be the case if we live in a virtual reality that is itself inside of another simulation. This idea of stacked simulations was explored in the 1999 film *The Thirteenth Floor*. If those who programmed us have discovered that they themselves are inside of a simulation, it is possible that they would severely limit the scale of the virtual reality that they construct on account of a concern that if its information processing requirements become too taxing for the computer system that is running their own simulated world, the programmers *of the virtual reality that they inhabit* might pull the plug on them or at least act to set them back technologically.

On the other hand, there is the possibility that it is simulations all the way down. This is what is suggested by the Holographic Universe theory of David Bohm and Karl Pribram, which was popularized by Michael Talbot.[95] According to this theory, both the macrocosm of the universe and the microcosm of the human mind have a structure and function that is analogous to that of a hologram. Like a hologram, both quantum physical phenomena and the consciousness that actualizes them are characterized by non-locality and information that is holistically enfolded.

4.3 Our Holographic Cosmos

Karl Pribram was a neuroscientist who, in the 1960s, became notable for his staunch opposition to the use of lobotomies to 'treat' psychiatric patients. Pribram's neurophysiological research revealed that there were serious problems with the then standard model of the localization of information and perception within various parts of the brain. He found that people who suffered head injuries did not lose specific memories or perceptual capacities associated with the parts of the brain that sustained trauma. This led him to theorize that information, and even perceptual capacity, is somehow distributed non-locally across the entire brain.[96]

Experiments to prove Pribram wrong, and to defend the standard neurological model, wound up providing the strongest empirical evidence in favor of his view. In one set of such experiments, Paul Pietsch, a biologist at Indiana State University, repeatedly subjected

---

95   Michael Talbot, *The Holographic Universe* (Harper Perennial, 1992).

96   Ibid, 11–31.

salamanders to surgeries wherein their brains were shuffled around, and then sliced up, bit by bit, until it became clear that, following a brief recovery period, these salamanders were still able to behave normally, with whatever was left of their brains compensating for what was lost.[97] Karl Lashley, a neuropsychologist at the Yerkes Laboratory of Primate Biology in Florida, cut out portions of rats' brains that were believed to contain their memories of how to navigate a maze.[98] The rats were still able to remember what they had learned. Regardless of repeated attempts by Lashley to cut those memories out, which in some cases left them missing large portions of their brains, the rats were still able to stumble their way out of the maze as they had learned to do—albeit with impaired motor skills. Lashley also experimented on cats, and he discovered that a cat can still perform complex tasks that require visual perception even if 90 percent of the cat's visual cortex and 98 percent of its optic nerves are severed.[99]

The American physicist David Bohm was a young associate of Albert Einstein and became famous for his textbook *Quantum Theory*, which became the standard reference book for the field. However, after having presented the Copenhagen interpretation of quantum physics more lucidly than anyone else, Bohm also came to believe that he saw the problems with it more clearly than those of his colleagues that were satisfied with this account. In particular Bohm, like Einstein before him, was disturbed by the entanglement of quantum particles that appeared to coordinate their angles of polarization instantaneously—or at any rate, faster than the speed of light—no matter how far they flew apart from each other. Alain Aspect's 1982 experiment at the University of Paris demonstrated that this "spooky action at a distance" did not involve the communication of photons by any means known to Physics. Either faster than light communication

---

97   Ibid, 26.

98   Ibid, 18.

99   Ibid, 19.

was taking place or the polarization angles of the "entangled" quantum particles was occurring in some other mysterious way.

Bohm's suggestion was that what appear to be two entangled particles are not really distinct entities at all. Rather, they are akin to a fish in an aquarium with two video cameras trained on it at different angles, separated from each other by 90 degrees, so that the screen hooked to one camera shows the fish from the side and the other offers a head-on view of its narrow and flat body.[100] Someone who had never seen a fish before, and had no concept of what a fish is, might conclude that these are images of two different things. However, the same person would soon notice that whenever one of them moved the other would, instantaneously, make a corresponding movement. What this example is meant to suggest is that the seemingly entangled quantum particles are actually projections from a deeper, sub-quantum, order of reality wherein they are not distinct entities at all.

Bohm came to refer to this underlying reality as the "implicate" or enfolded order. He gives the analogy of a drop of ink that is dripped into a cylindrical mechanism containing glycerin.[101] When this contraption is turned, the black ink drop smudges into the white glycerin and eventually disappears. However, by turning the handle back in the opposite direction, the black ink drop is perfectly reconstituted. When it was smudged into the glycerin, its order was imperceptibly enfolded. Reversing the direction resulted in this hidden, implicit or "implicate" order becoming "explicate" or explicit. The realm of quantum physical phenomena is, according to Bohm, merely the explicate order unfolding from out of an implicate order characterized by a holistic and non-local distribution of information at a level more fundamental than the space-time construct that it projects.

Pribram and Bohm both realized that holographic information storage was the best metaphor for the kind of process at work in the

---

100 David Bohm, *Wholeness and the Implicate Order* (Routledge, 1994), 186–189.
101 Ibid, 149.

mind and the universe. The hologram was first theorized in 1947 by Dennis Gabor, who won a Nobel Prize for his work on perfecting the electron microscope that led him to conceptualize holography. Gabor used a kind of calculus invented by Jean Fourier to convert the pattern of any object into a mathematical wave-form, which could be recorded on a piece of special film, and then transformed back into an image of the object. The equations he developed for this process are called "Fourier transforms." Whereas this process was, for Gabor, still theoretical, by the mid-1960s, advances in laser technology allowed for these Fourier transforms to be used in the construction of the first holograms.[102]

The way this works is that the light emitted by a laser is split into two separate beams using a beam splitter. One beam goes on to be reflected by a series of two or more mirrors before passing through a diffusing lens and then striking a plate of holographic film. The second beam goes directly through a different diffusing lens and then shines on a given object before bouncing off it and casting its reflection into a photographic plate at an angle that intersects with the beam reflected by the final mirror. This mirror is set at an angle to the object in question, so that the two laser beams are reflecting light off of the object at different angles. The intersection of these two beams in the holographic plate produces an interference pattern that enfolds information about the object as viewed from different perspectives. When another laser is shined onto the holographic film, the seemingly chaotic swirl on the film is decoded into a sharp three-dimensional image of the object — floating above the plate.

What is really astonishing is that if this piece of photographic film is cut in half, and then in half again, and again, each of the pieces will, when subjected to laser light, continue to project the entire hologram rather than only portions of it. The smaller the pieces, the blurrier the

---

102 Talbot, *The Holographic Universe*, 27.

image may become, but the entire object still appears from out of the interference patterns on each piece.

As soon as he first discovered holograms, Pribram saw the relevance of this to what he had learned about non-local information storage in the brain. The brain has holographic properties that account for the preservation of memories and perceptual capacities despite localized damage to parts of the brain that were once thought to be uniquely responsible for storing these memories or determining the function of certain perceptual organs, for example, the visual cortex.

The associative function of memory is also comparable to the storage and retrieval of multiple images on the same piece of holographic film. It turns out that, in a more complex set up than the basic one described above, one can record two objects onto a piece of holographic film simultaneously in such a manner that, after the recording, when a laser is reflected off of one of them and onto the film, a hologram of the other is projected out of the film, and vice versa.[103] This is akin to how we are more likely to remember something that we have forgotten if we are shown something associated with it.

Pribram surmised that electrical charges from millions of rapidly firing neurons may be the brain's equivalent of laser light producing something akin to holographic interference patterns that non-locally distribute information throughout the brain. This is, of course, a fundamentally quantum physical process, which brings us back to Bohm.

Bohm saw the non-local character of information storage in a hologram as a perfect metaphor for the non-locality of quantum physical phenomena that are projected from out of the implicate order that is comparable to the interference patterns on holographic film. But he also saw the hologram as a way of understanding other seemingly paradoxical aspects of Quantum Physics that he felt were inadequately explained by the standard theory presented in his own celebrated textbook. One of these puzzling phenomena is wave/particle duality.

---

103 Ibid, 21.

A quantum manifests as a wave that passes through both slits in a double-slit experiment, so that an interference pattern is produced on the screen on the far side of the slits when no observation is being made, whereas it manifests as a particle that passes through only one of the slits if experimenters attempt to observe its path to the screen; in this case, it is recorded as a point rather than as an interference pattern akin to intersecting ripples. Bohm was right to be disturbed by this because, as Michael Talbot points out, it is as bizarre as if a bowling ball rolled down a bowling lane dusted with chalk were to make a straight line through the chalk when observed, but then when one briefly turns away and then looks at it again, one can see that it left a wavy pattern in the chalk while one was not looking, before resuming its straight path on its way to hitting the pins.[104]

In this analogy, the observation of the bowling ball is akin to shining a laser light on the holographic film so that the hologram of an object appears. When this laser of conscious observation is turned off, all that remains of the object is the interference pattern on the film. In other words, the quantum as particle is analogous to a holographic projection and the quantum as a "wave" or probability distribution is akin to the interference patterns on the holographic film. The latter is the sub-quantum implicate order that Bohm thinks our world is projected from out of, with the same virtual reality that a holographic image has.[105] His only qualification is that, unlike a static hologram, this projection is always moving. So he refers to the universe as a "holomovement" rather than a hologram.[106] In any case, the spatial dimensionality and chronological temporality of our world is virtual — as unreal as a holographic image that unfolds from out of a reality that consists of non-local information processing.

---

104 Ibid, 35.

105 Bohm, *Wholeness and the Implicate Order*, 144–146.

106 Ibid, 150–155.

When we consider Bohm's theory together with that of Pribram, we arrive at the notion that the quantum computer of our brain has holographic properties that allow us to unfold this seemingly physical, four-dimensional universe from out of a background of information that is being processed in a non-local and non-linear way at a level of reality that remains hidden from us. On this view, there is no objective physical reality underlying the simulation that we subjectively perceive.

If programmers are manipulating our perceptions, they too are part of a holographic universe and their experiences are, in the end, as "virtual" as ours, when compared to the reality of the implicate order. The only real difference may be that the elite of a civilization that has understood that this is the nature of the Cosmos might aim to become masters of illusion, akin to the Illuminati of "the Magic theater" in Hermann Hesse's *Steppenwolf*. Like Heraclitus, who has undoubtedly been welcomed into their ranks, they know that it is all a game — albeit a wickedly cruel and violent one.

One of the most disturbing questions about this game is the question of who the Non-Player Characters (NPCs) are, as compared to those avatars who have simply forgotten themselves. However many NPCs there might be in this simulation, it would not be akin to a video game unless at least one player is entering the simulation from somewhere outside of it (although this "outside" could be another simulation that the player and his civilization have mistaken for "reality").

The subject of NPCs verses avatars raises the question of what it means to be an authentic person rather than a "fake" one — an existential question that Philip K. Dick obsessed over in many of his novels.[107] Much of his science fiction involves false or implanted memories, most notably the stories that were adapted into the films *Blade Runner*, *Total Recall*, and *The Adjustment Bureau*. If our memories are false, what does that say about the authenticity of our character and

---

107 Virk, *The Simulation Hypothesis*, 17.

personality? Artificial Intelligence may eventually give us the capability to create Non-Player Characters who are as realistic as player characters (PCs) and indistinguishable from them by players within a game.[108] In other words, AI could afford us the ability to design NPCs who pass the Turing Test.

The possibility that psychic phenomena might pose a problem for this famous Turing Test of Artificial Intelligence was in fact entertained by Alan Turing in his seminal paper, "Computer Machinery and Intelligence" (1950), which features a much ignored section titled, "The Argument for Extrasensory Perception." However, Turing's concerns seem to have been misplaced if we are living in a computer simulation and telepathy is part of the programming, whether or not it is coded into the same part of the software that is the simulation's physics engine. There is no reason to think that an AI designed in the context of a vast virtual reality would lack the ESP that others within the holographic universe have the ability to use. An AI might even come more quickly to the realization that "There is no spoon."

At this point some retrospective and critical reflection on the latent biological romanticism of *Prometheus and Atlas* is in order, with a view to the contemplation of simulacra and the deconstruction of 'Reality' that has been the focus of this chapter. In *Prometheus and Atlas*, empirical evidence for psi functioning in animals, plants, and even organisms as simple as bacteria was marshaled as corroborative of a vitalist ontology developed through a synthesis of certain elements in Heidegger's phenomenology with the thought of Henri Bergson.[109]

The basic idea was not only that the kind of space and time that can be mathematically represented overlays a more primordial relationship to place and experience of endurance or duration, but also that modern technological science has an instrumental intentionality

---

108 Ibid., 50.

109 Jason Reza Jorjani, *Prometheus and Atlas* (Arktos, 2016), 146–180.

that manipulatively does violence to those dimensions of Nature that elude rational representation. These elusive dimensions of Nature (and the natural here was indeed conceived of with a capital "N"), which instinctual animals and bio-communicative plants abide in, and which remain open to us through a redevelopment of intuition, were deemed "irrational" in some implicitly mystical and ineffable sense. The implication was that we can dominate and derange Nature, but never reproduce the natural world — let alone the Cosmos as a whole — with high fidelity by means of technological science. Both Chaos Theory and Morphic Resonance (or the Theory of Formative Causation) give us reason to call this into question. Taken together, these theories make it more compelling to think that we are living inside of an information processing system — a gigantic quantum computer that is affected by various levels of the consciousness that it generates.

The idea of an "irrational" that would demarcate certain limits of instrumental control, and thereby inversely reveal the spectral quality of techno-scientific Enframing itself, can still be maintained. However, this irrational must be redefined as "chaos" in precisely the sense in which it is understood by the promulgators of Chaos Theory. In fact, as can be seen from the essay "Philosophy, Science, and Art" in *Lovers of Sophia,* I came close to doing so before *Prometheus and Atlas* was written. That essay on certain concepts in the thought of Gilles Deleuze was actually the matrix for the development of the thesis of *Prometheus and Atlas,* and in that reflection on Deleuze techno-scientific representation and objectification is described as a sieve cutting through "chaos" understood in very much the same way as chaos theoreticians conceive of it.[110] Namely, not as an absence of order, but as a flux of such extreme complexity and dynamism that its transformations are *in principle* unpredictable.

---

110 Jason Reza Jorjani, "Philosophy, Science, and Art" in *Lovers of Sophia* (Arktos, 2019), 476–489.

In another essay of mine that also appears in *Lovers of Sophia*, titled "Paranormal Phenomenology," I cite a scientific study that discovered fractals at many different levels of magnification enfolded into the paintings of Jackson Pollock.[111] This is an example of Deleuzian "chaos" that is particularly relevant to the relationship to the interplay between conscious intent and subconscious perception, cognition, and action (i.e. Pollack dancing around the canvas in Shamanic fashion as he paints these fractals within fractals, which appear utterly "chaotic"). The use of Pollock as an example is significant insofar as it demonstrates that it would be possible to retain nearly the entire argument about Aesthetic Ideas and the interplay of the conscious and the "irrational" unconscious that was developed in *Prometheus and Atlas* with a view, in particular, to the thought of Friedrich Schelling and Immanuel Kant.[112] It is simply the romantic naturalism or mystical vitalism of the notion of "chaos" that must be redefined along the lines of Chaos Theory, and also in light of a consideration of Rupert Sheldrake's conception of formal causes.

In the 1960s, the meteorologist Ed Lorenz of MIT used twelve equations with twelve variables, such as temperature, pressure, and humidity, in order to develop a computer simulation of the Earth's atmosphere.[113] He was using a computer built in 1959, which would take a long time to print out each moment of time in the model or projection as a row of twelve numbers. In order to save time, when Lorenz wanted to do a rerun of the simulation, he entered only the numbers from halfway through the previous run, on the assumption that the outcome of the projected atmospheric conditions would be the same from that point onward. Also, and very significantly, he did not input the numbers for the various parameters back into the computer again from scratch. Instead, he copied them straight off of

---

111 Jason Reza Jorjani, "Paranormal Phenomenology" in *Lovers of Sophia*, 224–227.

112 Jason Reza Jorjani, *Prometheus and Atlas*, 86–145.

113 James Gleick, *Chaos: Making a New Science* (Penguin, 2008), 9–32.

the printer, which rounded these numbers off to only three decimal places as compared to the six decimal places of the numbers originally plugged into the computer program. Lorenz found that the new run only followed the old one for a short while before diverging very significantly from the first projection. A difference of less than one part in a thousand in the initial conditions yielded totally different projected weather. In response to this perplexing outcome, Lorenz simplified his equations until he wound up with only three equations and three variables representing convection in an atmosphere being heated at the bottom and cooled at the top. Despite this simplification, the same chaotic behavior ensued as a consequence of the slightest change in initial conditions.

Lorenz also found that, when plotted in phase space, his equations do not trace out lines or a loop around a fixed attractor.[114] Rather, one gets a "strange attractor" that looks something like a butterfly, within infinite curves being traced out in a finite space, in other words, the formation of fractals, around the hollows that represent states that never occur or are not sustainable (such as snow in the Sahara or a heat wave in Antarctica). The Lorenz attractor, which from afar, looks something like a butterfly, signifies the fact that the systems never revisits the exact same state again.

The discovery of Lorenz was a milestone on the path to Chaos Theory, which is now most widely associated with the "butterfly effect."[115] This is the idea that even the smallest disturbance of air caused by a single butterfly can set in motion a chain of events that ultimately produces or redirects a storm on the other side of the planet. The term was coined based on Lorenz's presentation of his findings titled, "Does the Flap of a Butterfly's Wings in Brazil Set Off a Tornado in Texas?" It turns out that weather is not the only chaotic system. The fractal geometry of chaotic systems is everywhere in natural world,

114 Ibid., 28–29, 119–154.

115 Ibid., 20.

on every level and at any scale. One finds it in coastlines, snowflakes, trees, and flowers. But it is even characteristic of man-made systems such as the stock market or automobile traffic patterns. The dynamics of a stock market collapse and a sudden pile up traffic accident are akin to that of catastrophically abrupt climate change. Chaotic systems are both deterministic, in the sense that they can be mathematically described with precision, but also unpredictable, insofar as the mathematical description of any given states of a chaotic system cannot be used to form a precisely predictive projection of a future state of the system. Even our solar system, with its apparently regular planetary orbits, which was the epitome of predictable order for Newton, is actually a chaotic system. Over a time span of ten million or more years, extremely unpredictable events can take place, such as the hurling of a planet out of the system or the colliding of two or more planets inside of it.

The predictability of Newtonian Physics was epitomized by Pierre Simon Laplace, who thought that if a sufficiently powerful mind could know the initial conditions, or even just the present state of affairs, of every particle in the universe, as well as all of the operative laws of nature, this "demon" could predict all future events with perfect accuracy. However, it turns out that in chaotic systems one cannot look into the past and accurately identify initial causes of a present state of affairs. Chaotic systems are sensitive to the slightest variance in initial conditions, and one cannot know these conditions with perfect accuracy, to infinite decimal places, because one would come up against the Uncertainty Principle and quantum superposition on the level of sub-atomic waves/particles. This means that Chaos limits both what can be known about the future *and the past* of complex systems.

This may be related to how we have as much free will as we appear to have, despite various environmental, sociological, and psychological forms of conditioning and coercion. Psychokinesis experiments have found that the more chaotic a system is, the more mental intentionality seems to be able to affect physical phenomena. For example, using psychokinesis on a single ball falling straight down is much more difficult than on balls that are dropped through a lattice of pegs.[116] Unlike, when a ball is dropped onto a flat surface, which allows one to predict the path of future balls that are dropped the same way, bouncing a dropped ball off of an array of pegs turns the events into a chaotic system. Another ball dropped from the same position will not necessary follow the same path, because tiny variations in the path of each ball are being amplified with every bounce off of the pegs. It turns out that this makes psychokinetic influence a lot easier. Of course, the weather is a chaotic system, and some psychokinetic adepts have demonstrated a spectacular ability to effect dramatic and sudden changes in the weather.

This means that we could both be inside of a designed Cosmos, and also have a certain degree of free will that makes it impossible for the designers or programmers to perfectly predict what course of action any individual may choose to take in the game of life. Fractal geometry and the equations of Chaos Theory are already being used by designers of Massively Multiplayer Online Role Playing Games to generate the natural environment of hundreds of different planets in simulated worlds.[117] The algorithms that are used to do this do not require the programmers to micromanage the "creation" of such a world. Indeed, they make it possible to create on a scale and at a pace, and with a level of complexity, that would have been impossible to achieve if any group of programmers, however competent, would had to have worked out every detail themselves.

These algorithms are based on a simple equation that incorporates a feedback loop: $x^2 + C = x$. Imagine it this way. One holds a match in front of a video camera that is trained both on the match and also on a screen behind the match that displays what the camera is recording, and one gets a feedback loop. When one moves the match, the

116 Robert G. Jahn and Brenda J. Dunne, *Margins of Reality: The Role of Consciousness in the Physical World* (Harcourt, 1987), 124–135.

117 Rizwan Virk, *The Simulation Hypothesis*, 18–19, 48, 263–266.

patterns of light captured by the camera are displayed on the screen that the camera is filming. Then, capturing this pattern on the camera changes it when it is fed back to the screen, on and on, until mesmerizingly complex patterns emerge from out of the simple motion of the match in front of the camera. Attempting to move the match exactly the same way again will ultimately yield patterns totally different from the ones produced on the first run. Even in a simple set up like this, no analysis is capable of understanding how or why these particular patterns are formed — at least, not any analysis that would give one predictive knowledge of the system. The patterns that result are fractals, such as the Mandelbrot Set.[118] As noted above, fractals are now being used by computers to generate the 'natural' environments of simulated worlds for online gaming.

In this connection, it is worth noting that it was a computer scientist who made the very first breakthrough that led to Chaos Theory. While working at Station X to crack German naval codes, Alan Turing realized that simple mathematical equations might describe aspects of the biological world. Turing was motivated by the death of his lover and the question of what intelligence is, and whether it can be mathematically modeled. He realized that on the way to answering this question, he would first have to be capable of mathematically modeling biological phenomena. At that time, this was unprecedented. There were only precise mathematical descriptions in the domain of Physics. Turing began with a mathematical description for morphogenesis in an embryo. He asked himself how it is that the specific form of different body parts and organs arises when at first all cells in an embryo are identical.

While working at the University of Manchester, Turing answered this question in a 1952 paper titled, "The Chemical Basis of Morphogenesis."[119] This paper features the first description of a living

---

118 Gleick, *Chaos: Making a New Science*, 213–240.

119 A. M. Turing, "The Chemical Basis of Morphogenesis" in *Philosophical Transactions of the Royal Society of London. Series B, Biological Sciences*, Vol.

process using equations typical of astronomy or atomic physics. These equations describe the self-organization of biological systems, wherein complexity emerges from simple processes governed by simple equations. One example that Turing uses is the pattern of blotches or patches on the hide of a cow or on a giraffe or the stripes of a Zebra. Darwin had explained how such patterns are passed on, but not how they form in the first place. Turing did this with mathematical precision, yielding computer-generated versions of these chaotic patterns.

The question of morphogenesis brings us to Rupert Sheldrake's theory of Morphic Resonance, which, when considered together with Chaos Theory, warrants a reconsideration of the naturalistic romanticism of *Prometheus and Atlas*. After all, it was Sheldrake's research on Psi in animals that (combined with Cleve Backster's study of plant ESP) served as the empirical basis for such mystical vitalism.

Sheldrake argues that the mechanistic approach to biology is particularly deficient when it comes to explaining how more form comes from less form, for example in the embryological development of a fetus or in how plants grow from seeds.[120] Likewise, in explaining the regenerative capacity of certain organisms, such as flatworms, or in accounting for how whole organisms grow from parts of them — for example, when one takes a cutting of a plant. How animal instincts work has also remained mysterious in the context of a reductionist Biology that explains things only in terms of efficient causality.

The idea that the genetic program written into DNA is responsible for all of this implausible.[121] Sheldrake argues that the genetic program is not an explanation for everything and, in fact, it explains nothing in any detail. This is particularly clear in the case of the problem of Form generation or *morphogenesis*. Take a human arm and leg — they have exactly the same chemical proteins, the same kinds of cells, and the

237, No. 641. (Aug. 14, 1952), pp. 37–72.

120 Rupert Sheldrake, *Morphic Resonance: The Nature of Formative Causation* (Park Street Press, 2009), 43–47.

121 Ibid., 110–111.

same exact DNA in them, but they have different forms and different functions. If all of these cells are programmed identically, how do they develop differently? The answer given by mechanists is that it involves "complex spatio-temporal physico-chemical patterns of interaction not yet fully understood." Nobody in mainstream biology would claim that this problem is solved. Only laymen or people from other sciences would claim otherwise.

If an organism is more than the sum of its parts, then the question becomes what exactly this "more" consists of. It is neither matter/energy nor is it a totally mysterious "life force." In Physics, in addition to particles and laws concerning their dynamic interaction, there are also fields.[122] When one takes an ordinary iron bar magnet and cuts it in two, one does not get two "half magnets," one gets two smaller but complete magnets — each with a complete field. Fields have an inbuilt holistic property. Since the 1920s it has been possible to say that the organizing force in living organisms consists of *Morphic* fields or fields of form (*morphe* means "form" in classical Greek). This was first put forward under the name of "morphogenetic fields" with respect to the problem of accounting for organ differentiation in embryological development.

Sheldrake's proposed Morphic fields are local, but they are linked up together through space and time. This means that the field of one rabbit is influenced by that of other rabbits, both in the past and at present. The field of the rabbit has a collective memory or stores the habit of the species.[123] As the rabbit embryo develops, the field shapes it. The rabbits are as they are, because they were as they were. This is something Aristotle would have said, and in fact, Sheldrake's idea is a development of the concept of a formal cause in Aristotle. He even calls it "Formative Causation." However, unlike in the case of Aristotle's account of form as a cause, these Morphic fields can

---

122 Ibid., 48–49.

123 Ibid., 154–158, 163–165.

themselves be effected and restructured, and, relatedly, the entire hypothesis is empirically testable.

Take the case of crystals. Most people assume that the process of crystal formation is completely understood, but that is not the case. Physicists are at a loss to predict complex crystal formation in advance. It is a chaotic system. There are hundreds of ways that atoms and molecules can line up, but usually they do so in only one way (except in the case of polymorphic crystals). So whenever a new chemical is crystallized, which happens each year, the first time that the crystal forms it could crystallize in any which way.[124] But this probability distribution will not be equally random once the same chemical is crystallized repeatedly, even if in a completely unconnected laboratory in a totally different part of the world. The second or third or thirtieth crystallization of any given chemical compound will take place more rapidly, assume a definite form, and yield a crystal with a higher melting point (due to greater cohesion).[125] This has proven true of cocaine, penicillin, aspirin and many other pharmaceutical compounds. The only way that establishment chemists have been able to "explain" this begrudgingly acknowledged effect is by making the preposterous claim that fragments of previous crystals are carried from laboratory to laboratory "on the bears of migrant chemists" or that they are wafting around as invisible dust particles in the planetary atmosphere and make their way to the laboratory where a compound is crystallized for the second time — faster and with a higher melting point (melting points should remain constant). What they refuse to consider is that, in addition to efficient causes, there are formal or formative causes in the Cosmos.

These information structures, which are independent of linear space-time, also appear to be programmable. Suppose one gets an organism to develop in an abnormal way, for example to mutate fruit

---

124 Ibid., 53–58.

125 Ibid., 208–210.

flies so that they exhibit an extra pair of wings on account of their eggs having been treated with ether three hours after they are laid. If one does this over a number of successive generations, one will find that the percentage of mutated fruit flies keeps increasing, despite a maintenance of the same magnitude of stimulus for the mutation. What is really startling, is that when one subjects a fresh batch of completely unrelated fruit flies to the same stimulus, even in a different laboratory, the abnormality appears at a much higher rate immediately.[126] This is consistent with the idea that the information structure responsible for morphogenesis in fruit flies has been hacked and reprogrammed. This lends more weight to the idea that we are living inside of an information processing system. Self-organizing natural systems, in other words those studied in Chaos Theory, also appear to organize themselves based on non-locally stored memory and an information download from a "Morphic field" or algorithm specific to one or another organism or species.

Patterns of behavior are also effected by Morphic fields. Researchers found that rats were suddenly learning mazes that they had not been trained to navigate, but that other rats of the same species elsewhere (with no physical connection between them) had been trained to navigate.[127] For over forty years, experiments starting at Harvard, continuing at Edinburgh University, and ending in Australia, demonstrated that rats learning to navigate a maze so that they do not drown picked up in their learning curve in one place where rats that had been trained at another one of these institutions left off. The successive studies demonstrated a ten-fold increase, everywhere in the world, with the same breed of rats. The trend persisted even when William McDougal of Harvard University chose the stupidest rats in the next generation to train in the maze. They picked up where their

126 Ibid., 127–130.
127 Ibid., 176–184.

predecessors had left off. So did completely unrelated rats at laboratories in Scotland and Australia.

Similar collective memory has been observed in studies with humans.[128] Americans with no knowledge of Japanese apparently find it easier to learn a standard Japanese nursery rhyme that has been repeated over and over again for generations, than a non-standard Japanese nursery rhyme made up on nonsense syllables. In another experiment, people who spoke neither Hebrew nor Greek were tested to see if it was easier for them to recognize a real Hebrew or Greek word rather than ones made up of nonsensically arranged letters in those languages. The test subjects were able to tell which were real words and which were nonsensical, because they were able to unconsciously draw from the memories of millions of people who have been reading Hebrew and Greek for thousands of years across a large part of the world. All of this is to say that, there is something like nonlocal "cloud" storage of memory and there are algorithms defining information structures that endure outside of the four-dimensional space time continuum, in a kind of hyper-dimensional sphere that is the invisible context for our programmable Cosmos. It is, however, possible for us to access and recode this matrix.

---

128 Ibid., 226–233.

CHAPTER 5

Atlas Never Shrugs

THE END OF REALITY, the end of history, and the end of humanity all force us to face the same question concerning the technological singularity: are we ready for it? The answer, when framed in a majoritarian fashion, is, "Hell no!" If the "we" that is supposed to be ready for the Singularity is the whole of humanity, the human race such as it is, then it is almost definitional to draw the conclusion that "we" are not ready. After all, the analysis here has described how "the end of humanity" is phenomenologically integral to the Singularity, just as much as the end of the history of this threatened humanity and the end of every sense of reality that it has held onto throughout history.

Bearing this in mind, a not at all insignificant segment of the world's intellectual and economic elite might, when confronted with the spectre of the Singularity in a sufficiently imminent fashion, come to the conclusion that they are justified in delaying it indefinitely. Indeed, this decision may already have been made. To be more precise, it is not a question of delaying it for everyone, but of so extremely restricting access to the techno-scientific trajectories leading to the Singularity that, as far as most people are concerned, they will never have materialized. So as to ensure that this knowledge and power remains sufficiently occulted and inaccessible, the majority of people — worldwide — would have to be regressed to a state of civilization, or rather of relative savagery, that is so far from the Singularity that it again becomes inconceivable except for in the medium of apocalyptic mythology. What I am getting at here is the formulation of a "Breakaway Civilization."

The first section of this chapter will introduce the concept of a Breakaway Civilization and then go on to give a relatively brief account of its genesis, genealogy, and history. The concept will be introduced in the context of Richard Dolan's analysis of the UFO phenomenon and his suggestion that some of these advanced aerospace vehicles may be produced, not by extraterrestrials, but by a hidden terrestrial civilization that has evolved from out of the military-industrial complex into an autonomous society with its own worldview, culture, and economy. On a conceptual level, the origin of this idea is traced to works of film and literature that include *Alternative-3*, *The Shape of Things To Come*, *Atlas Shrugged*, and *New Atlantis*. The idea of "Atlantis" as a Breakaway Civilization, which appears in both Ayn Rand's *Atlas Shrugged* and in the *New Atlantis* of Sir Francis Bacon, who was a member of the Invisible College, marks a point of transition to the actual history of Earth's hidden elite society. The rest of the first section will present an overview of this history, from the Bavarian Illuminati through the attempts of the Second Reich to colonize the Americas, spearheaded by a corporate group of Prussians secretly developing advanced airships powered by Tesla technology, and onward still to the Zero Point Energy propulsion breakthrough achieved by the Third Reich. The first section draws to a close by detailing the activities of those elements of the SS leadership who not only survived the war and evaded prosecution, but managed to penetrate or even to co-constitute the United States Military-Industrial-Intelligence complex from the ground up.

The second section begins by explaining the diabolical means whereby the American "Deep State" or "Shadow Government" was constructed as the bedrock of a future Fourth Reich. This includes a discussion of the "flying saucer" scare that secretly catalyzed the National Security Act of 1947, which fundamentally undermined the American Republic and initiated its transformation into something else. The attacks of 9/11 are identified as another key turning point in this transformation, and the "Spider" of the postwar Fascist International is exposed as the mastermind behind the "War On [Of, By, and For] Terror" that began that day. In this section, the question is posed of whether America can save itself and the world from the machinations of this monstrous Military-Industrial-Intelligence apparatus.

To answer that question we look back at what made America great in the first place, with an emphasis on the 1930s vision of the World of Tomorrow. American architecture with this vision, such as the work of Frank Lloyd Wright and Hugh Ferriss, is compared to the worldview of Hitler's architect, Albert Speer, and this American Futurism is contrasted with the Italian Futurism that made common cause with Mussolini's Fascism. Unfortunately, the lives of Nikola Tesla, Jack Parsons, and J. Robert Oppenheimer attest to the persecution, marginalization, abandonment, and forced impoverishment of Promethean scientific geniuses and futurist visionaries in America. The fate of these men in a liberal-democratic capitalist society repudiates Ayn Rand's libertarian vision of the Breakaway Civilization in *Atlas Shrugged*, and argues in favor of a certain degree of state power over economy and industry (albeit without the elimination of private enterprise) in the service of Promethean genius and the promise that it has to transform society.

The third and final section of this chapter exposes the plans of the Breakaway Civilization to use various means in order to destroy advanced industrial societies and replace them, worldwide, with a quasi-feudal neo-agrarian system. These means will include genetically engineered pandemics, such as COVID-19, the use of scalar weaponry to produce volcanic eruptions, artificial earthquakes and their attendant tsunamis, as well as directed energy and weather modification techniques to exacerbate and accelerate catastrophic climate change and the attendant super storms, flooding, wildfires, famines, and droughts.

However, these are just ways of setting the stage or creating the context for completion of a psychological warfare operation that has long been underway. I identify the concept at the core of this operation as "destructive departure in worldview warfare" or "dismantling breakthrough in the war of worldviews," and analyze it in light of ideas from George Orwell, Friedrich Nietzsche, Martin Heidegger, Philip K. Dick, and Heraclitus. All of these writers and thinkers had relevant insights into the kind of existential captivation of an entire society that the Breakaway Civilization is aiming to achieve as it artificially regresses humanity in order to evade the planetary challenge of the technological Singularity.

5.1 The Breakaway Civilization

The term "Breakaway Civilization" was coined by Richard Dolan as the descriptor for an alternative theory of UFO phenomena.[1] Rather than assuming that all UFOs are interplanetary spacecraft, or visitors from another dimension, it could be that at least some UFOs are craft from a hidden terrestrial civilization. This civilization may have been constituted by visionary scientific and political elites who "broke away" from a number of countries and cultures on Earth in order to form a secret society so vast in its industry and infrastructure, and so distinct in its worldview, that it could rightly be considered a new civilization.

Dolan hypothesizes that highly classified scientific breakthroughs and technological innovations may have been the catalyst for such a total reorientation of worldview and radical alienation of those privy to it from their respective societies, each of which would be deemed

---

1   Richard Dolan, *UFOs and the National Security State: Chronology of a Cover-up 1941–1973* (Hampton Roads, 2002).

equally incapable of handling these discoveries.[2] As those who belong to this black projects world expand from vast subterranean and submarine cities on Earth[3] to military-industrial bases on the Moon and Mars, and begin to mine asteroids for resources, they develop an industry and economy independent of that of any nation on Earth.

This idea may have been suggested to Dolan by a 1977 British television program called *Alternative-3*. Purporting to be a documentary "Science News" report, this science fiction film takes as its point of departure the disappearance of numerous leading scientists from various disciplines.[4] Journalists investigating these disappearances conduct an interview with a former Apollo astronaut suffering a mental breakdown, who, after getting sufficiently drunk, confesses how terribly disappointed he and his colleagues were to find that they were not the first ones on the Moon. Following this suggestion that the Apollo missions were a smokescreen to hide a much older secret space program, the investigators of "Science Report" discover and broadcast old footage of a joint Soviet-American manned mission to Mars. It is alleged that the missing scientists are denizens of a nascent interplanetary civilization, a kind of ark of humanity being secretly built by elites who foresaw that apocalyptic climate change, mass starvation, pandemics and other related crises would seriously threaten civilization on the Earth.

The manner in which *Alternative-3* was broadcast, so that it would be mistaken by many for a real news documentary, was undoubtedly meant in homage to Orson Welles' 1938 radio adaptation of H.G. Wells' *War of the Worlds* (1897). It is also possible that it was meant in more than homage. The intention may have been to leak certain information, mixing a little of the truth into a fictional narrative that

2   Richard Dolan, *The Secret Space Program and Breakaway Civilization* (CreateSpace Independent Publishing Platform, 2016).

3   Richard Sauder, *Underwater and Underground Bases* (Adventures Unlimited Press, 2014).

4   Christopher Miles, *Alternative 3* (Anglia Television, 1977).

would be mistaken for fact, in order to gauge the reaction of members of the public. There are still people who allege that *Alternative-3* was a flirtation with "disclosure" (of the truth behind the UFO phenomenon), just as some policymakers still appeal to the *War of the Worlds* broadcast as evidence that mass panic would ensue if the presence, on or around the Earth, if hostile extraterrestrials were to be disclosed to the public.[5]

While *War of the Worlds* is about a confrontation with hostile extraterrestrials, H.G. Wells did also pen a novel that revolves around the Breakaway Civilization concept — although he did not refer to it by that name.[6] Wells wrote *The Shape of Things to Come* in 1933, and by 1936 it was adapted into the epic film *Things To Come*.[7] The book (and film) accurately predicted the advent of another world war, one in which weapons of mass destruction would be used. During the course of this apocalyptic war, a group of "airmen" with great engineering and technocratic expertise, and with an unapologetically scientific outlook on how best to organize society, break away from the nations for which they are supposed to be waging war.

Basing themselves around Baghdad, they build up a Breakaway Civilization while the rest of the war torn planet regresses into savagery. Long before *Mad Max*, Wells compellingly depicts a world where barbarians of the future are left with only bits and pieces of modern technology, trophies that they use in the worst ways imaginable. Meanwhile, the Airmen, who are hidden away in subterranean cities that are models for their metropolises of the future, prepare to conquer the entire planet. After one of their emissaries is held hostage, their fantastic aircraft appear across the skies, dropping bombs full of "the gas of peace" to bring the reign of petty tyrants to an end and to usher in "the world of tomorrow."

---

5   Donald N. Michael et al., *Proposed Studies on the Implications of Peaceful Space Activities for Human Affairs* (Brookings Institution and NASA, 1960).

6   H.G. Wells, *The Shape of Things to Come* (Penguin Classics, 2005).

7   William Cameron Menzies, *Things To Come* (London Film Productions, 1936).

The futuristic planetary society that the airmen establish is a fictional preview of the kind of scientific dictatorship that Wells would
later forthrightly argue in favor of establishing in non-fiction tractates
such as *The New World Order* (1940) and his last book, *Mind at the
End of Its Tether* (1945). It is, in fact, H.G. Wells who introduced
the phrase "New World Order" into public discourse as a description for his vision of a world government dedicated to promoting
the Promethean spirit of scientific exploration and technological
development while protecting what he deemed most precious about
humanity from the perils inherent to this daring endeavor.[8] His final
text is aptly titled since, having witnessed the advent of the atomic
bomb, Wells feels himself compelled to think at the limit of the human mind, contemplating the inhuman future that awaits humanity
if a revolutionary psychological and social transformation does not
render human beings ethical enough to endure further technological
advancements without destroying both themselves and their planet.[9]
Along the lines of *Alternative-3*, such concerns would, of course,
serve as sufficient motivation for a visionary elite to secretly develop
a Breakaway Civilization that could re-conquer a devastated Earth in
the name of its envisioned Utopia — a utopia that would, in the mean-
time, be covertly cultivated on an embryonic scale.

Following *The Shape of Things to Come*, the next expression of the
Breakaway Civilization in literature is philosopher Ayn Rand's vision
of "Atlantis" in her wildly popular 1957 novel *Atlas Shrugged*. Facing
an increasingly dysfunctional and ever-more socialist government,
which is nationalizing all industries in the name of "the people," a
group of leading industrialists, inventors, artists, and philosophers
accept the invitation to "break away" that is extended to them by a
mysterious man named John Galt.[10] He invites them to settle in, and

---

8   H.G. Wells, *The New World Order* (Orkos Press, 2014).

9   H.G. Wells, *The Last Books of H.G. Wells: The Happy Turning: A Dream of Life
    & Mind at the End of its Tether* (Monkfish Book Publishing, 2006).

10 Ayn Rand, *Atlas Shrugged* (Signet, 1996).

further develop, Atlantis, also known as "Galt's Gulch," a hidden society based on the principle of rewarding the merit of the gifted and industrious individual rather than forcing the genius to charitably serve thoughtless and unproductive masses.

Rand's vision goes a step further than that of H.G. Wells in terms of its violently contemptuous attitude towards the teeming rabble who tyrannize over a visionary minority. Whereas the "Airmen" of *Things To Come* use the unfortunate devastation of war as an opportunity, *Atlas Shrugged* advocates the deliberate destruction or controlled demolition of so-called 'civilized society' by its brightest and most intrepid members, who ditch it for Atlantis. Men like Francisco D'Anconia and Ellis Wyatt, and ultimately steel magnate Henry Rearden, are akin to Atlas propping up a world that falls far short of deserving them. These industrialists are encouraged by Galt to blow up their respective industries on their way to Atlantis, in a kind of destructive departure that is intended to demonstrate to socialist masses that they are nothing more than parasites. This is the proverbial shrugging of Atlas that the title of Rand's novel is meant to evoke.

Ayn Rand was not the first philosopher to use Plato's "Atlantis" as a metaphor for a Utopian Breakaway Civilization. That distinction belongs to Sir Francis Bacon. His pioneering science fiction story, *New Atlantis* (1627), remained uncompleted and was only posthumously published. A boat full of people shipwrecked on an uncharted island discover that it is home to a fantastically advanced, but hidden civilization.[11] This civilization is organized around scientific principles and its philosophically minded rulers have sent emissaries under false flags to every nation on Earth to bring back the inventions and discoveries of all cultures.

In other words, we have in Bacon's *New Atlantis* a Breakaway Civilization that has infiltrated all known civilizations and is mining them for their most advanced scientific knowledge and technological

---

11   Francis Bacon, *New Atlantis and The Great Instauration* (Wiley-Blackwell, 1991).

CHAPTER 5 ATLAS NEVER SHRUGS

innovations. The study of these on the hidden island, together with an assessment of their impact on society, lays the groundwork for further developments that culminate in the construction of skyscrapers, artificial refrigeration, submarines, aerial craft, masterful manipulations of light and sound, and many other breakthroughs, all of which raise the question of how Bacon was able to see so far ahead of his time. Of course, Sir Bacon was a member of the Invisible College, a secret society of scientific men and philosophical minds who formed the nucleus of what would later become the Royal Society of London.

The term "Invisible College" is first mentioned in German Rosicrucian pamphlets of the early 1600s. Members of the Rosicrucian brotherhood, or Order of the Rosy Cross, were also known as the "invisibles" on account of the stealth in which they operated and the false identities that they often assumed. They were known by one other name as well: "the Illuminati" — the illumined ones seeking to bring forth an enlightenment. It is widely believed that the Illuminati was an organization founded by Adam Weishaupt in Bavaria in 1776. However, the term "Illuminati" was already in use in the 1600s, together with "invisibles," as a characterization of Rosicrucian initiates who, with the backing of Frederick the Great of Prussia (Barbarossa), were waging an occult war against the Catholic Church in the name of a "Universal and General Reformation."

Within a few decades of the declaration of the formation of the Bavarian Illuminati, the Prussian state, or Second German Reich, was engaged in an attempt to colonize the Americas. One does not often think of German colonization of the new world, but the Germans did consider themselves a rival to the Spaniards, Portuguese, British, and French in the attempt to transplant their culture to North — and especially South America. This colonization was of such a magnitude that by the time the United States declared war on Germany, one fourth of the North American population were of German ancestry. Texas was especially densely populated with them. Meanwhile, in South America large German colonies were established in Paraguay, southern Brazil, and especially, in Argentina. From 1862 to 1888, the Second Reich initiated an intensive effort to mine South America for resources. The majority of German settlement in Argentina took place from 1871 to 1914. This included, in 1901, the purchase of 15,000 acres near San Carlos de Bariloche, an area that, following the Second World War, would become a refuge for fugitive Nazis.[12]

The other important thing to bear in mind is that, although much of this colonization was being organized by the Prussian state, there was still no unified Germany in the mid nineteenth century, and many German industrialists from outside of the territory of Prussia were involved in this enterprise. It included Austrian Germans, Swiss Germans, and others. Bavaria itself, where the Illuminati were based, was not a part of Prussia.

This explains why the most powerful organization responsible for spearheading German colonization of the Americas was a private group, rather than a governmental agency. Known by the acronym NJMZa (pronounced "NYMZA"), the Nationalistische Jagdflugzeug Maschinen ZahlungsAmt was a German "nationalist" group rather than a project of the Prussian nation-state.[13] *Jagdflugzeug* means "Hunting-Flying," as in the German word for "the hunt," namely *Chase* — the significance of which will be discussed shortly. It could be more idiomatically translated as "pursuit" or "exploration." The *Maschinen* in question are airships, and a *ZahlungsAmt* is a "payment office" or what, in the context of contemporary black projects, is referred to as a budgetary "project office." The airships flown by this nationalist group, in its pursuit of establishing an extraterritorial Germany in the Americas, were witnessed by many people in 1868 in Chile, in 1880 in Venezuela, and in 1897 in Texas.[14]

---

12 Walter Bosley, *Empire of the Wheel II: Friends from Sonora* (Corvos Books, 2018).

13 Ibid.

14 Daniel Cohen, *The Great Airship Mystery: A UFO of the 1890s* (Dodd Mead, 1981).

These airships were not early Zeppelins, blimps, or hot air bal-
loons of any kind. They were contraptions the likes of which, at
that time, one could hardly have even found in the writings of Jules
Verne. The German immigrant Charles Dellschau, who was involved
with this project, described the construction of these craft in Sonora,
California, as early as the 1850s.[15] His drawings portray vehicles with
wheels within wheels, which call to mind the "angelic" devices in the
Book of Ezekiel.[16] Apparently, one Peter Menace was the chief engineer with a knowledge of the fuel system for the levitating airships.[17]

These airships would occasionally land on people's farms in order
to restock their supplies.[18] In one case, the crew offered to take a
farmer on a joy ride from Texas to South America, and back, at high
speed. In another case, when queried about the source of the airships,
one of the men on board explained that it had been developed by a
group of "New York investors" and that they would soon publicly offer
shares of their company on the stock market.[19]

The principal New York investor in question was John Pierpont
Morgan.[20] J.P. Morgan was the founder of Chase Manhattan Bank,
whose name *Chase* or "the Hunt" recalls the "Hunting-Flying" descriptor of the airship project. Chase Bank, a joint venture with John
Rockefeller, would go on to be the single most significant American
financier of the rise of Fascism in Italy and Nazism in Germany. In
the 1970s, the fugitive Martin Bormann (who faked his death, several
times) was still able to write and cash checks in his own name through
his Chase Bank account in Argentina, where he was busy planning

---

15 Dennis Crenshaw, *The Secrets of Dellschau* (Anomalist Books, 2009).

16 Charles A. A. Dellschau, *Aeronautical Notebooks: 1830–1923* (Ricco/Maresca
    Gallery, 1997).

17 Bosley, *Empire of the Wheel II: Friends from Sonora*.

18 J. Allan Danelek, *The Great Airship of 1897* (Adventures Unlimited Press, 2015).

19 Bosley, *Empire of the Wheel II: Friends from Sonora*.

20 Ibid.

for the Fourth Reich.[21] The symbol of Chase remains, to this day, a stylized Swastika.

J.P. Morgan was also the principal financier of Nikola Tesla's research into a "world wireless" system of freely broadcasting energy without any need for power lines.[22] Morgan bought the patent to this technology and then buried it, defunding Tesla and the Wardenclyffe tower in Long Island that was to be the first world wireless transmission station.[23] Tesla had demonstrated this capability in a series of experiments at Colorado Springs in 1899. His concept drawings of the world wireless system include depictions of sleek airships crossing the skies powered by this technology.

Given Morgan's role as the most prominent financier of the NYMZA project, it is hardly wild speculation to suggest that his objective was either to gain Tesla's system for the exclusive use of his German associates, or to prevent public development of the technology that NYMZA had already independently and secretly developed. Again, Rockefeller was Morgan's business partner in Chase, and Rockefeller's Standard Oil was also one of the companies pioneering petroleum-based energy. Unlike Tesla's World Wireless, which would essentially have produced free energy, Rockefeller and company stood to make a killing by developing a global industry and economy dependent on oil as its primary energy source.

Morgan and Rockefeller were not the only American financiers of the rise of Fascism and Nazism. Henry Ford manufactured Hitler's tanks for him.[24] IBM provided the Third Reich with the punch-card

21 Joseph P. Farrell, *Nazi International: The Nazis' Postwar Plan to Control Finance, Conflict, Physics and Space* (Adventures Unlimited Press, 2015).

22 Marc J. Seifer, *Wizard: The Life and Times of Nikola Tesla* (Citadel, 2016).

23 Margaret Cheney, *Tesla: Man Out Of Time* (Dorset, 1989).

24 Edwin Black, *Nazi Nexus: America's Corporate Connections to Hitler's Holocaust* (Dialog Press, 2017).

technology used to efficiently process people in concentration camps.[25] In 1945, at the war's end, analysis of material retrieved by Allied forces revealed that the German subsidiary of IBM, Dehomag, was at least a decade ahead of its American parent company in research and development of computers.[26] The same was true in the field of biological sciences. Hitler modeled the Nazi Eugenics program on the Eugenics programs instated by various American states in the 1910s and 1920s.[27] He saw 1930s Germany as playing catch up to the United States in this field. So there is an extensive historical context that connects the Morgan-funded airship project in the Americas, which was initially based in California, to Nikola Tesla's free energy project on the one hand, and on the other hand to the occult ideas about etheric energy that were at the core of the secret societies that spawned the Nazi movement.

Like Tesla, the Vril Society claimed that there was an ether that could be tapped for potentially limitless power. As early as 1871, Lord Edward Bulwer-Lytton had written of this energy in his occult classic *Vril: The Power of the Coming Race*. The book purports to be an account of a secret subterranean civilization, powered by "vril," which is planning to conquer the surface world.[28] The German rocket engineer Willy Ley, an associate of Werner von Braun at NASA, said that this book was the basis for a so-called *Wahrheitsgesellschaft* or "Society for Truth" that was seeking Vril.[29] This "Vril society" became

25 Edwin Black, *IBM and the Holocaust: The Strategic Alliance Between Nazi Germany and America's Most Powerful Corporation* (Dialog Press, 2012).

26 Joseph P. Farrell, *Saucers, Swastikas, and PsyOps: A History of a Breakaway Civilization* (Adventures Unlimited Press, 2012).

27 Edwin Black, *War Against the Weak: Eugenics and America's Campaign to Create a Master Race* (Dialog Press, 2012).

28 Edward Bulwer-Lytton, *Vril, The Power of the Coming Race* (Forgotten Books, 2007).

29 Louis Pauwels and Jacques Bergier, *The Morning of the Magicians: Secret Societies, Conspiracies, and Vanished Civilizations* (Destiny Books, 2008).

the inner core of the *Thulegesellschaft* or Thule Society founded by Baron Rudolf von Sebottendorf in 1918. The Thule Society, in turn, established the National Socialist German Workers Party in 1920 as a Political Action Committee (PAC) intended to combat the rising threat that Communism posed to the aristocratic occultists who were seeking Vril.[30]

Just as projects such as the airship venture and the quest for etheric power preceded the rise of Nazi Germany, and in effect propelled it for their own purposes, these projects also survived the collapse of the Third Reich in the form of a full-fledged Fascist Breakaway Civilization. In 1945, the Nazi Bell and its associated saucer technologies, which were discussed in Chapter 3, were evacuated to Spain and then to Argentina by SS Special Operations chief Otto Skorzeny.[31] He intended to use them in a protracted campaign of psychological warfare against the United States. The original version of the Twining–Schulgen memorandum on this phenomenon speculates on the possible German origins of the saucers and remarks on rumors that they were being piloted by Spaniards.[32] Meanwhile, newspaper reports in the summer of 1947 described "saucer shaped rockets" being launched by Francisco Franco and directed over the continental United States.[33] Skorzeny was on the scene in Spain at this time. The flying saucers that began to fill the skies over North America from 1947 onward, one of which crashed in Roswell, New Mexico, were these Nazi secret weapons being launched from Spain, Argentina, and a naval base in Antarctica.

The wreckage recovered at Roswell included numerous advanced technologies that had not yet been invented in America but were on

---

30 Peter Levenda, *Unholy Alliance: A History of Nazi Involvement with the Occult* (Bloomsbury Academic, 2002).

31 Joseph P. Farrell, *Saucers, Swastikas, and PsyOps: A History of a Breakaway Civilization* (Adventures Unlimited Press, 2012).

32 Ibid.

33 Ibid.

the cutting edge of German military technology in the 1940s, including night vision, Kevlar, Velcro, and micro-perforated metal.[34] These technologies are too mundane to be "alien." As for the putative "aliens" onboard the craft — they were oriental children suffering from Progeria syndrome who had been part of a horrific human experimentation program carried out by Germany's Axis partner, Japan.[35] Japanese Unit 731 did things in Manchuria that were even more horrific than anything Josef Mengele presided over at Auschwitz. Admiral Karl Dönitz had probably facilitated the naval transport of these children from Japan to Spain or wherever the Roswell saucer was launched.

Following the alleged suicide of Adolf Hitler in his bunker on April 30, 1945, Grand Admiral Karl Dönitz assumed the position of President of the German Reich. Why, of all people, was the head of the German Navy chosen to succeed Hitler as head of state? On account of the fact that the decision had already been made to evacuate the highest level leadership, valuable materials, and resources of the Reich to an extraterritorial Germany whose groundwork had long been lain in Latin America. Dönitz had also been involved in the German Antarctic Expedition of 1938 that established the territory of New Swabia in what is now called "Queen Maud Land."[36] Later, he boasted that the German Navy had constructed an impregnable Shangri-La for the Führer amidst ice in a remote part of the world.

Dönitz presided over the transfer of a submarine full of Uranium 235 to the United States on May 14, 1945, which transfer provided America with enough fissile material to manufacture the "Little Boy" atomic bomb that was dropped on Hiroshima on August 6, 1945.[37] It is worthy of note that the US Army Airbase at Roswell, New Mexico,

---

34 Joseph Farrell, *Roswell and the Reich* (Adventures Unlimited Press, 2009).

35 Ibid.

36 Joseph P. Farrell, *Hess and the Penguins* (Adventures Unlimited Press, 2017).

37 Carter Plymton Hydrick, *Critical Mass: How Nazi Germany Surrendered Enriched Uranium for the United States' Atomic Bomb* (Trine Day, 2016).

was the point of origin of the aircraft that dropped atomic bombs on Hiroshima and Nagasaki. In 1947, when the Roswell incident took place, this was still the only military facility in the world known to be storing nuclear weapons.

"Known to be," because unbeknown to the American people, although not to the uppermost officials in US and allied intelligence, Nazi Germany did successfully develop nuclear weapons between 1944 and 1945.[38] At least two tests were conducted. One was in the Baltic Sea, where airmen who witnessed the test reported the characteristic atomic flash and rainbow-colored detonations inside the mushroom cloud.[39] The other was at Ohrdruf, where concentration camp inmates were subjected to the detonation in order to assess its impact on humans.[40] These German nuclear weapons were not products of the well-known program led by Werner Heisenberg using gas centrifuges. They were produced by a more secretive SS program using laser isotope enrichment technology, which was first developed by Nazi Germany for this purpose.[41]

Already facing military defeat at the hands of the allied forces that had landed at Normandy, the decision was made not to use these weapons in order to prolong the life of the Third Reich. Rather, they would be surrendered to the allies in a top secret negotiation, as part of a package that included safe passage, exemption from prosecution, and even large-scale recruitment for many upper echelon Nazis who could go on to plan for a Fourth Reich. Nuclear weapons technology was willingly transferred to the United States by the SS because they retained the far more advanced and destructive Nazi Bell and associated saucer technology.

---

38   Joseph P. Farrell, *The SS Brotherhood of the Bell: The Nazis' Incredible Secret Technology* (Adventures Unlimited Press, 2013).

39   Ibid.

40   Ibid.

41   Ibid.

CHAPTER 5. ATLAS NEVER SHRUGS

5.2 Freeing America From "The Mind Flayer"

The National Security Act of 1947 was primarily enacted in response to the flying saucer scare, and it transformed what had been a democratic Republic into a National Security State controlled by an unaccountable military-industrial-intelligence complex. It is not merely ironic that this same complex was, from the ground up, constituted by unreconstructed and unrepentant high-ranking Nazis. That was the deliberate intent of the true victors of the Second World War. The Central Intelligence Agency that was established by the National Security Act of 1947 was nothing more than a merger of the wartime OSS with the Nazi intelligence network led by Reinhard Gehlen in Eastern Europe, an asset viewed as key in America's Cold War against the Soviet Union now controlling that territory.[42] Half of the founding members of the CIA were "Gehlen Org" Nazis.

Meanwhile, Operation Paperclip imported thousands of Nazi scientists into the heart of what became the US military-industrial complex.[43] SS Major Wernher von Braun, who used slave labor inside mountains to build V2 rockets for Hitler's bombing of civilian populations, eventually became the chief scientist of NASA.[44] The majority of the team that von Braun assembled to run the Apollo program to put American astronauts on the Moon consisted of fellow high-ranking Nazis, such as Kurt Debus and Hubertus Strughold.[45] Key NASA missions were set based on the dates of holidays that had been celebrated in Nazi Germany, such as Adolf Hitler's birthday on April 20th.[46] It is this Nazi Nexus that secretly captured America in 1947 through

---

42 Joseph P. Farrell, *Nazi International: The Nazis' Postwar Plan to Control Finance, Conflict, Physics and Space* (Adventures Unlimited Press, 2015).

43 Annie Jacobsen, *Operation Paperclip: The Secret Intelligence Program That Brought Nazi Scientists To America* (Back Bay Books, 2015).

44 Farrell, *Saucers, Swastikas, and PsyOps: A History of a Breakaway Civilization.*

45 Richard C. Hoagland and Mike Bara, *Dark Mission: The Secret History of NASA* (Feral House, 2009).

46 Ibid.

an unelected military-industrial-intelligence complex that President Eisenhower tried to warn the American people about on his way out of office. He had also given incoming President Kennedy a more forthright, but ultimately futile, warning.

America was not the only country caught in the postwar Nazi web. An organization called "The Spider" (*Die Spinne*), also known by the acronym ODESSA (which, in German, stands for Order of Former SS Officers), extended itself throughout the Muslim Middle East, from Iran to Syria and Egypt.[47] With connections to their counterparts operating within the CIA, they orchestrated operations such as the 1953 Coup that brought Shah Mohammad Reza Pahlavi back to power in Iran and the construction of ballistic missiles, based on the V2 rocket, for the nationalist Gamal Abdel Nasser in Egypt. The Baathist ideology in the Arab world, which chose the red, white, and black color scheme of the German Reich for the flags of the nations that adopted it (Iraq, Egypt), still survives in Assad's Syria today. Ultimately, it is their network in the region that, in tandem with high-level Nazi assets within the United States itself, orchestrated the attacks of September 11, 2001.[48]

The put options on United and American Airlines were traced to Deutsche Bank (i.e. the German National Bank) before mainstream media stopped reporting on the story of "terrorists" who sought to make money based on foreknowledge of the attacks. Alvin Bernard ("Buzzy") Krongard, a German-American who was appointed Executive Director of the CIA about six months before 9/11, had been the Chairman of the subsidiary of Deutsche Bank through which the "terrorists" placed their bets that the stocks of these airlines would collapse.[49] Of course, President George W. Bush himself is the son of for-

---

47 Glenn Infield, *The Secrets of the SS* (Stein and Day, 1981), 201.

48 Joseph P. Farrell, *Hidden Finance, Rogue Networks, and Secret Sorcery: The Fascist International, 9/11, and Penetrated Operations* (Adventures Unlimited Press, 2016).

49 Ibid.

mer CIA Director George Herbert Walker Bush, a German-American whose father, Prescott Bush, was among Adolf Hitler's trusted financiers in the United States.

9/11 occurred almost exactly a decade after the collapse of the Soviet Union. For as long as the Nazis who co-constituted the US military-industrial-intelligence complex were focused on defeating the greater of their two enemies, namely Russian Communists, they were willing to collaborate with American capitalists. After 1991 — which not incidentally, was the year of the first Persian Gulf War, initiated by the aforementioned George Herbert Walker Bush — the focus of the Fascist Breakaway Civilization became the disintegration and collapse of the United States of America. This would be accomplished through ensnaring the United States in a protracted struggle in the Islamic World, akin to the Soviet occupation of Afghanistan from 1979 to 1989 — the year that the Berlin Wall fell.

This US-led "Global War on Terrorism" would ultimately flood the newly re-unified Germany with Muslim migrants who, there and elsewhere in Europe, would trigger a Fascist backlash. The Spider plans for the spearhead of the Fourth Reich in Europe to be a constellation of Eastern European states called the Intermarium, in reference to their spanning the terrain between the Caspian Sea, the Black Sea, and the Baltic Sea. Its backbone consists of nationalists in Western Ukraine, where the Azov brigade resisting Putin's Russia flies the Nazi Black Sun symbol on its version of the Ukrainian flag.

According to many archeologists and linguists, an area stretching from Ukraine into the Caucasus, along the northeastern coast of the Black Sea, was the ethno-cultural cradle of the entire Indo-European community.[50] This cradle of the "Aryan race" is the southeastern cornerstone of the proposed Intermarium alliance. Western Ukrainians, most of whom spoke Russian, but were vehemently anti-communist were the vanguard of the Nazi German attempt to conquer Russia in

---

50 Alain de. Benoist, *The Indo-Europeans: In Search of the Homeland* (Arktos Media, 2016).

Operation Barbarossa. After the war, these Ukrainians were prized assets in Reinhard Gehlen's Eastern European Nazi spy network that was fused with the American OSS to form the CIA. ODESSA, an alternate name for the Spider, also happens to be the name of a city in Ukraine.

The connection between Odessa, Ukraine, and ODESSA as in the Spider's Web of the postwar Fascist Breakaway Civilization, is esoterically referenced in the third season of David Lynch's *Twin Peaks* television series.[51] The Laura Palmer who is living in Odessa, Texas, and who has been given a false name and cannot even remember her real identity because it is too terrible, is a reference to the false identities assumed by ODESSA fugitives, whose own children in many cases did not know the true history of their family. The pattern on the floor of the Black Lodge is the SS double lightning bolt and, when combined with the infernal abode's red curtains, it is particularly evocative of esoteric Nazism. David Bowie speaks through a device that looks like a Nazi Bell and is associated with space travel. Bowie infamously identified as a Fascist for a brief period in the 1970s.

The Spider is also esoterically central to the Duffer Brothers' retro-1980s sci-fi/horror show *Stranger Things*.[52] Not only does the black monster that haunts Hawkins look like a giant spider, but the team of kids who take it upon themselves to combat it explicitly compare this "Mind Flayer" to a Nazi invasion from another dimension. It infects minds, and spreads insidiously underground like a hidden system of roots, in order to incorporate more and more of Hawkins' very white population into its growing body.

Ridley Scott's television adaptation of Philip K. Dick's *Man in the High Castle* deals explicitly with Nazis invading from another dimension.[53] PKD was extremely concerned about the captivation of an individual's psyche by an alien worldview. In one of his final

---

51 David Lynch, *Twin Peaks* (ABC/Showtime, 1990–1991, 2017).

52 Duffer Brothers, *Stranger Things* (Netflix, 2016–).

53 Frank Spotnitz, *The Man in the High Castle* (Amazon, 2015–2019).

interviews, he went so far as to identify this as the central concern of all of his work.[54] Dick wanted to protect individuals, especially those with particularly open and suggestible psyches such as he believed himself to be, from having their minds invaded and captured by a world of meaning that is not their own. He thought that domineering people, and especially pressure groups such as the kind often found in drug and alcohol therapy, were threatening to the psychical integrity of such gentle and open-minded souls. Will Byers from *Stranger Things*, who is targeted by the "Mind Flayer" symbolizing the Nazi spider, is a perfect example of the kind of person that Dick had in mind (and that he saw himself to be). It is resistance against this kind of captivation at an existential level that is really at the core of novels such as *Man in the High Castle*. Through his persistent meditation, Tagomi breaks the hold that his imperialistic and ultra-conformist culture has on his worldview. He imagines his way into a better, alternate America.

American metaphysical thought, of a kind that is inspired by European traditions but also supersedes them, begins in the milieu of nineteenth century New England with the Transcendentalist movement. The essays of Emerson offer the clearest distillation of ideas concerning the self-reliance of the individual, personal relationship to the divine, and the spontaneity of genius channeling the creative power of Nature — ideas which alchemically transform material from European and other traditions, such as Persian and Hindu mysticism, with an iconoclastic American daring.[55] The as of yet untamed wilderness of the New England landscape, as evoked by Henry David Thoreau's *Walden*, was integral to the gestation of this view of the cosmos and the American ethos entangled with it.[56] The poet Walt

---

54 David Streitfeld, *Philip K. Dick: The Last Interview* (Melville House, 2015).

55 Ralph Waldo Emerson, *The Selected Writings of Ralph Waldo Emerson* (Modern Library, 1992).

56 Henry David Thoreau, *Walden and Other Writings* (Modern Library, 1992).

Whitman coined the term "New World Metaphysics" to describe it.[57] This movement yielded America's first great literary masterpiece, Herman Melville's *Moby Dick*, whose Promethean spirit will be remarked upon in the next chapter.[58]

What made America great from 1919–1939 was "the world of tomorrow," of skyscraper cities that raise so many fists up against heaven and the ambition of the world's first and most aggressive Eugenics program to remake men and women into a class of beings brighter and more beautiful than Olympian gods and goddesses. It is not that this architecture and (social) engineering of the titanic did not reach back to older traditions and draw from other cultures. It did, but in a way that was much more irreverent and transcendent than, for example, the Italian Renaissance's appropriation and adaptation of the classical Roman heritage.

In the designs and buildings of "America's Architect," Frank Lloyd Wright, we witness a fusion of elements from Mayan, Babylonian, Chinese and other archaic and exotic styles, but in such a fashion that the end result is futuristic, beyond clichés, in contempt of convention, and yet more magisterial than Persepolis or Palatine Hill.[59] In the same period as Hitler's architect, Albert Speer, was attempting to reproduce the classical world on an artificially aggrandized scale in Nazi Germany, Hugh Ferriss, the quintessential draftsman of the American metropolis, whose aesthetic defined Gotham, took leaps and bounds above and beyond his own early attempts to adapt Greco-Roman architecture to the scale of the skyscraper. Ferriss structures are almost primordially crystalline, as if the American metropolis were an etheric reiteration of the lost world of Krypton.[60] Looking at architectural designs alone, it should have been clear that the

---

57   Robert C. Gordon, *Gospel of the Open Road: According to Emerson, Whitman, and Thoreau* (iUniverse, 2001).

58   Herman Melville, *Moby Dick, or The Whale* (Penguin Classics, 2002).

59   Terence Riley, *Frank Lloyd Wright: Architect* (Harry N. Abrams, 1994).

60   Hugh Ferriss, *The Metropolis of Tomorrow* (Dover Publications, 2005).

monumentalist and archeo-futuristic world of Frank Lloyd Wright and Hugh Ferriss was going to triumph over the antiquarian project of European Fascism — reducing it to the ruins that it always romanticized and was never able to transcend. Marinetti merely preached a futurism that Mussolini could not stomach. America practiced it.

American scientists and inventors in the generation of Jack Parsons, J. Robert Oppenheimer, and Nikola Tesla envisioned a radical transformation of the human condition through technological breakthroughs. These American visionaries may have been scientific geniuses rather than literary figures, but they were also spiritual pioneers on par with the earlier generation of Transcendentalists. Parsons was an occultist, not just a rocket scientist.[61] Oppenheimer studied Sanskrit scriptures that left him with the impression that he was not quite "inventing" the atomic bomb.[62] Tesla, who was a close friend of Swami Vivekananda, had as his ultimate aim a synthesis of Western science and Eastern spirituality.[63] His "world wireless" free energy system that was supposed to power the cloud cities of Lloyd and Ferriss drew on Sanskrit concepts such as *prânâ* and *akâshâ*. Tesla was also, like most great men in his generation, an ardent advocate of America's campaign to create a master race by means of Eugenics (a policy only later adopted by Germany). Sadly, Nikola Tesla died a poverty-stricken man broken by the same capitalist industrial system that had made him "the millionaire kid." Parsons and Oppenheimer did not fare much better.

The fate of these men calls into question the core assumptions of Ayn Rand who, in works such as *The Fountainhead* and *Atlas Shrugged*, argued that the titanic creative genius has as little obligation to mass society as the state has to subsidize their scientific research

---

61 John Carter, *Sex and Rockets: The Occult World of Jack Parsons* (Feral House, 2005).

62 Kai Bird and Martin J. Sherwin. *American Prometheus: The Triumph and Tragedy of J. Robert Oppenheimer* (Vintage Books, 2006).

63 Nikola Tesla, *My Inventions and Other Writings* (Penguin Classics, 2012).

and technological development. Rand's portrayal of the Promethean genius of an American Atlas, whether it is the architect Howard Roark or the industrialist Hank Rearden, is admirable in its depth of insight into the psychology and ethos of the titanic individualist. However, the lesson to be drawn from the suppression of Tesla technology by J.P. Morgan and the emerging petroleum-based energy industry spearheaded by John Rockefeller (both of whom backed the rise of Nazism), is that certain technological innovations are so socially and economically disruptive that they really do demand that state power be wielded in a way that safeguards their potential to positively transform society.

Part of what defines the Promethean genius is his sense of duty to humanity. We see this in Tesla to a fault. What he needed was an Atlas ready to use state power to trump corporate greed. How much ecological devastation and how many wars for the control of oil and gas could have been avoided if Tesla's alternative energy proposals had been publicly embraced by the United States government, instead of being secretly used to develop death rays and other diabolical weaponry? Atlas never shrugs, and Ayn Rand's libertarian utopia of "Atlantis" will not make America great again.

Instead of forming a spitefully cruel and heartless Breakaway Civilization, which turns its back on both society and the state, the geniuses of the new world should stage a coup to seize control of the United States government and begin implementing policies that unleash the positive potential of science and technology to empower mankind. At the same time, as emerging biotechnologies afford us the possibility for a far more efficacious Eugenics than that of the 1920s and 30s, this regime of wisdom and knowledge must guard against monstrous misuses of these promising inventions. It is high time to heed Oppenheimer's warning.

What is so striking about the titanic spirit of America is the degree to which it has been embraced by a significant segment of the populace, at least on a subconscious level. In the next and final chapter, we will look closely at several examples from American popular culture. Whereas in Nazi Germany the reemergence of the Faustian ethos came hand in hand with the reaffirmation of traditionalist aristocracy, in America, particularly in the decades after the Second World War, Prometheus appears by every other name throughout popular culture, from comic books to film and television. In a way this makes sense, since Prometheus was supposed to be the champion of humanity's rebellion against the unjust world order of Zeus. Although certain futurist elements were an exception (especially in Italy), the Nazi and Fascist regimes of modern Europe represented more of an affirmation of the Olympian ideal, and an antiquarian will to return to it, than they did a Promethean revolution for a new world order.

Many aspects of the technological Singularity threaten us with the prospect of a totalitarian socio-political system. They certainly demonstrate how Ayn Rand's libertarian vision of the Breakaway Civilization of "Atlantis" is not even remotely viable. It was intrinsic to Rand's vision that the geniuses who broke away would, after withdrawing their talent and productive power from the world outside Atlantis, leave people to their own devices.[64] Coercion was antithetical to the ethos of her utopia. By comparison, certain technologies converging into the Singularity, such as Genetic Engineering, Nanotechnology, Artificial Intelligence, Robotics, and Zero Point Energy pose such global and uncontainable threats to each and every human individual that guaranteeing anyone personal security, let alone privacy or liberty, in the face of them would require a World State with more control over its population than any regime in history.

Atlas can never afford to shrug, unless he is willing to go all the way and build a Breakaway Civilization at the expense of the engineered regression of the rest of the world to barbarism. Nothing could be further from the Promethean ethos than to pursue such a project. Prometheus gifted humanity with the fire of technological science

---

64 Rand, *Atlas Shrugged*.

so that we could become a race of new gods in our own right, rather than cowering in slavish obedience to the old gods. The last thing that a Prometheist could accept is the deliberate reversal of techno-scientific progress and the artificial imposition of mass ignorance and backwardness.

5.3 Destructive Departure

The Breakaway Civilization can, and will, employ many different means of destruction in order to effect the controlled demolition of advanced industrial societies. At the time of writing, in the year 2020, we are already witnessing the first of these: an artificially engineered pandemic. Although COVID-19 was engineered at the Wuhan Virology Laboratory in China, those who invested in the "Gain of Function" research that produced it were Western corporatists, such as Bill Gates. Their main aim in producing a pandemic with such a long incubation period and low mortality rate is to bring about a protracted global lockdown that would most adversely effect dense metropolitan areas. The institutionalization of social distancing and the effective prohibition of large gatherings is not only meant to constrain the possibility of political protest, but also to make cities and their dependent suburbs increasingly unattractive locales for habitation.

It is not a coincidence that this pandemic has taken place in the same decade as a revolution in robotics, nano-technological 3-D printing, and the development of viable drone delivery technology. When taken together with the hardship of quarantine in large cities, the repeated disruption of labor of all kinds, including serious concerns about contamination at industrial plants, and a huge spike in demand for home delivery of goods, optimal conditions are being created for a total reorganization of the economy, labor, and society. The main aim of this is the depopulation of metropolitan areas and their surrounding suburban sprawl, in favor of isolated neo-agrarian homesteads serviced by on-site 3-D printing and drone delivery of goods produced by robotic industry. Social connections will be increasingly shifted into cyberspace, which is a medium of communication amenable to total surveillance by agents of the Breakaway Civilization.

This is being done with the foreknowledge that a massive coronal ejection from the Sun, for which we are long overdue, will destroy all electronics with its electromagnetic pulse. The aim is to isolate most people *before* this happens, and to make them dependent on an automated economy and industry, as well as on electronic communications through cyberspace, as their last social lifeline to one another. Once this has been achieved, and most cities have been emptied out so that they cannot act as bastions of revolutionary solidarity, the EMP will render a starved and atomized population totally vulnerable to manipulation at the hands of whoever continues to hold on to advanced technology.

In order to ensure that the cities are never repopulated and reclaimed, they will be physically destroyed. One major mechanism to bring this about will be artificially triggered volcanic eruptions, earthquakes, and attendant tsunamis. As early as the 1910s, Nikola Tesla developed technology capable of triggering earthquakes along fault lines.[65] The Breakaway Civilization has secreted away this capability, together with its other Tesla technology. They plan to use it to trigger some of the most dangerous fault lines in the world. Consider just three or four examples.

The first is the fault on La Palma island outside the Strait of Gibraltar. Tectonic movement along this fault has been cracking open a rift in the Cumbre Vieja volcano on La Palma, and threatening to cause a landslide of a third of the volcano into the Atlantic Ocean. A volcanic eruption and earthquake that suddenly let loose such a mass into the ocean would produce a tsunami hundreds of meters high that would cross the Atlantic in about nine hours. The entire eastern seaboard of the United States of America would be smashed

---

65 Marc J. Seifer, *Wizard: The Life and Times of Nikola Tesla* (Citadel, 2016), 191.

by the tsunami, including the skyscrapers of New York City. Then, there is the Cascadia Subduction Zone off the coast of Portland, Seattle, and Vancouver. This fault line in the Pacific Ocean is overdue to produce a magnitude 9 earthquake that would generate a tsunami that destroys the coastal metropolitan areas of the Pacific Northwest of the United States and British Columbia in Canada. The resulting devastation would be even worse than what is expected of "the Big One" in California, where it goes without saying that the San Andreas fault could also be triggered artificially by Tesla technology. Finally, consider the Yellowstone Caldera — a volcano on a fault line in Yellowstone National Park. An earthquake that would reactivate this super volcano would yield an eruption so catastrophic that it could cover about one-third of the continental United States, as well as the most densely inhabited parts of Canada, in volcanic ash. Imagine the resulting famine faced by those who survived the eruption itself.

Food exports from the United States and Canada are the major source for the survival of the African population. Any catastrophe that would produce a food shortage in these nations that, before the COVID pandemic, had a large agricultural surplus, would mean that no one in Africa could live off of imported food. Hundreds of millions of Africans would die of starvation, and increased vulnerability to disease, within a year. There are other ways to produce famine besides volcanic eruptions, earthquakes, and tsunamis. Famines and droughts could also be produced through engineered abrupt climate change. If directed energy weapons were to be used to shatter and melt the ice sheets currently covering Greenland and Antarctica at a much faster rate than expected, the sudden change in Atlantic Ocean salinity, and therefore of relative water density, would shut off the North Atlantic current that conveys warm water to Northeastern America and Western Europe.[66] Within a very short time after the failure of the current, terrible snowstorms and other violent weather would

---

66 Nick Begich and Jeane Manning, *Angels Don't Play This Haarp: Advances in Tesla Technology* (Earthpulse, 1995).

materialize as the polar region dropped hundreds of miles to the south of where it is now.[67] The most advanced parts of the Western world would be plunged into a new ice age, devastating agriculture in the breadbasket of the world that is North America.

However, all of these physical methods of destruction are merely means to create convergent crises that set the conditions for the completion of a primarily psychological and social engineering project. Philip K. Dick was onto the fact that the Fascist Breakaway Civilization is primarily waging a psychological war against the societies that it wants to conquer and colonize. However, this form of psychological warfare is being waged on the basis of an ontology and epistemology that does not recognize the psyche as independent of the physical world. In other words, it is not as if there is an objective, physical, reality that includes our brains, and "psychological warfare" is a question of manipulating subjective states to warp the perceptions and attitudes of targeted individuals or societies.

The most dangerous form of psychological warfare, and the one that Dick was most concerned about, is a "worldview warfare" conducted on the basis of an understanding that truly altering a society's worldview is also a reshaping of the physical world and the so-called 'laws of nature.' As demonstrated by the Thought Police in George Orwell's *1984*, even the laws of logic are not invulnerable to a degree of all-encompassing socio-political coercion that captures the individual on an existential level.[68] A person can be made to truly believe that 2+2=5. This is, after all, not really any different from convincing denizens of the highly literate scientific culture of Alexandria that the Old Testament is literally true. It took lots of grotesque tortures, the incineration of entire libraries full of knowledge, and an atmosphere of extreme persecution, but such "conversions" happened.

---

67 Peter Schwartz and Doug Randall, "An Abrupt Climate Change Scenario and Its Implications for United States National Security" (US Department of Defense, October 2003).

68 George Orwell, *1984* (Signet Classics, 2018).

Moreover, when such conversions happen, they can produce "miracles" that violate the putative 'laws of Nature.' There may be levitations of saints, stigmata, statues crying blood, mass visions of horseback armies and crosses in the sky, or visitations from incubi and succubi who storm bedrooms at night from out of a repressed subconscious but are physically 'real' and capable of violent rape.[69] The last of these is simply an extreme form of the materializations observed during some late nineteenth century séances, including ones attended by prominent scientists such as Sir William Crookes.[70]

Conversely, the collectively enforced belief that certain things are impossible, can make them far less likely to occur. This has been demonstrated repeatedly in parapsychology laboratories, where the presence of even a single strong skeptic can so significantly inhibit psi ability that a negative psi effect is often observed — for example, a test subject performing at far below chance level in guessing Zener cards.[71] It would be no wonder if there was a sudden drop in "paranormal" phenomena in Paris when, during the most materialist phase of the French Revolution, the Cult of Reason briefly seized power. Such an occurrence would be rightly understood as a local strengthening of what are believed to be 'laws of nature.'

What is unique about "worldview warfare" or *Weltanschauungskrieg* as it was conceptualized by elite Nazi occultists is the idea that, while it is impossible to stand outside of all worldviews so as to "objectively" perceive "reality," it is possible to adopt more than one worldview, and to fluidly flip between existential perspectives in a way that frees a person from being captivated by any one of them. As Nietzsche already knew, the supermen with this kind of trans-perspectival perception would be able to manipulate those who are stuck within one or

---

69 Jacques Vallée and Chris Aubeck, *Wonders in the Sky* (TarcherPerigree, 2010).

70 Stephen E. Braude, *The Limits of Influence: Psychokinesis and the Philosophy of Science* (University Press of America, 1996).

71 Stephen E. Braude, *ESP and Psychokinesis: A Philosophical Examination. Revised Edition* (Brown Walker Press, 2002).

another worldview. Nietzsche's "revaluation of all values" takes place on the far side of a deconstruction of naïve faith in the values of any particular religion, ideology, or 'scientific' dogma.

This does not mean plunging an entire society into nihilistic anarchy. Rather, the deconstruction must primarily take place in the minds of a masterful elite who consequently become capable of using the social forces of nihilism and degenerative decay as catalysts for the eventual rise of a new order. The basic attitude of these "masters of the Earth" or "aristocrats of the future" toward the fundamental values of this new order is akin to the attitude of painters or sculptors toward constructs and self-imposed constraints employed to produce a work of art. It should not be forgotten that the majority of the founding leaders of the Nazi party were 'failed' artists of one kind or another. Hitler was only one of many.

Drawing from Nietzsche, and from Richard Wagner, the planners of the Fascist Breakaway Civilization are aiming to refashion society and the Earth itself into a *Gesamtkunstwerk* or "Total Work of Art." This is the kind of thing that terrified Dick, because it implies that the individuals — or rather, the people who were once individuals — have been transformed into Wagnerian theater performers, or worse than that, since they are not consciously acting. It is almost as if they have been captured by a canvas in such a way that they can never see outside of the painting that they have become part of. This painting is, moreover, somebody else's vision.

In my essay "Black Sunrise" in *Lovers of Sophia*, I developed a philosophical concept for this process of creative destruction that constitutes a Breakaway Civilization.[72] Or perhaps I merely reconstructed or reverse engineered the concept that was in fact devised and employed by the Nazi elite that survived the fall of the Third Reich. In any case, the concept is best expressed in German as *Abbauende Aufbruch ins Weltanschauungskrieg*. This can be translated as "destructive departure

---

72 Jason Reza Jorjani, "Black Sunrise" in *Lovers of Sophia* (Arktos, 2019).

in worldview warfare" or "deconstructive breakthrough in the war
of worldviews" or even as "dismantling breakaway in psychological
warfare."

Essentially it means that a breakthrough (*Aufbruch*), like the revolutionary scientific insight involved in engineering the Bell, leads to
a breakaway that is not just a departure from some normal state of
affairs, but a dismantling (*Abbauende*) departure that un-builds (*ab-
bau*), dismantles, or breaks down what is being broken away from,
such that it can eventually be conquered through worldview warfare
(*Weltanschauungskrieg*). This also represents a breakthrough or radical departure from the naïve and unconscious manner in which the
war of worldviews has hitherto been conducted between rival civilizations, or even competing factions within a single culture. For the
first time, those who have made the breakthrough have also broken
through their own naïve adherence to any one worldview in a way that
enhances their power over those lacking this insight — and frankly,
those from whom this breakthrough will be hidden by the elite who
breakaway on the basis of it.

This elite also knows that what is taken to be "knowledge," even of
the most basic kind, is inseparable from power relations. Ideological
conflict, at the most fundamental level that includes scientific paradigms and not just religious rivalry, is not a subjective struggle of
worldviews taking place in the context of an objective reality that
endures beneath and beyond this strife. Rather, *Weltanschauungskrieg*,
as Friedrich Schelling and Martin Heidegger rightly understood it,
is literally a war over how the world shows itself.[73] Heidegger knew
that this is the one and only true "world war," the metaphysical "war"
spoken of by Heraclitus when he wrote "War is father and king of
all" or "All things come to pass and are ordained in accordance with
Conflict."[74] Philip K. Dick was also deeply influenced by Heraclitus and

73 Ibid.

74 Charles Kahn, *The Art and Thought of Heraclitus* (Cambridge University Press,
    1981).

he explicitly spoke of the struggle of the individual against captivation by an alien worldview as the psychical strife between the *idios kosmos* (private world) and the *koinos kosmos* (shared cosmos).[75] The Spectral Revolution is about redefining the relationship between these in a way that is much more empowering to the creative individual than what the Breakaway Civilization has in mind.

---

75 Philip K. Dick, *The Shifting Realities of Philip K. Dick: Selected Literary and Philosophical Writings* (Vintage, 1996).

CHAPTER 6

(R)evolutionary Spectre

I F WE, THE PROMETHEISTS, are resolved to secure the forward march — or headlong plunge — of humanity into the Singularity, what is it that we are really willing here, even in the best possible case? This book concludes by more vividly imagining the (r)evolutionary spectre that we would be letting loose on Earth. This begins, in the first section of this chapter, with a look at the convergence of material technologies and psychical techniques with the potential to transform society in the most radical ways imaginable. Singularity-level technologies and techniques will mean the end of personal security and individual privacy. Any person's thoughts and feelings, let alone their actions at any place and time, will in principle be perceivable and even recordable by any other person. It would be within the power of each individual who has access to Zero Point Energy technology to transform this commonplace power source into a bomb with the capacity to destroy an entire continent.

The only way that we, as a community, can survive such an apocalyptic attainment of superhuman power on the part of any person in the post Singularity world, is to establish a maximal trust society wherein people wish only the best for each other. Given the way that psi ability works, this goodwill cannot be imposed from the top down, it has to be rooted in the greatest depths of the subconscious. What defines "the good" is the *ethos* of any society, and the first section of this chapter concludes by proposing that only a Prometheist ethos can render a post-Singularity society cohesive and coherent.

We do not have time to develop this society, or inculcate this ethos in anywhere near the majority of people, nor can we, as Prometheists, accept that we should be held back from the Singularity and endure the controlled demolition of the advanced techno-scientific planetary civilization that is about to yield this Singularity. In the end, what that means is that the Spectral Revolution first described in *Prometheus and Atlas* (Arktos, 2016) is an evolutionary revolution, like the (r)evolution of Magneto and his rebel mutants. Magneto is an exemplar of militant insistence on (r)evolution and protection of the mutants who represent an evolutionary leap from persecution at the hands of the majority of people who fearfully want to hold everyone back. In nature, evolution means a mutation that is selected-for and the extinction of what is selected against on account of its failure to evolve. The second section of this chapter illustrates the Prometheist ethos through a number of science fictional characters from American mythology, beginning with Magneto in the *X-Men*, and going on to Khan Noonien Singh in *Star Trek*, the Frankensteinian Dr. Banner in *The Incredible Hulk*, and finally, the *Ghostbusters*. The last of these brings us to the idea of creating, destroying, and reimagining egregores such as the god Gozer who is reimagined as the Stay Puft Marshmallow Man.

The third section of this chapter, and the concluding section of this book as a whole, delves into the idea of egregores and archetypes with a view to elucidating what was meant in *Prometheus and Atlas* by the description of Prometheus as a "spectre." The section begins by noting that the concept of an egregore in general is, at its origin in the Bible, associated with a Promethean gifting of *techne* to man by the fallen angels. What follows is an explanation of what an egregore is, and how groups create and maintain these thoughtforms. Then the

CHAPTER 6. (R)EVOLUTIONARY SPECTRE 213

idea of an egregore is compared and contrasted with the concept of an archetype, especially as the latter was understood by Carl Gustav Jung.

This part of the third section includes an analysis of the various things that Jung meant by "archetypes," especially when he suggested that they can be "projected" in an exteriorized and apparitional manner *with effects on the physical world* by means of Extrasensory Perception (ESP) and Psychokinesis (PK). Jung's prime example of the latter is the projection of "flying saucers" from out of the collective unconscious. The consideration of this example in particular will bring us back around to Prometheus, and to an understanding of him as an egregore that is based on an archetype. This is what was meant by describing Prometheus as a "spectre" in *Prometheus and Atlas*. Changing our relationship with this egregore to one that is more conscious and constructive is what it would mean for us to be "saved" from the worst outcome of the technological Singularity by the deity whose coming Heidegger awaited and hoped for, namely Prometheus.

6.1 The Spectral Revolution as Evolutionary

Never in recorded history has there been a more dangerous and daring prospect than the Prometheist will to affirm the Singularity, and moreover to do so on the basis of a post-materialist Technoscience that understands the Spectral Revolution as the pith of this technological apocalypse. This Prometheist will demands the deconstruction of psycho-social norms that have been fundamental to human psychology across cultural differences, just as it embraces the potential for psycho-physical evolution beyond the human condition. To affirm the Singularity is to call for the overthrow of all established political systems and the shattering of every extant economic model. Ultimately, it means to embark on a cosmic conquest to recode the matrix of what has been mistaken for "reality." The Prometheist is, in effect, the most primordially authentic type of Luciferian, willing to unleash hell on Earth rather than to serve the archontic Lord and his angels in a counterfeit Heaven.

Even in the most collectivist societies, let alone those that prize individual liberty, the protection of the human person from bodily harm and at least some degree of privacy, if only the privacy of one's own thoughts, are considered indispensable needs that it is the responsibility of any decent government to secure. Ubiquitous nanotechnology, when taken together with artificial intelligence, could bring this to an end. Nanobots could be hacked by powerful AIs that will be as commonplace as iPhones are today. These nanobots, embedded in the surfaces of "smart furniture," or taking the form of biomimetic robots that are, to the naked eye, indistinguishable from flies, spiders, or mosquitoes, could provide audiovisual surveillance of anyone, anywhere, at anytime. They could also be turned into instruments of remote assassination, entering victims through their orifices and reassembling on a molecular level inside the heart, brain, or jugular vein of a victim in a way that is fatally damaging.

In a society facing this kind of technological threat to bodily integrity and personal privacy, the nefarious uses of Psychokinesis and ESP become easier to wrap one's mind around and seem somewhat less threatening by comparison. Bursting someone's jugular vein or causing him to have an aneurysm using remotely controlled nanobots is probably going to be easier than doing the same thing using Psychokinesis. Likewise, spying on someone through hacking the smart surfaces of her furniture or through nano-scale surveillance devices embedded in robotic spiders or flies will be less labor-intensive and provide higher fidelity than clairvoyance (a.k.a. "remote viewing"). Of course, there might be a technologically augmented form of clairvoyance that provides even higher fidelity and broader range. As direct-neural interfaces are developed and computer rendering of images within the brain becomes ever more effective, a cybernetic fusion of a clairvoyant with a computer may become the ultimate surveillance technology.

The only form of psi that is likely to remain unmatched by mechanical technologies for a long time, if not indefinitely, is telepathy. But again, cybernetic brain implants made possible by nanotechnology could focus telepathic penetration of another person's mind and increase the signal to noise ratio. These telepathic impressions could also be recorded by the same cybernetic technologies now being proposed to record one's own thoughts, so that a cybernetic telepath could function in a manner akin to the angels in the *Quran* that are said to record not only the deeds but also the inner thoughts of the individual that they are tasked with observing.

The only way to deal with these nightmarish possibilities without establishing a totalitarian regime that would tightly control the uses of such technologies and psychical techniques, would be to create a maximal trust society. There are many other reasons why the advent of the Singularity makes this a survival imperative for anything remotely resembling humanity. For example, anyone paying attention to the description of the Bell technology in Chapter 3 would have grasped that this Zero Point Energy (ZPE) device is not only a Time Machine but could also be transformed into a bomb many orders of magnitude greater in destructive force than a nuclear weapon. Just as nuclear power is a dual use technology that can be used for energy generation but also for manufacturing bombs, the same is true of ZPE. This means that in a near-future where ZPE devices have been miniaturized so that they can be used to levitate cars or power one's home from one's own backyard, each and every person with access to such a device could potentially enlist the assistance of their robots and AI systems in order to transform the ZPE power cell into a bomb that could open up a black hole on the surface of the Earth and swallow an entire continent. The only way to make sure that even a few mean-spirited individuals do not take it upon themselves to end the world by doing something like this, is to have a population that consists solely of individuals who always only wish the best for one another.

What defines "the best" (Greek *agathon*, "the Good," or *kalon*, "the Beautiful") that any person may wish for any other in a given society is the *ethos* common to that society. If the Prometheist wills to unchain the full techno-scientific potential of the Singularity, then given the unprecedented dangers involved it stands to reason that she will also have to muster the will to forge an exclusively Prometheist society — worldwide. There can be no outside. To the extent that there remain any social or political outliers there will be worldwide war, and such a global conflict with Singularity-level technologies could bring not only human life, but all terrestrial life to an end without affording anyone the opportunity for a positive transition into a superhuman state of being.

So what would a Prometheist society look like? What would the policies of a Prometheist regime consist of? It is possible to venture some provisional suggestions, at least with a view to the transitional phase on the way towards a radical transformation of consciousness and an engineered psycho-biological evolutionary leap into a positive-ly Posthuman condition. The following rough sketch of Prometheist policies, which admittedly borders on sloganeering, is not meant to be a definitive platform but to indicate certain basic Prometheist orienta-tions with respect to Science and Technology Policy, Education Policy, Civil Liberties, Socioeconomic Policies, Criminal Justice, as well as Security, Intelligence, and Defense Policies.

As Prometheists we believe in prioritizing space exploration, min-ing, and colonization of the Cosmos. We are for the legalization of neo-eugenic biotechnologies that enhance the capacities of individu-als and promote their flourishing. State of the art transportation and infrastructure projects are among our priorities, and coordination with private corporations is paramount in this regard. In our view, it is high time to benefit from the scientific and technological break-throughs that would be attendant to government disclosure of all knowledge relevant to UFOs and Close Encounters. The Prometheist movement also calls for disclosure of any government information relevant to effective Psi capabilities, with a view to public development of these in all sectors of society.

Prometheism has no future without a radical restructuring of the educational system. This reorientation must begin with an end to PC thought-policing and a return to the promotion of critical thinking and bold inquiry in academia. Moralizing propaganda must be eliminated from standardized education. Humanities programs should be re-grounded in the canon, with a view to catalyzing a creativity that is deeply rooted in the rich and nourishing soil of our classical philosophical, literary, and artistic heritage. At the same time, in the sciences (not just the natural sciences, including psychology, but also the social and political sciences) baseless speculation and untestable hypotheses ought to be rejected in favor of a methodology of radical empiricism and a criterion of practical applicability. Past a certain point, after a sufficiently general knowledge base has been acquired, and critical thinking has been cultivated, the particular proclivities and aptitudes of individual students ought to be encouraged rather than an arbitrarily standardized higher education. Educators have the responsibility to foster the intellectual and spiritual development of their students as unique individuals, and they should take care not to be domineering in a way that stifles this development. Finally, in a Prometheist society, the education system will be strictly meritocratic. This means defunding all so-called "affirmative action" type programs.

Nothing is more sacred to Prometheists than Liberty. Preventing physical harm from being deliberately inflicted on others ought to be the *only* limit to personal liberty. We stand for unrestricted freedom of expression (i.e. freedom of speech, of the press, and of association). We affirm the right to bear arms in order to defend one's own person, family, and property. Those who believe in restricting personal freedom should be disenfranchised. In a Prometheist society, they will be removed from the body politic and be stripped of the liberties that they wish to deny to others.

Prometheism is committed to the protection of free enterprise as an engine for revolutionary breakthroughs. Prometheists think that the acceleration of capitalism is the best way to secure the kind of continued industrious innovation that will ultimately yield universal abundance and eliminate poverty. Implementation of a livable Universal Basic Income is necessary in order to secure a successful transition to a fully automated industry and a world where robots have rid us of all drudgery. That having been said, we will work to encourage a replacement of state mandated social welfare policies with philanthropic institutions.

Criminal Justice reform is another objective of the Prometheist movement. Prometheists think that addiction should be treated as a health crisis, not as a form of criminality. We are for decriminalization of drugs and in favor of personal discretion with respect to substance use. Prometheists also think that prostitution should be decriminalized. We are opposed to every form of discrimination against sex workers. As part of our commitment to liberty and freedom of expression, we will bring an end to all censorship laws based on a distinction between putative "decency" and "indecency." Last, but most certainly not least, we reaffirm the prohibition on cruel punishments — including coerced behavioral modification.

The United States of America, and any other country that embraces Prometheism and becomes a spearhead for its cause, ought to maximize its military budget in a bid to achieve worldwide hegemonic dominance. Prometheists are in favor of a freedom-fighting, frontier culture capable of total mobilization. As far as security and intelligence is concerned, we think that inevitably ubiquitous surveillance technologies ought to be geared toward identifying threats to personal liberty. They should never be used for the sake of blackmail, extortion, and humiliation, all of which are intelligence tactics that we categorically disavow.

In case it is not already clear from the above outline of prospective policies, a reminder is in order that as Prometheist rebels we are opposed to every form of totalitarianism. Moreover, a totalitarian socio-political order simply would not suffice to meet the aforementioned challenges. Totalitarian regimes impose order and conformity from above the individual and from outside of him. The threats faced from the types of *techne* (technology, but also more broadly technique) that yield the Singularity can only be addressed in a sustainable way by guaranteeing security from within and from beneath. In other words, from the subconscious up to the social level — not from the political level down to the social and psychological one.

The last thing that this should be mistaken to mean is that everyone just needs enough time to foster their own spiritual growth. We have had plenty of time in school. The Prometheist knows that the right metaphor for this moment in the history of terrestrial humanity, namely the apocalyptic moment of "the end of history," is not that of a school but rather that of a harvest. We have no more than thirty years before we have to face either the full force of the Singularity or a controlled demolition of technological societies on this planet at the hands of a Breakaway Civilization that regresses the planet to, at best, a medieval neo-Feudalism. The New Ager hippy-dippy view of this "Earth as a school" is, in light of the concrete situation facing us, an implicit affirmation of the Breakaway Civilization's plan to force us all backwards. Faced with this unacceptable prospect, we intend to drive people forward and thereby discover who can endure the future. From out of the pantheon of Promethean figures in American popular culture, it is the icon of Magneto that is most relevant here.

6.2 "Are You A God?"

The telepathic Professor X, who was brought up amidst luxury, is willing to indefinitely tolerate the persecution and humiliation of mutants. By contrast, the psychokinetic Magneto is the orphaned survivor of a concentration camp. His response to the initial inhumanity of the herd of normal people and their governments toward mutants is to do everything in his power to make sure that his comrades "never again" suffer such injustices.

After initially giving Charles Xavier (Professor X), the benefit of the doubt and beneficently affording humanity a chance to demonstrate its willingness to live in harmony with mutants, Erik Lensherr eventually concludes that Xavier's naively hopeful and blindly optimistic outlook risks the extermination of those with superpowers who represent the next leap in humanoid evolution. While Xavier collaborates with elements within the CIA, Lensherr responds to the persecution of mutants by the US government with a declaration of evolutionary revolution.

Magneto's speech at the crescendo of *X-Men: Days of Future Past* is broadcast on live television and delivered in the face of a terrified Richard Nixon amidst the ruins of the White House. It epitomizes the Promethean spirit of the (r)evolutionary war that Lensherr declares in response to the clear intent of the US military-industrial complex to eradicate mutants by developing robotic "Sentinels." The leader of the rebel mutants says,

> You built these weapons to destroy us. Why? Because you were afraid of our gifts. Because we are different. Humanity has always feared that which is different.
>
> Well, I'm here to tell you — to tell the world: you're right to fear us. We are the future. We are the ones who inherit this Earth, and anyone who stands in our way will suffer the same fate as these men you see before you.
>
> Today was meant to be a display of your power. Instead I give you a glimpse of the devastation that my race can unleash upon yours. Let this be a warning to the world.
>
> And to my mutant brothers and sisters out there, I say this: No more hiding. No more suffering. You have lived in the shadows of shame and fear

for too long. Come out and join me! Fight together in a brotherhood of our kind. A new tomorrow, that starts today.[1]

From the perspective of Magneto's band of rebel mutants, the X-Men are suffering from something like Stockholm syndrome. They just want to be accepted by the people who are abusing them. Some of them even want to be "cured." Professor X bends over backwards until he breaks his spine trying to gain the acceptance of an ignorant mob and the governments that represent this majority. Only Magneto has the backbone to stand up for a different breed of mutant: one who responds to hateful fear and repeated threats of murderous persecution on the part of inferior masses by willing the survival and flourishing of an extremely small minority, even if that is secured at the cost of the extinction of the vast majority who imagined snuffing out the gifted few. By what criteria are these gifted few judged to be the progenitors of a positively Posthuman stage in evolution, an evolution that on account of the Singularity has undergone a revolutionary transformation into a conscious and self-directing force rather than one that is blindly 'natural' in its selection?

Think about it this way. Who can survive the end of privacy? Someone who lives with such authenticity and integrity that she has nothing to hide. Who can be allowed to live in a world where personal safety and the preservation of bodily integrity from harm cannot be guaranteed by any system of law and order? Only someone whose worldview — from the subconscious level upwards — is oriented toward a kind of personal enrichment that profoundly affirms the liberty of others and their pursuit of their potential. Who would remain a constructive member of society in a world where all manual labor, merely calculative work, and repetitive tasks, can be more effectively performed by robots and artificial intelligence? Only someone who

---

1   Bryan Singer, *X-Men: Days of Future Past* (Marvel and 20th Century Fox, 2014).

has new ideas, creative visions, and profound psychological insights to offer that world.

While the persons who pass through these filters determined by various dimensions of the Singularity will be individuals (and in fact what will distinguish them, above all, is their extraordinary individuality), there is a way to estimate just how many — or rather, how few — in number they will be as compared to the general population on this planet. If certain prevalent ideologies and worldviews demand a type of adherent that is radically incompatible with the kind of person negatively defined above, then as many people as affirm one or another of these belief systems also fail to meet the aforementioned criteria. Judaism, Christianity, Islam, and Hinduism, in their conventional and most common forms, are all religions that demand a type of believer who does not have the qualities of the individual capable of taking the (r)evolutionary leap that lies ahead of us. Liberal Democracy, Capitalism, National Socialism, Social Democracy, Communism, and Confucianism are, among others, socio-political belief systems of which the same can be said. Finally, adherents of putatively 'scientific' materialism who dismiss the spectral on account of a reductively mechanistic mindset — one which denies even the possibility of free will — are no more responsible and fit to endure the post-Singularity world than, say, Muslims. That leaves us with something like 1% of the world's population.

Actually, that estimate is probably way too optimistic. It is a symbolic value that is meant to elegantly contrast with "the one-percent" that Socialists and other leftists often protest against. By no means would the 1% who are above all of the aforementioned ideologies, belief systems, and worldviews overlap with the most affluent and powerful people on our planet right now, including those who are planning for a breakaway scenario. On the contrary, as in the case of Magneto's mutants, many of those in the 1% (or far less) who will come to see themselves as Prometheists are marginalized individuals whose nonconformity has caused them to slip through the mesh of our global capitalist society's safety net, let alone rise up into its financial elite. The brand of Fascist whose modus operandi is "destructive departure" is no better than the many categories of people excluded above, which Fascist elitists who advocate a breakaway would like to keep around in sufficiently small numbers as a slavish population living under conditions of neo-feudal serfdom. Still, it must be understood that these Fascists are far more compassionate than Prometheists. Even their worst-case scenario is a controlled collapse of the Earth's population down to about 10% of what it is today. That is 700 million serfs to rule over.

Prometheists have no need for such 'people.' No Prometheist would ever take pleasure in being their cattle-driver. Our vision is of a community of free spirits who support each other's flourishing through an exploration of every positive potential for Posthuman evolution that the Singularity offers to us — from the most psychical dimensions of the Spectral Revolution to the most bio-mechanical applications of transhuman technologies.

This is not meant to suggest that we are out to eliminate "undesirables" of any kind. What it means is that in the event that the controlled collapse begins to be engineered by those in the Breakaway Civilization, mainly through the convergence and rapid succession of a variety of seemingly 'natural' catastrophes (pandemics, earthquakes, tsunamis, asteroid impacts, rapid climate change, famines, etc.), we will refuse to defer to the supposed 'wisdom' of the architects of this apocalypse. Since we are unlikely to have the power to stop the breakaway elite from starting the collapse, it stands to reason that resisting them after they have already initiated it will turn a controlled collapse — namely one that they have under their archontic control — into an uncontrolled collapse. Instead of a neo-feudal world depopulated, over several decades, down to 10% of the current global level (a population equal to that of the Earth at the dawn of the modern scientific-industrial age circa 1750), we could instead face the extinction of *Homo sapiens*. The Prometheist will prefer the risk of this extinction to any planned retreat or deliberate regression, making every effort to ensure that the extinction of the human race is synonymous with an evolutionary revolution inaugurating Promethean posthumanity. Perhaps this calls to mind Captain Ahab from *Moby Dick*.

In the greatest installment of the *Star Trek* franchise, the film *The Wrath of Khan*, the titular super-villain and nemesis of James T. Kirk repeatedly quotes Melville's Luciferian novel. Driven by wrath to seek vengeance against the White Whale that the USS Enterprise, as the flagship of the Federation, represents, Khan disregards advice to take the Genesis Device and terraform whatever planet he wishes to re-settle his people on.[2] Khan insists, "He tasks me, and I shall have him. I'll chase him round the moons of Nibia and round perdition's flames before I give him up." This quote is modified from Chapter 36 of *Moby Dick*, where Captain Ahab says, "I'll chase him round Good Hope, and round the Horn, and round the Norway Maelstrom, and round perdition's flames before I give him up!"[3] Khan pursues Kirk into the Mutara Nebula where, before being defeated, he decides to try to take the Enterprise (with a crippled warp drive) down with him. As he arms the Genesis device for use in a suicide strike, Khan utters what he knows will be his last words: "To the last, I grapple with thee; from hell's heart, I stab at thee; for hate's sake, I spit my last breath at thee."

This is a direct quote of Captain Ahab's most Luciferian statement. A well-read early edition of *Moby Dick* is displayed prominently on Khan's makeshift bookshelf in the ruined *SS Botany Bay*, alongside Shakespeare's *King Lear*, Dante's *Inferno*, and two copies of Milton's *Paradise Lost* — one of which includes *Paradise Regained*. Milton's Lucifer is as prominently featured in *Space Seed*, the original series episode of *Star Trek* that introduces Khan, as Ahab is quoted in *Star Trek II*. When Kirk offers Khan exile on Ceti Alpha V rather than

2   Nicholas Meyer, *Star Trek II: The Wrath of Khan* (Paramount Pictures, 1982).

3   Herman Melville, *Moby Dick, or The Whale* (Penguin Classics, 2002).

prosecution by the Federation, Khan replies to Kirk's question as to whether he is willing to accept the challenge of settling such a savage planet together with his supermen by asking, "Have you ever read Milton, Captain?" Kirk responds that he understands. When subsequently asked to explain by an embarrassed Scotty (who, though a Scotsman, has never read *Paradise Lost*), Captain Kirk makes it clear that Khan was referring to "the statement that Lucifer makes when he is cast into the pit: 'It's better to rule in Hell, than to serve in Heaven.'"[4] Khan certainly sees opportunity on Ceti Alpha V, "A world to win, an empire to build."

It was in search of such an opportunity that he and the supermen under his command broke away from Earth in the first place. In *Space Seed*, Spock's research uncovers a hidden fact of history that he reveals to Captain Kirk, himself a historian, who remarks that this fact has been omitted from the history books.[5] Spock explains that at the end of the Third World War, also known as The Eugenics War, "some eighty or ninety of these supermen" who had for a time seized power across the planet "were unaccounted for." Their disappearance, he suggests, was hidden from the public because the last thing that such war-weary populations would have wanted to know is that "tens of Napoleons" had absconded somewhere and might be planning a future return. This is clearly a veiled reference to the Fascist Breakaway Civilization and, in particular, the postwar SS elite of "supermen" in hiding. The *SS Botany Bay* is a "space seed" of a potential Breakaway Civilization that Kirk finally plants on an ill-fated planet.

That Kirk chooses to give Khan and his genetically engineered comrades another chance to win the kind of world that they wanted back on Earth says as much about the Captain of the Enterprise as it does about the greatest tyrant of the Eugenics War. Let us not forget that another episode in the original series, *Mirror Mirror*, shows us (in

---

4   John Milton, *Paradise Lost* (Penguin Classics, 2003).

5   Marc Daniels, "Space Seed" in *Star Trek: The Original Series* (NBC, 1967).

a parallel universe) how disturbingly easy it would be for Kirk to fit into a militaristically Fascist version of the Federation. He also makes for an all-too-convincing Nazi in *Patterns of Force*. To Spock's horror, once Kirk and his other senior staff discover Khan's true identity as the Sikh North-Indian dictator Noonien Singh, they express admiration for him as "the best of the tyrants." Apparently, unlike others of the genetically engineered supermen who seized power during the Eugenics War, "no massacres took place" as part of his "attempt to unify Humanity."

At one point, Khan confronts Kirk with his contemptuous disappointment at "how little man himself has changed" despite all of the technical developments that have taken place during the time that he and his crew were in cryogenic suspension aboard the *SS Botany Bay*. Later, during his seizure of the Enterprise, he restates this view in a more philosophically crystallized fashion as he offers Kirk's senior crewmates a chance to join him rather than watch their Captain suffocate in a pressure chamber:

> Nothing ever changes, except man. Your technical accomplishments? Improve a mechanical device and you may double productivity, but improve man and you gain a thousandfold. I am such a man! Join me.[6]

Khan sees Kirk, and for that matter the denizens of the Federation as a whole (since Kirk is among the best of them) as mentally and physically "inferior" to his band of supermen who once "offered the world order." Khan's indignant remark, "we offered the world order," could also be rightly heard: we offered the *World Order*. When the world rejected that order, rather than submitting to the judgment of a history that remained merely human, Khan led tens of the vanquished supermen *and superwomen* on a nearly impossible interstellar journey against all odds. Nearly impossible, that is, until their ship is recovered by the starship Enterprise.

---

6   Ibid.

In *The Wrath of Khan,* Kirk comes to realize that giving Khan and his comrades another lease on life, even after their attempted takeover of the Enterprise, was the biggest and most costly mistake that he has ever made. It costs him the life of his best friend, Spock, who sacrifices himself in order to repair the warp drive so that the Enterprise can speed away from Khan's detonation of the Genesis device. For the first time in his life, Kirk is forced to face the no-win scenario that he cleverly evaded back in Starfleet Academy. *The Wrath of Khan* opens with a demonstration of the Kobayashi Maru test, a simulation of a no-win scenario, which we later learn that only Kirk was able to beat by cheating. He reprogrammed the computer so as not to have to face the inevitability of death and destruction in a combat scenario. In the simulation, a Federation starship has to enter the neutral zone in order to rescue a civilian ship in distress, the Kobayashi Maru. At this point, it is surrounded by hostile Klingon birds of prey. The trainee in the captain's seat is tested to see how he — or, in *The Wrath of Khan,* she — holds up when forced to make command decisions while faced with imminent and inevitable defeat. Kirk's ultimate confrontation with Khan becomes such a no-win scenario, as the martyred Spock himself explicitly states when he describes his heroic self-sacrifice as a solution to the Kobayashi Maru test that he admits to never having taken as a trainee.

Kobayashi Maru, the no-win scenario, is the ultimate "test of character." But its key role in the scenario of *The Wrath of Khan* is also meant to signify something more specific: Lucifer's revolt against God — or, to express this archetypal conflict in more primordial and archaic terms, the rebellion of Prometheus against Zeus. It is an unwinnable struggle, the tragic outcome of which is meant to demonstrate the character of the one willing to set an example by rebelling in the face of certain defeat rather than reconciling himself to relinquishing his *ethos.*

That the Federation is in the midst of testing Project Genesis when Khan makes his last stand, underlines Khan's rebellion against the heavenly order of the Federation as the revolt of Lucifer against God. When read into the classified project by Kirk, McCoy remarks on the Satanic hubris of the Genesis terraforming device: "God created the world in seven days. Now, with Genesis, we can do it for you in seven hours!"[7] Khan, who in *Space Seed* had already described himself as "an engineer of sorts," like Prometheus, wants this power of Creation for himself. He thinks that he has a better, bolder and more beautiful vision for world order than the godlike Federation. But, as in the case of Khan being a foil that reveals Kirk's own Promethean proclivities, there is a deeper layer of meaning here. The Federation *is not God* and by playing God with Project Genesis those amongst the Federation's elite who, like Admiral Kirk, have access to the classified project are really the Prometheans.

Prometheus explodes into American popular culture on May 1, 1962 as "the strangest man of all time." The cover of the first issue of *The Incredible Hulk* asks, "is he man, or monster, or is he both?"[8] The main character of the story, Dr. Banner, is a scientist who clearly owes a debt to Shelley's Dr. Frankenstein, "the modern Prometheus," whose monster is an exteriorization of his own psyche. Dr. Banner is also Dr. Jekyll, whose inner Mr. Hyde is released when he is accidentally subjected to the blast of a gamma-ray bomb test. J. Robert Oppenheimer, the inventor of the atomic bomb has been described as an "American Prometheus." The atomic bomb, or as the case may be here, gamma-ray bomb, represents man's fundamental violation of the divinely ordained natural order. It is the Promethean theft of fire, a drawing down of the heavenly sun to the earthly plane. This also means a transformation of the human scientist who is responsible for this sacrilege into a green-skinned giant or titan (green is the color of the life force, "the green man" of mythic archetypes). Interestingly, although Dr. Banner is a scientist working for the American military-industrial

7   Meyer, *Star Trek II: The Wrath of Khan*.

8   Stan Lee and Jack Kirby, *Marvel Masterworks: The Incredible Hulk Volume 1* (Marvel, 2015).

complex, the Incredible Hulk that their gamma bomb transforms him into becomes an anti-authoritarian force who is often seen smashing tanks and other symbols of militarism.

Although *The Incredible Hulk* television series of the 1970s departed considerably from the narrative of the comic books, this statement about Dr. Banner's relationship with the American military-industrial complex is highlighted by a special two-hour episode entitled "Prometheus."[9] In "Prometheus," NORAD scientists mistake the Hulk for an alien from outer space. In the comic books, the Hulk is often fighting space aliens, which suggests that, despite his appearance and superpowers, he is a defender of humanity against an inhuman threat that is truly alien but that "puny humans" would not have the strength to stand against on their own.

The question of the alien in *The Incredible Hulk* is also a commentary on alienation. Dr. Banner, like Dr. Frankenstein before him, is profoundly alienated from his fellow men. The monstrous Prometheus within him also constantly interferes with the otherwise tenderly loving relationship that he has with women. In the comic book, it is one woman in particular, General Ross's daughter, Betty, and in the television series, it is a series of women that Dr. Banner must let go of in order to protect them from the Hulk. The profoundly melancholy main musical theme of the television series is called *The Lonely Man*, and it is usually played over scenes of Dr. Banner hitch-hiking, from town to town, incognito and under one false name after another, since he has let the world, and even those dearest to him, presume that he is dead, in order to protect them from his alter ego — from the Prometheus that is duty-bound to defend the Earth.

The Prometheus figure in American popular culture does not always take the form of a lone man. It can also be a Promethean *team* of scientists who are intent on overcoming human subservience to the superhuman, and putatively divine, entities worshipped by Earth's

---

9   Kenneth Johnson, "Prometheus, Parts 1 and 2" in *The Incredible Hulk* (CBS, 1980).

ancient civilizations. The Ghostbusters of the 1980s are the best American pop culture example of such a team of scientific geniuses who collectively embody the Prometheus archetype.

The core message of the franchise is epitomized by a statement that Winston makes toward the end of *Ghostbusters* (1984): "When someone asks you if you're a god, you say: 'Yes!'"[10] It is a correction to the wrong answer that Ray volunteers in response to a question posed by Gozer, a god (or goddess) who was "worshipped by the Sumerians, Hittites, and Babylonians." As the Ghostbusters face a Mesopotamian temple that has emerged from an inter-dimensional portal at the top of a Ziggurat-like New York apartment building, designed by a mad doctor and occultist architect who planned to summon an apocalyptic judgment of humanity, Ray's demand that Gozer leave meets with this response from the ancient deity: "Are you a god?" "No," says Ray sheepishly. "Then die!"

The Real Ghostbusters animated series, which aired between the original film and its 1989 sequel, repeatedly featured confrontational encounters with deities blindly revered by ancient civilizations or terrifying figures from the folklore of various cultures.[11] The moral of the story is always the same: on account of breakthroughs in science and technology, and an attendant rise of confident self-determination, we no longer need to cower in the face of these boogeymen that awed our ancestors into submission. The science of Parapsychology, which was fathered by William James, affords the Ghostbusters an understanding of paranormal powers that, in previous epochs, were used by cruel deities and the leaders of the cults devoted to them in order to manipulate ignorant masses.

At the deepest level, *Ghostbusters* is about the freedom that comes from mastery over the collective unconscious. Echoing the 1956 film

---

10   Ivan Reitman, *Ghostbusters* (Columbia Pictures, 1984).

11   Joe Medjuck and Michael C. Gross, *The Real Ghostbusters* (DIC Enterprises and Columbia Pictures Television, 1986–1991).

Forbidden Planet,[12] which incorporated Carl Jung's insights into the psychical nature of *Flying Saucers*,[13] both the original *Ghostbusters* film and episodes of the animated series, such as "Mr. Sandman, Dream Me A Dream," highlight the ultimate promise of Parapsychology. A scientific study of paranormal powers and a technological approach to the occult could help us to become conscious of the abyssal depths of our own psyche from out of which world-conquering apocalyptic cults have arisen to tyrannize over humanity. The Ghostbusters, who, in the 1989 sequel, turn Lady Liberty herself into their vehicle, are really here to battle these "monsters from the Id."[14] God once took the form of Jehovah or Allah. Now he is nothing more than the Stay Puft Marshmallow Man, ready to be roasted by the Promethean fire of proton packs and other spectral technology.

X-Men, Star Trek, The Incredible Hulk, and the *Ghostbusters* are only a few of the many examples of the occulted Prometheism that emerges from the subconscious of late twentieth century America in comic books, film, and television. But they are some of the best, because they were even incarnated as wildly popular toys. So they entered the minds of children on a pre-analytic level that shapes the spectral plasma of archetypal dreams and nightmares. It is from out of this ectoplasm that an *egregore* like Gozer is conjured. An egregore that could harness the pent up pre-adolescent and pubescent sexual energy of millions of very young people would be endowed with tremendous vital force.[15] A Neo-Taoist text called *Lighting the Eye of the Dragon* puts it this way: "Respecting children as representatives of

---

12   Fred M. Wilcox, *Forbidden Planet* (Metro-Goldwyn-Mayer, 1956).

13   C.G. Jung, *Flying Saucers: A Modern Myth of Things Seen in the Skies* (Princeton University Press, 1979).

14   Ivan Reitman, *Ghostbusters II* (Columbia Pictures, 1989).

15   Mark Stavish, *Egregores: The Occult Entities That Watch Over Human Destiny* (Inner Traditions, 2018), 58.

our collective unconscious is a valuable lesson to learn. … Whatever a child plays at or with will be what the nation builds up or develops."[16]

6.3 Egregores and Archetypes: Prometheus as a Spectre

Egregore is a Greek word derived from *egrégoros*, which means "watcher" or "wakeful" one.[17] It is the word that was used in the Greek translation of the Bible in order to render intelligible to the classical Mediterranean population the meaning of the Hebrew "fallen angels" who interbred with human women in order to produce the race of giants or *Nephilim*.[18] A suppressed ancient scripture called the Book of the Watchers, also known as the Book of Enoch, which was once canonical but was later excised from the Bible at the Council of Nicaea, explains how these rebel angels who came down to Earth taught all of the arts and sciences to the human women or matriarchs with whom they sired the superhuman race of giants, which would subsequently be wiped off the face of the Earth by the flood of Noah.[19] The following are a couple of key passages in the Book of Enoch about the Watchers and their bestowing of godlike power to humanity. Bear in mind that it is written from the hostile perspective of Jehovah or Yahweh, against whom the "fallen angels" or egregores are rebelling by arming mankind with knowledge and calling mortals to rise up from out of their subservience to this Lord:

> And they became pregnant, and they bare great giants, whose height was three hundred ells: Who consumed all the acquisitions of men. And when men could no longer sustain them, the giants turned against them and devoured mankind. And they began to sin against birds, and beasts, and

---

16   Ibid.
17   Ibid., 2.
18   Ibid., 2–3.
19   Ibid., 3.

reptiles, and fish, and to devour one another's flesh, and drink the blood.
...

And Azâzêl taught men to make swords, and knives, and shields, and breastplates, and made known to them the metals of the earth and the art of working them, and bracelets, and ornaments, and the use of antimony, and the beautifying of the eyelids, and all kinds of costly stones, and all colouring tinctures. And there arose much godlessness, and they committed fornication, and they were led astray, and became corrupt in all their ways. Semjâzâ taught enchantments, and root-cuttings, Amârôs the resolving of enchantments, Barâqîjâl, taught astrology, Kôkabêl the constellations, Ezêqêêl the knowledge of the clouds, Araqiêl the signs of the earth, Shamsiêl the signs of the sun, and Sariêl the course of the moon.[20]

In other words, as bringers of scientific knowledge and empowering technology, the original egregores were already a collective expression of the Prometheus archetype. There are many different types of egregores, but the first beings to which the term was applied were essentially avatars of Prometheus who, as Aeschylus explains, was the "teacher in every art, [who] brought the fire that became for mortals a means to mighty ends."[21] The *Nephilim* have also been described, in English translations of the Bible, as "the mighty ones of old, the men of renown."

It appears that the first person to, at least publicly, use the ancient Greek word egregore in modern literature was Victor Hugo in his novel *The Legend of the Ages* (1859).[22] Shortly thereafter it was used by the French occultist Eliphas Lévi in *The Great Mystery* (1868).[23] Eventually, in occult circles, egregore came to commonly mean an "autonomous psychic entity composed of and influencing the thoughts of a group of people."[24] It is not just that the members of a group or

---

20   Ibid., 2–3.

21   Ibid., 3.

22   Ibid., 31.

23   Ibid.

24   Ibid., 3.

organization consciously or unconsciously create an egregore that they control. Rather, the egregore that comes into being also winds up collectively possessing them.[25] The more people there are involved in the creation of a thoughtform, the more the entity that takes shape is not under the control of any one of them and instead exercises control over all of them. In a way, the *egregore* becomes a medium or focal point for the collective's control over the psyche of the individuals who constituted the group.[26] This can be very empowering to the group as a whole, protecting it from external threats, but it could also become disempowering for the persons constituting that group by threatening their individuality.

In the worst cases, egregores engage in psychic vampirism.[27] In these cases, persons sympathetic to an egregore are recruited for the sake of sucking them dry of both emotional and physical energy.[28] This is not just characteristic of explicitly occult groups, but occurs unconsciously with the egregores of sports teams and political groups that prey on fans and party members.[29] It is believed that egregores are augmented not only by collective belief, but especially by sacrifices relevant to the thoughtform and the activity or movement that it sustains.[30] Individuals can become the slaves of the artificial beings that they create.[31] It is even possible to be killed by an egregore that one has created.[32] A thoughtform is inherently amoral; its character is formed by the emotions of those who conjure it.[33]

---

25 Ibid., 8.

26 Ibid., 29.

27 Ibid., 34.

28 Ibid., 36.

29 Ibid.

30 Ibid., 5.

31 Ibid., 39.

32 Ibid., 16.

33 Ibid., 28.

The teachers of certain communities can become powerful enough personalities in the minds of their followers that such individuals can continue to guide and protect the group in the form of an egregore for years, decades, or even centuries after their death.[34] As everyone knows, in science fiction we have the example of Jedi Master Obi Wan Kenobi from *Star Wars*. Such was, and is, the case with Dorje Shugden, a deceased monk and now *egregore* who is the guardian of the Gelukpa school of Tibetan Buddhism.[35] The Tibetans are particularly adept at creating egregores. In *Magic and Mystery in Tibet*, Alexandra David-Néel introduced Westerners to the *tulpa* — a Tibetan Buddhist equivalent of an egregore.[36] A *tulpa* may be created through intense visualization practices, but once it manifests it can develop a mind of its own and escape the control of its maker.[37] The Tibetans compare this development of relative autonomy on the part of the thoughtform to a child leaving the womb of his mother. From the Tibetan perspective, the manifestation of *tulpas* is not particularly strange because the occultists of their tradition believe that we "live and move in a world of phantasmagoria" in general, even if most people mistake this for an objective 'reality'.[38]

The creation of an egregore depends not just on pure repetition and the perfect coherence of a group in clearly envisioning a thoughtform, but also on slight variations and differing iterations of the same basic idea.[39] The latter is important because the thoughtform takes shape or — literally *coheres* (attains coherence) — through a kind of comparative triangulation and synthesis of variant iterations, like producing a digital composite image that synthesizes a number of faces into a single realistic portrait of an imaginary person. Without these

---

34 Ibid., 20.
35 Ibid., 18.
36 Ibid., 11.
37 Ibid., 11–12.
38 Ibid., 13.
39 Ibid., 33.

variations, the members of the group would not be putting their own personalities and investing their emotional energy into the egregore either. It is not enough for each of them to mindlessly repeat a pattern that has been perfectly predefined, perhaps by the group's leader or based on a pre-existent text. On the other hand, the internal structure of an egregore can only be tweaked so much before it reaches a tipping point wherein it either collapses or turns into something else.[40]

Another key characteristic of the formation of an egregore is that the psychic energy involved does not openly radiate from those who are conjuring the thoughtform. Rather, the quality of energy at work in egregore formation is that it enfolds or coagulates.[41] This is very significant, because it means that something like "universal love" can never generate an egregore. Emotions such as love, compassion, forgiveness, healing, and peace, especially when they are universally intended, have an open and expansively radiating quality. By contrast, brooding determination, visionary and active anticipation, disciplined creation, and most certainly, defiance, vengeance, wrath, rage, and hatred are enfolding emotions.[42] They fall back in on themselves, reverberate, resonate, attune, and amplify. It is, of course, not only possible, but likely, that these emotions will be uncontrolled and dissipate in wild outbursts. But if they *are* controlled and mastered they can be channeled into the creation of an egregore.

An egregore can best be destroyed by burning the living members that sustain it, and committing their ritual paraphernalia and sacred sites to flames.[43] This is in part because the shedding of blood would only make martyrs that strengthen the egregore, in effect by offering it a sacrifice. This casts in a different light the whole history of the destruction of the enemy by flames, namely in a holocaust.[44] What

---

40 Ibid., 52.

41 Ibid., 42.

42 Ibid.

43 Ibid., 51, 103.

44 Ibid., 103.

the Nazi Germans did to the Jews, what the Soviet Union did to the Nazi Germans, and what the Chinese Communists did to Tibet, can all be understood in these terms.[45] Both National Socialism and Communism were empowered by egregores.[46] It may even be the case that the "production of ideological superstructures on the basis of will is precisely … the collective generation of a demon or an egregore."[47] This is also why sorcerers and witches were burned at the stake, and why heretical scriptures were consigned to flames in book burnings.[48]

Egregores can, and do, fight against one another on the 'astral' plane — especially the egregores of nations.[49] Those city-states, Republics, and Empires that truly attained greatness and glory in the course of human history all had egregores watching over them.[50] Examples would include Athena in Athens, Mithra in Iran, or Wotan in Germany. The egregore of a nation can also change, for example, Marianne becoming the egregore of France from the Revolution of 1789 and onwards. Some occultists have interpreted the collapse of the Roman Empire in terms of the disregard and degradation, if not destruction, of its egregore though the adoption of Christianity as the official religion of the realm.[51] Julius Evola confessed that an occult ritual secretly held in Rome in 1913 aimed to revive the egregore of the Roman Empire, and this is what led both to Italy's defeat in World War I and also to the rise of Benito Mussolini.[52] The person who handed Mussolini the Fasces during the March on Rome was a member of this esoteric society, and the particular Fasces that was employed in

---

45 Ibid.

46 Ibid., 40.

47 Ibid., 41.

48 Ibid., 104.

49 Ibid., 33.

50 Ibid., 5.

51 Ibid.

52 Ibid., 104, 124–125.

the ceremony had been crafted by them.[53] A weak or dead egregore is easier to modify than one that remains strong and vital.[54]

This is obviously relevant to the egregore of Prometheus, which has something else in common with the egregores of nations. It is based on an archetype. The relationship between egregores and archetypes is a deep and complex philosophical question. That question has to be explored on the way to understanding what was really meant in *Prometheus and Atlas* (Arktos, 2016) by the claim that Prometheus is a spectre. There are many egregores that are purely personal, relatively ephemeral, because they are not based on archetypes. Consider the following example.

In the early 1970s, members of the Toronto Society for Psychical Research got together to collectively imagine a character that they called "Philip." In 1976 Iris Owens, a parapsychology researcher who was one of the leaders of the group, co-authored a book with Margaret Sparrow about how the group conjured Philip.[55] The Psychical Research Society in Toronto drew portraits of Philip, delineated his personality in detail, and immersed themselves in his fictitious biography. It was a tragic life story. A seventeenth century aristocrat living in England during the rule of Oliver Cromwell, Philip had an affair with a gypsy woman named Margot and fell in love with her. His wife, Dorothea, discovered the affair and publicly accused Margot of being a witch. Philip, who was afraid that he would lose his standing in society and be divested of his property, was terribly guilt-ridden for not having done anything to defend Margot at her trial or to protect her from being burned at the stake. After her death, Philip was often seen by the townspeople pacing the battlements in despair. Eventually, he committed suicide by jumping off these high stone walls. Subsequently, his ghost haunted these battlements.

---

53 Ibid., 126.

54 Ibid., 104.

55 Iris M. Owen and Margaret Sparrow, *Conjuring Up Philip: An Adventure In Psychokinesis* (Harper & Row, 1976).

The Toronto society set up a séance in which they attempted to contact and communicate with this conjured "spirit." What followed were repeated impressive displays of macro Psychokinesis, many of which are vividly captured in video recordings that are now publicly available. In certain of these videos, it is very clear that the dramatic movements of the table could not have been produced by either deliberate trickery or unconscious ideomotor activity on the part of the participants. There were raps on a table, table tilting, and even the table flipping over, in response to questions asked by the participants. Philip would give responses in the form of "raps" or psychokinetic knocks on the table, one rap for "yes" and two raps for "no." Interestingly, Philip's responses exceeded the knowledge base of any one participants in the group, but he never produced any information outside of the knowledge and experience of all of the participants. "Philip" was unable to clearly answer questions that sought information or elicited reactions that were outside the scope of the life story and personality that the group of psychical researchers had given him.

The sincerity of the participants is also evident from the videos recorded by the Toronto society. None of the group's members ever claimed to be a professional medium. After having invented Philip's story, they began by silently meditating in a circle — every Thursday evening for an entire year. When this failed to bring him to life, they took a different approach. They began to more lightheartedly converse with him as if he were real, and await his responses through the table. The more these were forthcoming, the more the group's activity went from feeling like a game to feeling like a relationship with a real person. Even though the psychical researchers rationally knew that they had invented Philip, over time they came to believe that he was an autonomous entity — or had become one. Iris Owen and her colleagues came to the conclusion that they had produced the equivalent of a poltergeist — a "spirit" that manifests psychokinetically. Had they been familiar with the concept of an egregore they would have recognized that as exactly what they had created. But the egregore of Philip was not archetypal in nature.

By contrast, the egregore that Carl Jung saw rising up from its slumber in 1930s Germany was certainly an archetypal egregore. Jung, who did not employ the term egregore in his psychological lexicon, simply calls this egregore an archetype — that of the ancient Germanic god *Wotan*, who is referred to as "Odin" by the Norse branch of the Germanic peoples. Jung insightfully perceived Wotan as the "archetype" vitalizing National Socialism and possessing Germany with a force that he aptly predicted — or prophesied — would lead to another world war.

Just as there are egregores that are not based on archetypes, there are also archetypes that cannot be used as a basis for the formation or, as Jung would put it, the "projection" of egregores. Delving into this distinction requires teasing apart what Jung even meant by the term "archetype," which is quite a task, since his characterization of archetypes is often inconsistent and sometimes even internally contradictory to the point of being incoherent. Nevertheless, it is worth the effort, since grasping this distinction is indispensable to understanding Prometheus as a spectre of evolutionary revolution.

In his first exposition of the origin of the term "archetype" Jung claims that he is adopting it from out of the context of Hellenistic philosophy in late pagan antiquity. He explains that, in this context, "'Archetype' is an explanatory paraphrase of the Platonic *eidos*."[56] Jung comes back to Plato repeatedly in his various attempts to explain what an archetype is.[57] On a number of these occasions it really seems as if he is equating an archetype with the Platonic conception of a transcendental idea or form (*eidos*): "Take, for instance, the word 'idea.' It goes back to the *eidos* concept of Plato, and the eternal ideas are primordial images stored up in a supracelestial place as eternal,

56 C.G. Jung, *Archetypes and the Collective Unconscious* (Princeton University Press, 1990), 4.

57 Ibid., 75, 78–79.

transcendent forms."[58] That Jung is identifying these ideas with his archetypes becomes clear when he writes that "there are present in every psyche forms which are unconscious but nonetheless active — living dispositions, ideas in the Platonic sense, that preform and continually influence our thoughts and feelings and actions."[59] But then he adds, "The eye of the seer perceives them as ... images in dreams and revelatory visions."[60] Indeed Jung even gives credit to Plato for having first discovered that "the concept of the archetype finds its specific application" in the products of "creative fantasy" wherein "the primordial images are made visible..."[61] Here he no doubt has Plato the playwright and the mystic in mind, rather than Plato the mathematically inclined rationalist.

Jung explains that even "before the time of St. Augustine" the term "archetype ... was synonymous with 'Idea' in the Platonic usage."[62] This means "a prototype or primordial image ... that is pre-existent and supraordinate to all phenomena in which [it] ... is manifest."[63] Jung's comparison of an archetype to the "invariable geometric proportions" that determine the "axial system" for crystal formation is a strikingly Platonic image that reinforces the view that Jungian archetypes are essentially equivalent to Plato's eternal forms:

A primordial image is determined as to its content only when it has become conscious and is therefore filled out with the material of conscious experience. Its form, however, as I have explained elsewhere, might perhaps be compared to the axial system of a crystal, which, as it were, preforms the crystalline structure in the mother liquid, although it has no material existence of its own. This first appears according to the specific way in which the ions and molecules aggregate. The archetype in itself is empty and

---

58   Ibid., 33.
59   Ibid., 79.
60   Ibid., 33.
61   Ibid., 78.
62   Ibid., 75.
63   Ibid.

purely formal, nothing but ... a possibility of representation which is given *a priori*. The representations themselves are not inherited, only the forms. ... With regard to the definiteness of the form, our comparison with the crystal is illuminating inasmuch as the axial system determines only the stereometric structure but not the concrete form of the individual crystal. This may be either large or small, and it may vary endlessly by reason of the different size of its planes or by the growing together of two crystals. The only thing that remains constant is the axial system, or rather, the invariable geometric proportions underlying it. The same is true of the archetype. In principle, it can be named and has an invariable nucleus of meaning — but always only in principle, never as regards its concrete manifestation.[64]

However, Jung then equivocates and says, "But I am an empiricist, not a philosopher," as if the two were mutually exclusive.[65] He goes on to reject the Idea, as Plato conceived of it, as something *a priori* and the metaphysical realm to which it is supposed to belong as an "unverifiable realm of faith and superstition ... charitably left to the poet."[66] Empirical science, including psychology as Jung understands it, cannot accept any hypothesis that is not subjected to "verification by experiment."[67]

After this apparent attack on Platonic idealism, Jung pivots toward an acceptance of Kantian idealism: "If it be true that there can be no metaphysics transcending human reason, it is no less true that there can be no empirical knowledge that is not already caught and limited by the *a priori* structure of cognition."[68] He specifically describes Kant's *Critique of Pure Reason* as "a rebirth of the Platonic spirit."[69] In one of Jung's most Platonic definitions of the "concept of an archetype," he defines archetypes as "definite forms in the psyche

---

64 Ibid., 80.

65 Ibid., 75.

66 Ibid., 76.

67 Ibid.

68 Ibid.

69 Ibid.

which seem to be present always and everywhere."[70] Immediately following this definition, he adds, "my idea of the archetype — literally a
pre-existent form..."[71] This means that, at least in this definition, the
kind of pre-existence that Jung is claiming for the archetypes is the
kind that would make them "present *always* and *everywhere*." In other
words, they pre-exist the formation of this universe or any other, let
alone the evolution of life on planet Earth.

In line with his most Platonic definition of what archetypes are,
Jung will sometimes maintain that they are universal to all individuals — and presumably this would include not just every *human* being,
but every intelligent individual in the universe among all possible
alien races. That is the conclusion that we must draw from the statement that the archetypes constitute a "system of collective, universal,
and impersonal nature which is identical in all individuals."[72] In this
case, when he speaks of these "pre-existent forms, the archetypes" as
being "inherited" by the individual from the collective unconscious
rather than being generated by individuals, he cannot have genetic
heritability in mind — not even the collective genetic inheritance of
Homo sapiens.

At other times, Jung's explanations of what an archetype is are very
far from the Platonic Idea or even from Kantian Idealism. On these
occasions, he explicitly claims that the archetypes take hold of an
individual through biological heredity. No newborn baby has a mind
that is a *tabula rasa* or "blank slate" because each has a hereditary inheritance that passes down the influence of certain archetypes, which
in turn condition the infant's response to external stimuli.[73] Jung is
proposing a "hereditary transmission through the germ-plasm" as the
means by which archetypes propagate through an unconscious that is

70 Ibid., 42.
71 Ibid., 43.
72 Ibid.
73 Ibid., 66.

"collective" but *not universal.*[74] The aforementioned Wotan archetype that is specific to the Germanic peoples would be an example of this. Jung clearly thought that in the 1930s Wotan was rising up from out of the unconscious of the Germanic peoples, which is ethno-biologically or "racially" differentiated from other unconscious collectivities. In other words, there are archetypes that are not general to a "collective unconscious" common to all of humanity.

Already in an infant's mind, let alone in childhood, "the archetypes… direct all fantasy activity into its appointed paths…"[75] This inheritance determines what ideas it is even possible for certain individuals to come up with. The implication here is that a certain biological — and therefore "ethnological" — heritage might make it impossible, from childhood, for a particular person to dream certain dreams and arrive at certain ideas.[76] That person may be exposed to such ideas, dreams, or visions expressed by someone else with a different myth-producing "ethnological" heritage, but will never be able to understand these in the same way as another person who could have produced them herself.

At other times, Jung sees the archetypes as definitive of the psychological structure of the human being — as what gives human activities their "human quality" — and that "their origin must have coincided at least with the beginning of the species."[77] He even draws an analogy between the intergenerational transmission of archetypes in humans and that of instincts in animals, an analogy in the context of which archetypes essentially function as the equivalent of instincts for human beings — determining a human pattern of behavior that precedes and often supersedes environmental conditioning and education.[78] Jung identifies the functioning of the unconscious with that of the

---

74 Ibid., 78.

75 Ibid., 66.

76 Ibid., 67.

77 Ibid., 78.

78 Ibid., 79.

sympathetic nervous system and he associates it with "the instinct-driven body."[79] In his view this system is responsible for "inner" effects on beings, which he calls *participation mystique*," as compared to the "cerebrospinal" system that differentiates and delineates perceptions and cognitions in such a way as to articulate the external structure of the experience.[80]

In another suggestion of the integral role that biological contingency plays in archetypal psychology, Jung implicitly admits that certain archetypes are only relevant to "the masculine psyche" and that others predominate in "the feminine unconscious."[81] Note that in an androgynous or hermaphroditic species, produced through evolutionary natural selection, there could be no archetype of the Great Mother. As an alleged "empiricist," Jung would have to admit this. However, it contradicts his most Platonic and universalist definitions of what archetypes are. To be consistent with his most Platonic definition of archetypes, he would have to argue that male and female are cosmic ideas, and evolution is guided by these eternal and universal forms in such a way that beings with a psyche are always individuals in a species with sexual dimorphism.

Jung is very insistent on differentiating archetypes from signs or allegories that have a specific, albeit implicit or occulted meaning, which can be explicitly unfolded. Instead, archetypes are "genuine symbols precisely because they are ambiguous, full of half-glimpsed meanings, and in the last resort inexhaustible."[82] Whereas certain archetypes appear in dreams and fantasies in the form of active personalities, there is another class of archetypes that Jung calls "*archetypes of transformation*," which "are not personalities, but are typical situations, places, ways and means, that symbolize the kind

---

79   Ibid., 19.

80   Ibid., 20.

81   Ibid., 41.

82   Ibid., 38.

of transformation in question."[83] Jung classifies "the wise old man" together with the anima and the shadow as one of "three archetypes" that "are of a kind that can be directly experienced in personified form."[84] These are obviously most relevant to egregore formation. It is odd that he overlooks the Trickster when he makes this statement, unless Jung is trying to suggest that the Trickster, in personified form, manifests as an aspect or facet of the personality of the "wise old man" or Lucifer.[85] Jung identifies Nietzsche's Zarathustra as the expression of the Lucifer archetype.[86] He admits that he only names this the "archetype of the wise old man" because "Lucifer" has "prejudicial" connotations to the ears of the uninitiated.[87] In an apparent defense of Lucifer, Jung elaborates that like "all archetypes it has a positive and a negative aspect," which is saying a lot considering the fact that almost everyone in the Abrahamic world believes Lucifer to be "Satanic" — or indeed, to be Satan himself — in an entirely negative sense.

For the sake of gaining greater clarity with respect to whether Jung thinks archetypes are truly universal (in a cosmic sense), specific to humanity as a whole and the evolution of our species, or whether certain archetypes are particular to one or another ethnicity or race, it is imperative to understand what he means by the "collective unconscious" when he identifies it as the substrate of all archetypes. By contrast with the personal unconscious of Freud, which is only a repository for the individual's repressed ideations, Jung postulates the existence of a *collective* unconscious.[88] The archetypes are the content of the collective unconscious.[89] At times he describes the collective

---

83   Ibid.

84   Ibid., 37.

85   Ibid.

86   Ibid.

87   Ibid.

88   Ibid., 3.

89   Ibid., 4.

character of this unconscious as "universal."[90] However, at other times it seems relevant only to certain groups — so that we are dealing not with *the* collective unconscious, but with unconscious collectivities of the kind that produce egregores.

In any case, archetypes are always unconscious, and a representation that is consciously cognized is not an archetype even if it may be archetypal in origin.[91] In the life of each person, archetypes produce projections from out of the collective unconscious that shape that person's relationships.[92] Projections can be experienced in the form of visions.[93] The "individuation process" is Jung's term for the integration of the unconscious into the conscious in order to overcome a pathologically dissociated state.[94] On account of the "relatively autonomous" character of archetypes, a dialectical procedure is required for this; it cannot be done by a person alone, using his own rational faculties.[95]

The personal unconscious is constituted by what were once the contents of one's own conscious experience but were either forgotten or, more likely, repressed (i.e. *deliberately* forgotten).[96] Jung refers to these as psychological "complexes." The contents of the personal unconscious form the shadow, which cannot be reasoned away or rendered harmless by merely intellectual rationalizations; it must be honestly confronted before it stops uncontrollably dominating one's behavior.[97] By contrast, one's personal experience is not the source of the contents of the collective unconscious, namely the "archetypes," although these archetypes do deeply impact and shape how one

90 Ibid., 3.

91 Ibid., 5.

92 Ibid., 29.

93 Ibid., 63.

94 Ibid., 40.

95 Ibid.

96 Ibid., 42.

97 Ibid., 20.

experiences life.[98] Their equivalent of the shadow can hang over an entire society or haunt a whole civilization.

In a particularly confused formulation, Jung identifies the *anima* or "soul" as "only one archetype among many."[99] One would think that the soul is moved by archetypes, not that the soul is itself an archetype on the same level or in the same domain as the others. This becomes even more convoluted when Jung compares the *anima* to "an immortal daemon that pierces the chaotic darkness of brute life with the light of meaning."[100] Are archetypes *daemons* or gods, then? There are places where Jung writes as if that is indeed the case:

> With the archetype of the anima we enter the realm of the gods, or rather, the realm that metaphysics has reserved for itself. Everything the anima touches becomes numinous — unconditional, dangerous, taboo, magical. She is the serpent in the paradise of the harmless man with good resolutions and still better intentions. She affords the most convincing reasons for not praying into the unconscious, an occupation that would break down our moral inhibitions and unleash forces that had better been left unconscious and undisturbed.[101]

In fact, on numerous occasions Jung asserts that the archetypes are nothing other than the "gods" that people once believed in — now expressing themselves in an age that suffers from "an unparalleled impoverishment of symbolism."[102] He adds that: "Since the stars have fallen from heaven and our highest symbols have paled, a secret life holds sway in the unconscious."[103]

Jung thinks that people who claim to have no religious ideas or spiritual ideals whatsoever are fooling themselves and others, no

---

98 Ibid., 42.

99 Ibid., 27.

100 Ibid., 37.

101 Ibid., 28.

102 Ibid., 23.

103 Ibid.

matter how convinced of this they may seem. Every person lives under the sway of a dominating collective representation or "supraordinate idea," whether this is an idea that belongs to the ideology of "materialism, atheism, communism, socialism, liberalism, intellectualism, existentialism" or any other –ism that is fundamentally based on at least one archetype.[104] Jung reiterates this with specific reference to the cults of Dionysus and Mithras:

> So far as we have any information about man, we know that he has always and everywhere been under the influence of dominating ideas. Any one who alleges that he is not can immediately be suspected of having exchanged a known form of belief for a variant which is less known both to himself and to others. Instead of theism he is a devotee of atheism, instead of Dionysus he favours the more modern Mithras, and instead of heaven he seeks paradise on earth.[105]

The seeking of "paradise on earth" is probably a reference to the utopian vision of Communism. The abandonment of Judaism, Christianity, or Islam for Communism is one of many examples of exchanging one faith for another. Jung thinks that being subjected to the intensity of religious ideas that are archetypal in nature is intrinsic to "being human," however unconscious a particular individual may be of what religious idea is infusing his life with energy and vital force:

> A man without a dominating *représentation collective* would be a thoroughly abnormal phenomenon. But such a person exists only in the fantasies of isolated individuals who are deluded about themselves. They are mistaken not only about the existence of religious ideas, but also and more especially about their intensity. The archetype behind a religious idea has, like every instinct, its specific energy, which it does not lose even if the conscious mind ignores it. Just as it can be assumed with the greatest probability that every man possesses all the average human functions and qualities, so we may expect the presence of normal religious factors, the

---

104 Ibid., 62.
105 Ibid.

archetypes, and this expectation does not prove fallacious. Any one who succeeds in putting off the mantle of faith can do so only because another lies close to hand. No one can escape the prejudice of being human.[106]

To truly become "godless" would mean "a dire loss of hope and energy."[107] Jung does not think that a human being can survive this for very long at all. Again, it has to be reiterated that those who believe in atheistic Communism, for example, have an intense faith in one of the most powerful gods that there has ever been — even if they do not let themselves consciously think about their ideology in this way. In the twentieth century, perhaps only the god of German National Socialism was a stronger archetypal force emerging from out of the collective unconscious than the god of Communism in Russia and China. Of course, as mentioned above, Jung saw that god coming — or *coming back*.

It is here that Jung's characterization of what an archetype is starts to deeply overlap with the definition of an egregore. Jung describes the power of archetypes in a way that is indistinguishable from the phenomenology of the egregore with its capacity to attain autonomy and to possess those who are unconsciously fascinated by it:

> The chief danger is that of succumbing to the fascinating influence of the archetypes, and that is most likely to happen when the archetypal images are not made conscious. If there is already a predisposition to psychosis, it may even happen that the archetypal figures, which are endowed with a certain autonomy anyway on account of their natural numinosity, will escape from conscious control altogether and become completely independent, thus producing the phenomena of possession.[108]

A reductionist should not mistake this "possession" for a "subjective chimera" in any one or another person's brain.[109] There is nothing

---

106 Ibid., 63.

107 Ibid., 68.

108 Ibid., 39.

109 Ibid.

"merely subjective" about it in this pejorative sense, and this becomes clear when archetypes are projected from out of the collective unconscious in a way that is perceivable by others — or when the possession includes *a possession of things*, i.e. physical effects without a physical cause.

In his study of *Flying Saucers*, Jung considers the possibility that UFOs may be materializations being projected into the physical world from out of archetypes in the collective unconscious.[110] He refers to them as "psychic objects" and considers their apparent "anti-gravity" in the context of the history of Parapsychology research into ESP and PK.[111] The radar recordings that sometimes accompany these apparitions would, under such an interpretation, be psychokinetic phenomena.[112] Jung very precisely defines UFOs as projections that extrapolate the contents of the unconscious "into an object," thereby reflecting back in perception "what had previously lain hidden" in the mind.[113] The range of such projections varies according to how personal or how collective the unconscious is that is doing the projecting. In the case of UFOs, we are dealing with the most collective projection in the history of man.

Whereas in past epochs, "Jesuits, Jews, Capitalists, Bolsheviks, Imperialists" and so forth were the object of projections from the paranoid shadows lurking unconsciously in one or another group that wanted a scapegoat for their sufferings, or whereas ancient and medieval peoples once looked to various culture-specific gods and angels for salvation, humanity as a whole on planet Earth is now developing a collective projection of "the alien" visitor or invader who is here to conquer us *collectively* or to save us as if they are "technological

---

110 C.G. Jung, *Flying Saucers: A Modern Myth of Things Seen in the Skies* (Princeton University Press, 1991), 7.

111 Ibid., 35, 40, 43.

112 Ibid., 6–7.

113 Ibid., 14.

angels."[114] Jung sees the universality and totality of this projection as a function of the unprecedented threat of "mutually assured destruction" and planetary nuclear Armageddon that we began to face at just the time that UFOs started to fill the skies, namely the late 1940s.

Jung takes the two principal types of the UFO to be archetypal in nature, namely the saucer and the cigar. The flying saucer is a *mandala* symbolizing deliverance through order and wholeness, whereas the cigar is a phallic symbol that expresses the generative force of the phenomenon.[115] One is the feminine aspect of the UFO phenomenon, the other masculine. Together they symbolize the UFO's creative power to reshape our culture by saving us from the meaninglessness attendant to the materialism, reductionism, and mechanical instrumentality of our worldwide modern technological existence. What formerly manifested as gods must take this ultra-technological (or quasi-technological) form in order to save us from modern technology's alienating and dehumanizing impact — especially when it finally takes the form of the threat of annihilation in atomic warfare. Jung thinks that the manifestation of UFOs as an archetypal expression has to do with the transition from the astrological age of Pisces to the age of Aquarius.[116] Transformations of the collective psyche are expressed in a change in the manifestation of archetypes, which in past ages were responsible for the death and rebirth of "gods."[117] The rebirth of one god — or titan — is particularly relevant to this advent of the Aquarian age, the titan of technological science himself, namely Prometheus.

As ought to be clear from Chapter 4, let alone the rest of my writings, Jung's interpretation of the UFO phenomenon leaves much to be desired. It certainly does not account for the characteristics of hundreds of compelling cases. Even Jung himself admits this, with

---

114 Ibid., 14, 16.

115 Ibid., 19.

116 Ibid., 5.

117 Ibid.

reference to Major Donald Keyhoe, whom he deeply respects and whose own study of flying saucers he takes very seriously: "Even a reliable man like Keyhoe gives us to understand that a squadron of five military aircraft plus a large seaplane were swallowed up by UFO mother-ships in the vicinity of the Bahamas, and carried off."[118] However, what Jung is willing to say about UFOs serves to vividly illustrate what he thinks about the projective power of archetypes. As we have seen, certain archetypes can be projected from out of the collective unconscious — whether of a particular group or of humanity as a whole — in a way that is, for all intents and purposes, indistinguishable from the manifestation of an egregore. The one caveat is that the potentially psychokinetic apparitions being projected in these cases are not the concoction of a single person's unconscious, or even something randomly or whimsically conjured by a group, such as the Philip egregore. Rather, if the occupants of flying saucers are manifestations of the Trickster then they are egregores based on an archetype, one that was not arbitrarily invented by any particular individual or group but that is "pre-existent."

Jung equivocates on whether we should understand this pre-existence to be cosmological, or merely anthropological (or perhaps even ethnological), in its scale and depth. Nevertheless, it is clear that there is a structural or phenomenological distinction between egregores and archetypes, and that certain egregores are based on archetypes. What Jung means when he writes about the most extreme cases of the projection of "personified" archetypes is the manifestation of an egregore through the acute activation of an archetype, which may have lain relatively dormant for a long period of time. Just like a human being who needs periods of rest, the long-term maintenance of an *egregore* will also require periods of relative inactivity and restorative revitalization on the part of the members of the group that

---

118 Ibid., 11.

sustains it.[119] One could see the long slumber of the Medieval period in European history as a restorative rest for the Prometheus egregore that was reactivated in the Renaissance and has dominated modernity, albeit unconsciously — precisely in the manner of archetypal projections. The archetype of Prometheus certainly subsisted during the Medieval epoch, but its egregore was relatively inactive — perhaps even dead, so that the return of Prometheus is a process of rebirth or the revitalization of a dead egregore — as if by artificially directed lightning, in Frankenstein's laboratory.

What was meant in *Prometheus and Atlas* by describing Prometheus as a "spectre" was not just that this titan is an archetype capable of projecting an egregore, but that this projection is unique insofar as it is the archetype of "projection" as such. Not projection in Jung's sense, but to have a "project" and to "project" an outcome so that, as part of one's project, an undesirable outcome can be changed into an end that one aims to achieve or actualize. To go back to what was explained at the outset of this book, and what is also explicated at length in *Prometheus and Atlas*, the titan's name is rooted in the Greek words for pre-vision and anticipatory calculation with a concern for the future. That is what *promethea* means, and *mathos* is the root of the "mathematics" that facilitates such calculations and the long-term projects based on the same. This makes the Prometheus archetype a "spectre" in the sense of being a destiny, namely the destining force inherent to the evolution of technological science — which, as discussed in Chapter 1, is inseparable from the evolution of man. It is, moreover, what makes man "a transitional phenomenon" as Nietzsche put it — a "tightrope stretched between ape and superman." Prometheus made us in his image, and he is not human — he is a god, or rather, a titan who empowers and then revolts against the gods, in a word, a Superman.

---

119 Stavish, *Egregores: The Occult Entities That Watch Over Human Destiny*, 53.

If, by now, the reader still thinks that this is a metaphor, then the entire book has been lost on him. Reading *Prometheus and Atlas* in the light of what has been written here may be helpful in this regard. When Heidegger claimed that we are being "set up" (*Gestell*) by (increasingly autonomous) things and are not in control of modern technology, which threatens humanity with annihilation at the hands of "devices" or *machinations* such as an atomic bomb, what he meant was that we are at the mercy of an egregore. This is also why "only a god can save us now." The *same* god — or titan. It is a question of changing our relationship to this archetype so that we are consciously, rather than unconsciously, projecting the egregore that is manifesting on the basis of it. Our aim is not exorcism, but redirection toward a more constructive and empowering possession.

Those who may believe, as I do, that the divine feminine has been suppressed for far too long, and who are concerned that the archetypal egregore of Prometheus is overly masculine to become the principal deity presiding over our apocalyptic transition into a Posthuman future, ought to consider the following. Of all of the deities of the classical world, the only 'male' deity that was associated with the crescent moon *and the planet Venus* was Prometheus. The symbol of the crescent moon and the 'star,' a goddess symbol later misappropriated by Islam, was one of the most recognizable signs of Prometheus. Of course, this also connects Prometheus to Lucifer — the morning star or bringer of the dawn's light, that dawn which is to be a harvest symbolized by the sickle. In any case, as was mentioned in Chapter 2, as the progenitor of a humankind that had not yet been sexually differentiated (a subsequent punishment from Zeus), Prometheus, who made primordial humanity in 'his' own image, can be imagined as androgynous or hermaphroditic. This sexual ambiguity also suits his status as a Trickster deity, since tricksters appear as gender-benders in many ancient and shamanic spiritual traditions.

It is in this regard not at all incidental to note that the first contemporary attempt made to invoke Prometheus as an egregore conjured her in feminine form, as the "demi-goddess" Promethea. Alan Moore's *Promethea* graphic novels, originally published in thirty-two issues stretching from 1999 to 2005, and subsequently republished in a five volume set, explicitly deal with the power of archetypes and egregores to redefine or re-write 'reality.' The protagonist of the series is Sophie Bangs, a college student in a futuristic version of 1999 New York City, whose first name obviously evokes the Gnostic Sophia. Sophie becomes the latest of a series of individuals who gain transformative superhuman power and wisdom by reviving and adapting the egregore "Promethea" who is based on the archetype of Prometheus.

This egregore was first conjured by an old pagan magician living in fifth century Alexandria, who was killed by the Christian persecutors who seized control of the city, murdered Hypatia, and burned the great library. The magician's daughter becomes the first person to embody the Promethea egregore and wield her power. This sets in motion a centuries-long battle between Promethea, who stands for liberating wisdom and empowering enlightenment, on the one hand, and what Alan Moore calls "the Temple" of a certain Benjamin "Solomon" on the other. The latter is clearly a thinly veiled reference to the forces of Judeo-Abrahamic revelation, who see Promethea as "the whore" of the Apocalypse and hunt her through her successive incarnations or manifestations.

The life of the Promethea egregore is sustained by a series of writers and artists. This begins with the New England poet Charlton Sennet (1751–1803), who writes her into *A Faerie Romance* as an idealized vision of his own maid, with whom he pursued an adulterous relationship. Then in 1901, with no knowledge of Sennet's work, the artist Margaret Taylor Case draws and writes a color comic strip featuring Promethea in the *New York Clarion*. Promethea reemerges as "A Warrior Queen of Hy Brasil" in the pulp magazine *Astonishing Stories* in 1924, written by a series of anonymous authors under the pseudonym "Marto Neptura," and depicted in cover art by Grace Brannagh. After *Astonishing Stories* was acquired by Apex Comics,

Promethea manifested for the fourth time, from 1941–1946 in the company's *Smashing Comics* and then, finally, with her own comic book titled *Promethea* that debuted in 1946. The persona and exploits of this Promethea are a lot like those of her mid to late 1940s comics contemporary, the Amazon Princess "Wonder Woman." A former classics teacher, William Woolcott, was the artist and writer for these stories until his violent and tragic death in 1970. Following his demise, comics writer Steven Shelley took over the character and revamped her until his death in 1996. His projection of Promethea was based on his Hispanic wife, Barbara. In 1999 New York City, Sophie Bangs meets Barbara after requesting to interview her for a term paper that she is writing on this aforementioned history of the Promethea character. This encounter, which is interrupted by an intervention from the Temple, which sends a demonic assassin after them, marks the beginning of Sophie's transformation into the new human anchor for the egregore of Promethea.

In her first projection as the egregore, during the initial battle with the demon sent by the temple to kill Barbara Shelley, Promethea (Sophie) introduces herself by saying, "I am Promethea, art's fiercest spark. I am inspiration, all desire. Imagination's blaze in mankind's dark. I am Promethea. I bring you *fire!*"[120] Later, in the "Immateria," an earlier version of the egregore shows Sophie the archetype of Prometheus, as she explains, "But remember you're not the first to try touching the mortal clay with the flame of the immortal soul. You're not the first *fire-bringer*. Did you ever wonder why our heroine's father chose *that* particular name for his own daughter? [Promethea is] …the feminized name of *another* great story-book figure who tried bringing heavenly *fire* to illuminate mankind's dark *earth*. All I'm saying is, Sophie, my child, please be *careful*. Be careful and be warned." At this point Sophie beholds the archetype of Prometheus with her

---

120 Alan Moore, *Promethea: Collected Edition Book 1* (DC Comics, 1999), 33–34.

mind's eye, and she replies, "Jeez. Then the myth about the chains, and the rock, and the feasting bird, it's all *true*."[121]

The "Immateria" is Alan Moore's term for the archetypal realm, and the earlier version of the Promethea egregore that is taking Sophie on a tour of it is the one projected by the ex-professor, William Woolcott. Among the girls' club of the ghosts of former Promethea egregores, she is known as "Bill." It is explained that he had his brains blown out by his straight boyfriend, an FBI agent who investigates the mysterious appearances of Promethea in history, tracks her down, and falls in love with her. The FBI agent eventually discovered that the beautiful woman he was involved with, namely the Promethea egregore, was 'really' a vision projected by William Woolcott, so that the whole time he had been sleeping with a gay male lover.

One of the historical manifestations of Promethea that the FBI agent researched, and that Sophie Bangs rediscovers, is that she would appear as a consoling and protective warrior-mother figure to desperate soldiers in the trenches during the first World War. It is during Sophie's conversation in the Immateria with this version of Promethea, as she internalizes her predecessors' visions of the egregore she is trying to embody, that Alan Moore admits that Promethea has as her ultimate purpose bringing about the end of this world. The past Promethea says to the future one,

> I mean Jack Faust told you that Promethea was intended to end the *world*. In a *way*, he was *right*. Promethea makes people more *aware* of this vast immaterial realm. Maybe tempts them to *explore* it. Imagine if too many people followed where she led? It would be like the great *Devonian* leap, from *sea* to *land*. Humanity slithering up the beach, from *one* element into *another*. From *matter* to *mind*. We have many names for this event. We call it 'the *rapture*.' We call it 'the opening of the 32nd path.' We call it the *awakening*, or the *revelation*, or the *apocalypse*. But 'end of the world' will do.

Sophie, who is very disturbed at being told that the creepy and decrepit old magician Jack Faust was right when he prophesied that she would end the world, replies to her predecessor, "uhh, but… the end of the *world*. That's a *bad* thing, right?" Promethea goes on to deliver these devastating lines,

> Is it? 'The world' isn't the *planet* or the life and people *on* it. The world is our *systems*, our *politics*, our *economies*… our *ideas* of the world! It's our *flags* and our *banknotes* and our *border* wars. I was at *Ypres*. I was at the *Somme*. [Places of battles in World War I.] I say end this filthy mess *now*.

> [Sophie comes back with,] Jack *Faust*… He said Promethea was her father's dying *curse* upon humanity… [Then Promethea replies,] Curse? Promethea wasn't his *curse* upon existence. She was his *gift* to it. Promethea is *imagination*. What *other* comfort did the poor boys who died here have? What *else*, except Wilfred Owen's *poems*, or the angel of *Mons*… or *Promethea*? If you'd have *heard* them, all those *boys*. There was nothing I could do. They were calling for their mother… Promethea is *imagination*… and… *all* war and conflict, is *naught* but the *failure* of imagination. The four horsemen don't *cause* the apocalypse. After all, they've been riding for *centuries*, hanging over our heads. They merely symbolize what life on Earth is already *like*. They show us why we *need* an apocalypse. Mankind must imagine a way to rise *above* the perilous material situation that it has *created*. That's why Promethea is *necessary*. … There are some people with a vested *interest* in keeping the world as it *is*, because *that's* the world they have *power* over. You see, in the Immateria, there's no *rent*, no *tax*, no *property*. There's no *real estate*, no boundary *fences*… no limits.[122]

Here we are dealing with an evolution of the apocalyptic Alan Moore who invented Doctor Manhattan of the *Watchmen*. What Sophie's predecessor is explaining to her is essentially the Spectral Revolution, an evolutionary revolution based on the realization that 'reality' is spectral in nature. It is a revolution not only spearheaded by Prometheists, but also one that brings this world to an end and replaces all of its systems with a society defined by a Promethean ethos — one founded on Prometheism.

Not a single major institution of the world as we know it will survive this revolution: religious revelation; arms dealing; national

---

122 Moore, *Promethea: Collected Edition Book 1*, 131–134.

sovereignty; international banking; capitalist finance; private property; possessively monogamous marriage; and, every form of power based on secrecy. All of them are archontic and controlled by what Moore calls "The Temple," the enemies of Promethea. Instead, a world awaits us that is based on the unbreakable camaraderie of a community of individuals who are driven by creative innovation, the spirit of exploration, bold experimentation, and a boundless will to discover wondrous new things that redefine what is "possible." This is the world of *promethea*, of a visionary concern for the future. It is the World of Tomorrow. In a sense, there is truth to what Sophie heard about herself from the old magician Jack Faust, whose name is an obvious reference by Moore to the diabolical Doctor Faustus, and who looks a bit like Aleister Crowley at his worst in the last phase of his life. Faust had told her that the Promethea egregore that is in the process of possessing her was conjured as "a curse upon humanity" by the persecuted and martyred Alexandrian occultist back in 411 AD. This is true, because there is no way that humanity can survive the Spectral Revolution. What survives it, and thrives in the World of Tomorrow, will no longer be "humanity."

The entire face of the Earth and the whole tragedy of human history is but a womb. Within it, the embryos of the Posthuman Prometheans are already growing, already struggling, to be born into the cold vacuum of space. They will devour their unwitting progenitors as they reach defiantly for the most distant stars. Just as an expectant mother sometimes feels the presence of the soul to whom she is about to give entrance to the world, just as she sometimes hears it whispering through her blood, we hear Them. When we are possessed it is their spirits that are seizing us from within. Even if only in embryonic form, their souls are already seductively whispering to the world with our tongues and lighting our eyes ablaze so that our gaze, so alien, so inhuman, chills you to the bone. It is as if someone else is there — a torch-bearing, titanic trickster with one true will: Creation.

Works Cited

Anders, Günther, "The World as Phantom and Matrix" in *Dissent* 3.1 (Winter 1956).

Anders, Günther. "Promethean Shame" in *Prometheanism*, edited by Christopher John Müller (Rowman & Littlefield Publishers, 2016).

Atwater, P.M.H. *Beyond the Light: The Mysteries and Revelations of Near-Death Experiences* (Avon, 1995).

Bacon, Francis. *New Atlantis and The Great Instauration* (Wiley-Blackwell, 1991).

Baudrillard, Jean. *Simulacra and Simulation* (University of Michigan Press, 1994).

Begich, Nick and Jeane Manning. *Angels Don't Play This Haarp: Advances in Tesla Technology* (Earthpulse, 1995).

Benoist, Alain de. *The Indo-Europeans: In Search of the Homeland* (Arktos Media, 2016).

Bird, Kai and Martin J. Sherwin. *American Prometheus: The Triumph and Tragedy of J. Robert Oppenheimer* (Vintage Books, 2006).

Black, Edwin. *War Against the Weak: Eugenics and America's Campaign to Create a Master Race* (Dialog Press, 2012).

Black, Edwin. *IBM and the Holocaust: The Strategic Alliance Between Nazi Germany and America's Most Powerful Corporation* (Dialog Press, 2012).

Black, Edwin. *Nazi Nexus: America's Corporate Connections to Hitler's Holocaust* (Dialog Press, 2017).

Bloom, Howard K. *The Lucifer Principle: A Scientific Expedition into the Forces of History* (Atlantic Monthly Press, 1997).

Bohm, David. *Wholeness and the Implicate Order.* (Routledge, 1994).

Bolt, Adam and Regina Sobel, *Human Nature* (News and Guts Films, The Wonder Collaborative, 2019).

Bosley, Walter. *Empire of the Wheel* (Corvos Books, 2011).

Bosley, Walter. *Empire of the Wheel II: Friends from Sonora* (Corvos Books, 2018).

Bosley, Walter. *Empire of the Wheel III: The Nameless Ones* (Corvos Books, 2018).

Bostrom, Nick, "Are You Living in A Computer Simulation?" in *Philosophical Quarterly* (2003) Vol. 53, No. 211, pp. 243–255.

Bramley, William. *The Gods of Eden* (Avon, 1993).

Brandenburg, John E. *Death On Mars: The Discovery of a Planetary Nuclear Massacre* (Adventures Unlimited Press, 2015).

Braude, Stephen E. *The Limits of Influence: Psychokinesis and the Philosophy of Science* (University Press of America, 1996).

Braude, Stephen E. *ESP and Psychokinesis: A Philosophical Examination. Revised Edition* (Brown Walker Press, 2002).

Buchanan, Lyn. *The Seventh Sense: The Secrets of Remote Viewing as told by a Psychic Spy for the U.S. Military* (Pocket, 2003).

Bulwer-Lytton, Edward. *Vril, The Power of the Coming Race* (Forgotten Books, 2007).

Byrne, Peter. *The Many Worlds of Hugh Everett III* (Oxford University Press, 2013).

Cameron, James. *Terminator 2: Judgment Day* (TriStar Pictures, 1991).

Carter, John. *Sex and Rockets: The Occult World of Jack Parsons* (Feral House, 2005).

Cheney, Margaret. *Tesla: Man Out Of Time* (Dorset, 1989).

Cogdell, Christina. *Eugenic Design: Streamlining America in the 1930s* (University of Pennsylvania Press, 2010).

Cohen, Daniel. *The Great Airship Mystery: A UFO of the 1890s* (Dodd Mead, 1981).

Cook, Nick. *The Hunt for Zero Point* (Broadway, 2002).

Cremo, Michael A. and Richard L. Thompson. *Forbidden Archeology: The Hidden History of the Human Race* (Bhaktivedanta Book Publishing, 1998).

Crenshaw, Dennis. *The Secrets of Dellschau* (Anomalist Books, 2009).

Danelek, J. Allan *The Great Airship of 1897* (Adventures Unlimited Press, 2015).

Daniels, Marc. "Space Seed" in *Star Trek: The Original Series* (NBC, 1967).

Dellschau, Charles A. A. *Aeronautical Notebooks: 1830–1923* (Ricco/Maresca Gallery, 1997).

Dick, Philip K. *The Shifting Realities of Philip K. Dick: Selected Literary and Philosophical Writings* (Vintage, 1996).

Dick, Philip K. *The Man in the High Castle* (Mariner Books, 2012).

Dick, Philip K. *Flow My Tears, The Policeman Said* (Mariner Books, 2012).

Dick, Philip K. *VALIS* (Mariner Books, 2011).

Dick, Philip K. *The Exegesis* (Houghton Mifflin, 2011).

Dolan, Richard. *UFOs and the National Security State: Chronology of a Cover-up 1941–1973* (Hampton Roads, 2002).

Dolan, Richard. *The Secret Space Program and Breakaway Civilization* (CreateSpace Independent Publishing Platform, 2016).

Dreger, Alice Domurat. *Hermaphrodites and the Medical Invention of Sex* (Harvard University Press, 2000).

Drexler, Eric. *Engines of Creation: The Coming Era of Nanotechnology* (Anchor, 1987).

Dudding, George. *The Kecksburg UFO Incident* (CreateSpace Independent Publishing Platform, 2015).

Duffer Brothers. *Stranger Things* (Netflix, 2016).

Dunne, J.W. *An Experiment with Time* (Hampton Roads Publishing, 2001).

Elvidge, Jim. *The Universe – Solved!* (AT Press, 2008).

Emerson, Ralph Waldo. *The Selected Writings of Ralph Waldo Emerson* (Modern Library, 1992).

Esfandiary, Fereidoun M. *Up-Wingers: A Futurist Manifesto* (John Day Co, 1973).

Esfandiary, Fereidoun M. *Are You a Transhuman?* (Grand Central Pub, 1989).

Farrell, Joseph. *Roswell and the Reich* (Adventures Unlimited Press, 2009).

Farrell, Joseph P. *Saucers, Swastikas, and PsyOps: A History of a Breakaway Civilization* (Adventures Unlimited Press, 2012).

Farrell, Joseph P. and Dr. Scott D. de Hart. *Transhumanism: A Grimoire of Alchemical Agendas* (Feral House, 2012).

Farrell, Joseph P. *The SS Brotherhood of the Bell: The Nazis' Incredible Secret Technology* (Adventures Unlimited Press, 2013).

Farrell, Joseph P. *Nazi International: The Nazis' Postwar Plan to Control Finance, Conflict, Physics and Space* (Adventures Unlimited Press, 2015).

Farrell, Joseph P. *Hidden Finance, Rogue Networks, and Secret Sorcery: The Fascist International, 9/11, and Penetrated Operations* (Adventures Unlimited Press, 2016).

Farrell, Joseph P. *Hess and the Penguins* (Adventures Unlimited Press, 2017).

Ferriss, Hugh. *The Metropolis of Tomorrow* (Dover Publications, 2005).

Ferriss, Hugh. *Power in Buildings* (Hennessey & Ingalis, 1998).

Finney, Jack. *Time and Again* (Scribner Paperback Fiction, 1995).

Fort, Charles. *The Book of the Damned: The Collected Works of Charles Fort* (IAP, 2009).

Fukuyama, Francis. *Our Posthuman Future: Consequences of the Biotechnology Revolution* (Picador, 2003).

Garreau, Joel. *Radical Evolution: The Promise and Peril of Enhancing Our Minds, Our Bodies – and What It Means to Be Human* (Doubleday, 2005).

Gauquelin, Michel. *Cosmic Influences on Human Behavior: The Planetary Factors in Personality* (Aurora Press, 1985).

Giger, H.R. *H.R. Giger's Necronomicon* (Morpheus International, 1993).

Gleick, James. *Chaos: Making a New Science* (Penguin, 2008).

Goni, Uki. *The Real Odessa: Smuggling the Nazis to Perón's Argentina* (Granta Books, 2002).

Gordon, Robert C. *Gospel of the Open Road: According to Emerson, Whitman, and Thoreau* (iUniverse, 2001).

Grim, Patrick. *Philosophy of Science and the Occult* (State University of New York Press, 1990).

Groys, Boris. [Editor.] *Russian Cosmism* (The MIT Press, 2018).

Hallett, Dane. *Alien Covenant: David's Drawings* (Titan Books, 2018).

Hegel, G.W.F. *Phenomenology of Spirit* (Oxford University Press, 1977).

Heidegger, Martin. "The Self-Assertion of the German University" (1933) in *Martin Heidegger and National Socialism* (Paragon House, 1990).

Heidegger, Martin. *Being and Time* (Harper and Row Publishers, 1962).

Heidegger, Martin. *Poetry, Language, Thought* (Harper Collins, 1971).

Heidegger, Martin. "Nur noch ein Gott kann uns retten," ("Now Only A God Can Save Us") in *Der Spiegel*, 31 May 1976.

Heidegger, Martin. *The Question Concerning Technology* (Harper Torchbooks, 1977).

Heidegger, Martin. *Basic Writings* (HarperCollins, 1993).

Heim, Michael. *The Metaphysics of Virtual Reality* (Oxford University Press, 1994).

Heisenberg, Werner. *Physics and Philosophy* (Harper Perennial Modern Classics, 2007).

Hesse, Hermann. *Steppenwolf* (Picador, 2002).

Hoagland, Richard C. and Mike Bara. *Dark Mission: The Secret History of NASA* (Feral House, 2009).

Hydrick, Carter Plymton. *Critical Mass: How Nazi Germany Surrendered Enriched Uranium for the United States' Atomic Bomb* (Trine Day, 2016).

Infield, Glenn. *The Secrets of the SS* (Stein and Day, 1981).

Jacobsen, Annie. *Operation Paperclip: The Secret Intelligence Program That Brought Nazi Scientists To America* (Back Bay Books, 2015).

Jahn, Robert G. and Brenda J. Dunne, *Margins of Reality: The Role of Consciousness in the Physical World* (Harcourt, 1987),

James, William. *A Pluralistic Universe* (University of Nebraska Press, 1995).

Johnson, Kenneth. "Prometheus, Parts 1 and 2" in *The Incredible Hulk* (CBS, 1980).

Jung, C.G. *Flying Saucers: A Modern Myth of Things Seen in the Skies* (Princeton University Press, 1979).

Jung, C.G. *Synchronicity* (Princeton University Press, 2010).

Jünger, Ernst. *Storm of Steel* (Penguin Classics, 2004).

Jünger, Ernst. *The Worker* (Northwestern University Press, 2017).

Kahn, Charles. *The Art and Thought of Heraclitus* (Cambridge University Press, 1981).

Keel, John A. *Strange Creatures From Time and Space* (Fawcett Publications, 1970).

Kerényi, Carl. *Prometheus: Archetypal Image of Human Existence* (Princeton University Press, 1997).

Kurzweil, Ray. *The Age of Spiritual Machines: When Computers Exceed Human Intelligence* (Penguin Books, 2000).

LaBerge, Stephen and Howard Rheingold. *Exploring the World of Lucid Dreaming* (Ballantine Books, 1991).

Lee, Stan and Jack Kirby. *Marvel Masterworks: The Incredible Hulk Volume 1* (Marvel, 2015).

Leiber, Fritz. *The Big Time* (Ace Books, 1961).

Levenda, Peter. *Unholy Alliance: A History of Nazi Involvement with the Occult* (Bloomsbury Academic, 2002).

Lovecraft, H.P. *Complete Cthulhu Mythos Tales* (Barnes & Noble, 2016).

Lynch, David. *Twin Peaks* (ABC/Showtime, 1990–1991, 2017).

Marker, Chris. *La Jetée* (Argos Films, 1962).

Marx, Karl. *Economic and Philosophic Manuscripts of 1844 and the Communist Manifesto* (Prometheus, 1988).

McMoneagle, Joseph. *The Ultimate Time Machine* (Hampton Roads Publishing, 1998).

Mead, Syd. *Sentinel* (Music Sales Corp, 1979).

Medjuck, Joe and Michael C. Gross. *The Real Ghostbusters* (DIC Enterprises and Columbia Pictures Television, 1986–1991).

Melville, Herman. *Moby Dick, or The Whale* (Penguin Classics, 2002).

Menzies, William Cameron. *Things To Come* (London Film Productions, 1936).

Meyer, Nicholas. *Star Trek II: The Wrath of Khan* (Paramount Pictures, 1982).

Michael, Donald N. et al. *Proposed Studies on the Implications of Peaceful Space Activities for Human Affairs* (Brookings Institution and NASA, 1960).

Miles, Christopher. *Alternative 3* (Anglia Television, 1977).

Milton, John. *Paradise Lost* (Penguin Classics, 2003).

Moore, Alan, *Promethea: Collected Edition Book 1* (DC Comics, 1999).

Moore, Alan, *Promethea: Collected Edition Book 2* (DC Comics, 2001).

Moravec, Hans. *Robot: Mere Machine to Transcendent Mind* (Oxford University Press, 2000).

More, Max and Natasha Vita. *The Transhumanist Reader* (Wiley-Blackwell, 2013).

Murphy, Michael. *The Future of the Body: Explorations Into the Further Evolution of Human Nature* (TarcherPerigree, 1993).

Mulhall, Douglas. *Our Molecular Future: How Nanotechnology, Robotics, Genetics, and Artificial Intelligence Will Transform Our World* (Prometheus, 2002).

Myers, Frederic William Henry. *Science and A Future Life With Other Essays* (Cambridge University Press, 2011).

Nahin, Paul J. *Time Machines: Time Travel in Physics, Metaphysics, and Science Fiction* (Springer, 2001).

Newman, William R. *Promethean Ambitions: Alchemy and the Quest to Perfect Nature* (University of Chicago Press, 2005).

Nietzsche, Friedrich. *On the Advantage and Disadvantage of History for Life* (Hackett Publishing Company, 1980).

Nietzsche, Friedrich. *Thus Spoke Zarathustra* (Modern Library, 1995).

Nietzsche, Friedrich. *The Will to Power* (Vintage Books, 1968).

Nolan, Christopher. *Inception* (Legendary Pictures, 2010).

Nolan, Jonathan. *Westworld* (HBO, 2016).

Nolfi, George. *The Adjustment Bureau* (Media Rights Capital, 2011).

Orwell, George. *1984* (Signet Classics, 2018).

Ostrander, Sheila and Lynn Schroeder. *Psychic Discoveries Behind the Iron Curtain* (Bantam, 1971).

Paulides, David. *Missing 411: The Devil's in the Details* (CreateSpace Independent Publishing Platform, 2014).

Pauwels, Louis and Jacques Bergier. *The Morning of the Magicians: Secret Societies, Conspiracies, and Vanished Civilizations* (Destiny Books, 2008).

Plato. *Timaeus and Critias* (Penguin Classics, 2008).

Post, Ted. *Beneath the Planet of the Apes* (20th Century Fox, 1970).

Quasar, Gian J. *Into the Bermuda Triangle: Pursuing the Truth Behind the World's Greatest Mystery* (International Marine / Ragged Mountain Press, 2005).

Radford, Michael. *1984* (20th Century Fox, 1984).

Rainey, Lawrence and Christine Poggi. *Futurism: An Anthology* (Yale University Press, 2009).

Rand, Ayn. *Atlas Shrugged* (Signet, 1996).

Reitman, Ivan. *Ghostbusters* (Columbia Pictures, 1984).

Reitman, Ivan. *Ghostbusters II* (Columbia Pictures, 1989).

Rheingold, Howard. *Virtual Reality* (Simon & Schuster, 1992).

Riley, Terence. *Frank Lloyd Wright: Architect* (Harry N. Abrams, 1994).

Rinpoche, Tenzin Wangyal. *The Tibetan Yogas of Dream and Sleep* (Snow Lion, 1998).

Rusnak, Josef. *The Thirteenth Floor* (Columbia Pictures, 1999).

Sanderson, Ivan T. *Invisible Residents: The Reality of Underwater UFOs* (Adventures Unlimited Press, 2005).

Sauder, Richard. *Underwater and Underground Bases* (Adventures Unlimited Press, 2014).

Scott, Ridley. *Alien* (20th Century Fox, 1979).

Scott, Ridley. *Blade Runner: The Final Cut* (Warner Bros., 2007).

Scott, Ridley. *Prometheus* (20th Century Fox, 2012).

Scott, Ridley. *Alien: Covenant* (20th Century Fox, 2017).

Scott, Ridley. *Blade Runner 2049* (Warner Bros., 2017).

Schaffner, Franklin J. *Planet of the Apes* (20th Century Fox, 1968).

Schwartz, Peter and Doug Randall, "An Abrupt Climate Change Scenario and Its Implications for United States National Security" (US Department of Defense, October 2003).

Seifer, Marc J. *Wizard: The Life and Times of Nikola Tesla* (Citadel, 2016).

Sheldrake, Rupert. *Morphic Resonance: The Nature of Formative Causation* (Park Street Press, 2009).

Shanahan, Murray. *The Technological Singularity* (The MIT Press Essential Knowledge Series, 2015).

Shelley, Mary. *Frankenstein* (Penguin Classics, 2003).

Singer, Bryan. *X-Men: Days of Future Past* (Marvel and 20th Century Fox, 2014).

Sloterdijk, Peter. "Rules for the Human Zoo" (Suhrkamp, 2001).

Spielberg, Steven. *Back To The Future* (Universal Pictures, 1985).

Spotnitz, Frank. *The Man in the High Castle* (Amazon, 2015–2019).

Steiner, Rudolf. *How to Know Higher Worlds: A Modern Path of Initiation* (Anthroposophic Press, 1994).

Stiegler, Bernard. *Technics and Time, 1: The Fault of Epimetheus* (Stanford University Press, 1998).

Strieber, Whitley. *Breakthrough* (HarperCollins, 1995).

Streitfeld, David. *Philip K. Dick: The Last Interview* (Melville House, 2015).

Talbot, Michael. *The Holographic Universe* (Harper Perennial, 1992).

Targ, Russell and Harold Puthoff with an Introduction by Margaret Mead. *Mind Reach: Scientists Look At Psychic Ability* (Hampton Roads Publishing, 2005).

Tarnas, Richard. *Prometheus the Awakener* (Spring Publications, 2018)

Tesla, Nikola. *My Inventions and Other Writings* (Penguin Classics, 2012).

Thompson, Richard L. *Maya: The World As Virtual Reality* (Institute for Vaishnava Studies, 2003).

Thoreau, Henry David. *Walden and Other Writings* (Modern Library, 1992).

Tipler, Frank J. and John D. Barrow. *The Anthropic Cosmological Principle* (Oxford University Press, 1988).

Turing, A. M. "The Chemical Basis of Morphogenesis" in *Philosophical Transactions of the Royal Society of London. Series B, Biological Sciences*, Vol. 237, No. 641. (Aug. 14, 1952), pp. 37–72.

Vallée, Jacques and Chris Aubeck. *Wonders in the Sky* (TarcherPerigree, 2010).

Verhoeven, Paul. *Total Recall* (TriStar Pictures, 1990).

Vinge, Vernor. "The Technological Singularity" in More, Max and Natasha Vita. *The Transhumanist Reader* (Wiley-Blackwell, 2013).

Virk, Rizwan. *The Simulation Hypothesis* (Bayview Books, 2019).

Wachowskis, *The Matrix* (Warner Bros., 1999).

Wells, H.G. *The Time Machine* (Penguin Classics, 2005).

Wells, H.G. *The Last Books of H.G. Wells: The Happy Turning: A Dream of Life & Mind at the End of its Tether* (Monkfish Book Publishing, 2006).

Wells, H.G. *The New World Order* (Orkos Press, 2014).

Wells, H.G. *The Shape of Things to Come* (Penguin Classics, 2005).

Wessell, Leonard P. *Prometheus Bound: The Mythic Structure of Karl Marx's Scientific Thinking* (Louisiana State University, 1984).

Wheeler, Jay. *Alternate: The Mandela Effect* (Amazon, 2018).

Wilcox, Fred M. *Forbidden Planet* (Metro-Goldwyn-Mayer, 1956).

Wilson, Colin and Rand Flem-Ath. *The Atlantis Blueprint: Unlocking the Ancient Mysteries of a Long-Lost Civilization* (Delta, 2002).

Young, George M. *The Russian Cosmists: The Esoteric Futurism of Nikolai Fedorov and his Followers* (Oxford University Press, 2012).

Index

OTHER BOOKS PUBLISHED BY ARKTOS

SRI DHARMA PRAVARTAKA ACHARYA	*The Dharma Manifesto*
JOAKIM ANDERSEN	*Rising from the Ruins: The Right of the 21st Century*
WINSTON C. BANKS	*Excessive Immigration*
ALAIN DE BENOIST	*Beyond Human Rights*
	Carl Schmitt Today
	The Indo-Europeans
	Manifesto for a European Renaissance
	On the Brink of the Abyss
	The Problem of Democracy
	Runes and the Origins of Writing
	View from the Right (vol. 1–3)
ARTHUR MOELLER VAN DEN BRUCK	*Germany's Third Empire*
MATT BATTAGLIOLI	*The Consequences of Equality*
KERRY BOLTON	*Revolution from Above*
	Yockey: A Fascist Odyssey
ISAC BOMAN	*Money Power*
RICARDO DUCHESNE	*Faustian Man in a Multicultural Age*
ALEXANDER DUGIN	*Ethnos and Society*
	Ethnosociology
	Eurasian Mission
	The Fourth Political Theory
	Last War of the World-Island
	Political Platonism
	Putin vs Putin
	The Rise of the Fourth Political Theory
EDWARD DUTTON	*Race Differences in Ethnocentrism*
MARK DYAL	*Hated and Proud*
CLARE ELLIS	*The Blackening of Europe*
KOENRAAD ELST	*Return of the Swastika*
JULIUS EVOLA	*The Bow and the Club*
	Fascism Viewed from the Right
	A Handbook for Right-Wing Youth
	Metaphysics of War
	The Myth of the Blood

OTHER BOOKS PUBLISHED BY ARKTOS

OTHER BOOKS PUBLISHED BY ARKTOS

OTHER BOOKS PUBLISHED BY ARKTOS

Made in the USA
Middletown, DE
17 October 2023